DEVELOPMENT TODAY

A FUND RAISING GUIDE FOR NONPROFIT ORGANIZATIONS

by Dr. Jeffrey Lant

Published by JLA Publications
A Division of Jeffrey Lant Associates, Inc.
50 Follen Street, Suite 507
Cambridge, Massachusetts 02138
(617) 547-6372

DEVELOPMENT TODAY
A FUND RAISING GUIDE FOR NONPROFIT ORGANIZATIONS

Dedication:

I dedicate this book to the thousands and thousands of non-profit personnel who over the years have used this resource and my fund raising methods to raise the money they need to do so much good work. I am deeply sensible of the continuing honor they do me and thank them most heartily for their trust and friendship.

TABLE OF CONTENTS

INTRODUCTION

A Letter From the Author, Dr. Jeffrey Lant

Dear Friend,

Welcome to the new fifth edition of one of the most popular books in America on one of the least popular subjects in America: fund raising. **DEVELOPMENT TODAY** is now being used successfully by thousands of organizations nationwide to raise the capital, project and operating funds they need at a time when the competition for such funds has never been more intense.

I know.

In my capacity as development counsel to a wide range of organizations around the nation and as a trainer in fund raising and organizational development techniques to hundreds more, I have worked with the executive directors, trustees and staff of nonprofit organizations to make sure they know exactly what they need to know to make their fund raising activities successful. Having done this for many years, I have a very clear sense of what it takes to raise money — and the things nonprofit personnel often find it so difficult to do.

DEVELOPMENT TODAY aims to deal with both areas by providing you with the exact technical information you need to raise the funds you must have and by giving you techniques to overcome your own reluctance (and that of the people you'll be working with) towards raising money.

I know you probably hate fund raising, that you approach the subject with distaste, anxiety and an acute desire to get it over with as quickly as possible. I know the people you'll be working with probably feel the same way. No wonder!

Fund raising is a time-consuming, slow-moving, intrusive, and often frustrating process. It's also a crucial activity in the kind of country we have where approximately one million organizations rely in some measure on voluntary support — the kind of support **DEVELOPMENT TODAY** will help you get.

Until now nonprofit personnel — be they trustees, executive directors or staff — have had very little assistance with the task of raising funds expeditiously and inexpensively, of getting the kind of help they need to get on with a job they so often dislike. This is not to say that there is limited fund raising literature. Quite the contrary. But all too often this literature is maddeningly theoretical, or, even worse, it stops just at the moment you need very practical guidance.

DEVELOPMENT TODAY is my attempt to correct matters. I wrote **DEVELOPMENT TODAY**, the first volume of the JLA Publications Nonprofit Technical Assistance Series, to make generally available the kind of pragmatic, tested, thoroughly utilitarian advice we've been offering our clients for years. I know the kinds of problems which arise in the fund raising process, and in **DEVELOPMENT TODAY**. I deal with them. Here's just some of what you'll find:

- A planning process which ensures success
- Determining the right level of capital, project and operating fund raising objectives
- Getting the Board of Directors to contribute
- Involving the Board in the fund raising effort
- Deciding which corporations and foundations to apply to, and for how much
- Gathering links to funding sources
- What to do with the links when you've got them
- Making a "No!" into a "Yes!" if a corporation or foundation declines your proposal
- Organizing an annual fund raising effort
- Creating the Coordinating Committee to supervise it
- Crafting persuasive fund raising documents at low cost
- Mounting successful special events
- Identifying Leadership Gift prospects
- Motivating and training volunteers
- Undertaking successful solicitation visits
- When and how to use direct mail
- Techniques for ensuring the success of a Capital Campaign
- When and how to use professional fund raising counsel and other technical assistance consultants.

This book, of course, is designed so you can implement a successful fund raising effort yourself. If, however, you decide to seek professional fund raising counsel to assist your efforts, I want you to know my firm is at your service. You will find further information about what we do at the end of this book along with my helpful Sure-Fire Small Business Success Catalog. I've designed this catalog to help you solve a wide variety of business and organizational development problems. Please take the time to review it and if you are not on my mailing list, please let me know as this catalog is updated quarterly.

In conclusion, let me take this opportunity to urge you to begin by reading **DEVELOP-MENT TODAY** from cover to cover. Once you have done so, start at the beginning once again, pen, paper and calendar in hand, to begin to organize your fund raising effort. Each page is punctuated with precise, thorough directions on what needs to be done, who should do it and when it needs to be accomplished. The more closely you are able to follow these guidelines, the greater your likelihood of success in getting the funds you need.

If your fund raising effort stalls for any number of nagging reasons (which I have collectively named the "Dog Ate My Homework" Syndrome), return to **DEVELOPMENT TODAY** to find the appropriate technique to get things going again. For that is the essence of successful fund raising: persistent effort towards the desired objective. **DEVELOPMENT TODAY** provides you with the tools you need so that your effort will be both persistent — and successful.

Now go to it! The people who rely on your organization for the services you provide are counting on you to raise the money you need and so continue to help them. For isn't this what it's all about? Helping other people? Keep this in mind when you are feeling drained and irritated, when the process seems stalled and when the money seems beyond your reach. Many people (including those who benefit from what you do but who have not yet seen the wisdom of supporting it) are counting on you. With **DEVELOPMENT TODAY** (and its companion volume **THE COMPLETE GUIDE TO PLANNED GIVING**) in hand you will not fail them!

After you've used this book to get the money you need, drop me a note to let me know how well you've done. I love success stories, especially yours.

Yours for development success,

Jeffrey

Cambridge, Massachusetts
September, 1992

CHAPTER I

THE PLANNING PROCESS

As an administrator of a nonprofit organization, your job is to gain support from as broad a base as possible for a constituency whose significant needs might otherwise go unmet. During times of economic uncertainty and hardship, your job is likely to be a difficult one. You must ask for funds from sources which may be decreasingly able to provide them. You may get discouraged. But with the proper attitude and a thorough, considered method, fund raising can be both easier and more effective.

Assuming The Right Attitude

The right attitude is a confident, positive one. In fact, such an attitude is an essential first step to any fund raising effort. Without it, you should question the desirability of seeking funds at all.

Such an attitude may prove difficult to adopt. After all, very few people actually *like* asking for money. Most feel embarrassed about it. They consider asking for money an almost vulgar intrusion into the personal affairs of family members or friends. In our culture, money has traditionally been regarded as a very private matter; awkwardness and hesitancy to discuss it are, therefore, perfectly understandable. Also, most Americans are schooled to believe that people who don't ask for "hand-outs" are more virtuous than those who do.

It is important to acknowledge and then dispense with these obstacles. Asking for money is one of the critical ways your organization will survive to do its good work. So be it. Without nonprofit organizations, American life would be significantly altered and immeasurably impoverished. Not least because many millions of citizens unable fully to care for themselves would lack necessary advocates.

Thus, to overcome your natural hesitancy remember that you ask for money to serve others — including the people who themselves give the money. The act of solicitation is an act of citizenship and humanity and must be regarded as such.

Communicating this essential attitude to agency administrators, staff, board members and volunteers will make a fund raising effort run more smoothly. It is the job of the executive director and chairman of the board to promote fund raising as an active, positive means of expressing concern and facilitating beneficial community change.

The Plan

Even the best attitude in the world, however, cannot insure a successful fund raising result. A thorough fund raising plan is an absolute necessity.

First Steps

The January board meeting of your organization is the most effective time to introduce your fund raising plans. At this meeting the chairman of the board may profile the current and anticipated fiscal situations of the organization, solicitating the view of appropriate experts (such as the agency's treasurer, executive director and an outside development consultant) as to why a fund raising effort is both timely and necessary.

He will then outline what will be expected of each board member throughout the year: each will be expected both to contribute financially and to serve prominently on a fund raising solicitation committee. The chairman may well present the Time Line to the board (see the appendix of this book). He will also introduce the members of the Needs Assessment and Development Planning Committee (if not previously done) and outline their tasks over the next several months. At the close of this meeting, the chairman should call for either a "sense of the board" or a formal resolution that the board endorses the development concept and will work diligently to implement the tasks as they are conceived and set. This will be set forth in the minutes of the meeting and serve as a policy guideline. Note: it is important that any absent members of the board be told of this decision, asked for their consent, and pressed for their cooperation. No one must later be allowed to say he was uninformed of what was forthcoming and expected.

The January board meeting is an acceptable but not ideal time for the chairman to appoint the Needs Assessment and Development Planning Committee. Rather, this small, critical group should begin meeting in December, and its members be appointed a month or so beforehand. As it is virtually inevitable that the holiday season will interfere with the early work of this committee, it is a good idea to try and have its first meeting in late November or early December.

The Needs Assessment And Development Planning Committee

The Needs Assessment and Development Planning Committee works as an autonomous entity within the organization. During the months the board is finishing up its current year's work, this committee is hard at work planning for the next one. Periodic reports of its activities and findings must be made to the board by the committee's chairman.

The Needs Assessment and Development Planning Committee is created by the board of directors, is composed of directors, and reports only to the board. It is designed as a small working group of four or five members which must perform several critically important tasks. It is best composed of your accountant (whose chief function is as a business planner), the treasurer of the organization, who oversees all disbursements; a banker, whose general knowledge of finance and whose contacts in the financial world may prove helpful; the chairman of the board, and someone who is familiar with agency programs. The executive director serves this committee not as a full, voting member but rather as an internal consultant. He or she advises the committee and recommends which staff members should appear before it as in-house consultants and experts in specific programs.

The Needs Assessment and Development Planning Committee must begin meeting in January at the latest. The executive director should make available a staff liaison for this committee. The liaison will see that notes are kept of all meetings, gather necessary information and documents, schedule meetings, and perform related staff duties.

The Needs Assessment and Development Planning Committee must complete six major tasks between its first meeting in early January and the last meeting of the board in June. These six tasks are:

- Analyze the organization's service area
- Arrive at a suggested overall fund raising goal for the next fiscal year
- Present this goal to the board with specific capital, program, and operating fund raising objectives
- Advise the board on how these three objectives can be met both in terms of overall strategy and specific fund raising sources
- Gain the board's adherence to the plan(s)
- Draft a Five Year Plan for the organization.

Knowing Your Service Area

Most funds in this country are raised locally for local projects. Many agencies have no problem in establishing that they are local and that they serve the neighborhood. It is often, indeed, clear from their very names that they do so — the *Melrose* YMCA, the Girls Club of *Fall River*, &c. For such organizations fund raising outside the community will be rare and usually for major capital purposes only or demonstration projects.

Other organizations, however, must spend some time establishing 1) the areas they formally exist to serve, and 2) the places from which clients are actually drawn. The information gathered, particularly about item 2, may have a significant bearing on future fund raising.

Organizations usually have less problem determining the formal areas they are expected to serve than the areas from which clients are in fact drawn. The former are often set forth in a goals statement or organizational charter; if not, it is the responsibility of the board and its Needs Assessment and Development Planning Committee to make the service area plain.

Once this area has been determined, the Committee must gather relevant statistical information showing the exact extent of an agency's work in specific communities. For instance, a special needs adoption agency may claim that its service area is the eastern half of Massachusetts. However, it may in fact draw 40% of its clients from Boston and another 40% from just 6 surrounding communities. This information becomes important in later assessing what funding sources might be approached — and for how much money.

Institutional funding sources, like many individuals, often want only to support local projects. They generally define their giving areas strictly so that grant seekers will be comfortably excluded from consideration. The objective, usually unstated, of particularly institutional donors is to define their giving area starkly and hence reduce legitimate applicants. *Your* task is to show that your agency performs local service, even though your headquarters may be far away. It is the job of the Needs Assessment and Development Planning Committee to collect the necessary information showing where local service has been performed and to what extent, and thence to factor in funding sources from areas which might not otherwise be considered in a fund raising effort.

Organizations should always be creative about expanding the area where they perform service and from which they may seek funds. Take the special needs adoption agency above-mentioned, for instance. The children served may come from state facilities of various kinds; indeed, given the nature of the child welfare system these children may have been associated with various facilities. Funding sources in these communities will probably feel distinctly limited interest in this information. What *may* interest them, however, is knowing where the parents of these children are located, particularly if programs are run which will help these parents provide better service to the difficult special needs population. Thus, if a significant number of adoptive parents came from one area, it might make sense to pursue some funding in that area, particularly for projects benefitting the local people. It is the task of the Needs Assessment and Development Planning Committee to gather the information that will allow such a decision to be made.

The Competition Folder

Once you have defined your marketing area, the next step is to analyze your competition within that area. The objective of this analysis is either to affirm your unique, non-competitive service or to discover very convincing reasons why overlapping or competitive services of the same type are needed within one community.

Since your organization must establish its uniqueness from others, you must get to know your competition as well as funding sources inevitably will. The best way to do this is to open either one Competition Folder or else a series of smaller competition folders on each of your distinct programs. This folder will be a place to keep data on the activities and programs of all *profit* as well as nonprofit organizations whose work resembles yours either in whole or in part.

This folder should be organized and updated by a designated staff representative. It should include:

- the full name, address, and phone number of other organizations
- the names of their directors and pertinent information about them
- their annual reports
- public relations materials such as brochures, &c.
- other pertinent documents, such as development proposals and internal reports
- information about special events, including programs, tickets, press releases, and the like
- newspaper articles about their activities
- announcements of grants and contracts as taken from local newspapers, newsletters, &c.

You may very well discover that there are, within your marketing area, several organizations whose services may be similar to yours. The next step in developing the Competition Folder is to complete a full analysis of each of these organizations. To do this, you must ask yourself:

- Program by program, what does this agency do?
- How many people does it serve?
- What is their universe or marketing area (both formally and in actual fact)?
- How much does each program cost per client?
- What is this agency's public image?

The result of compiling such thorough data is that you will be able to use to your advantage what I call the "Implied Comparison Test." The idea, of course, comes from television commercials. It is an *implied* comparison rather than an explicit one because much of the information will be subtly used to your benefit. For example, in a situation where resources are scarce, if you find out that a competitor is being criticized because of wasteful use of money, you can stress your fiscal accountability. If criticism has been heard of their inactive board, stress your own board's intense level of commitment. If you learn that their books have long gone unaudited, you can emphasize that yours are audited annually and that everything is in apple pie order.

When you present your organization in this way to a funding source which is very likely to have much, if not all, the information you do (and perhaps even more!), the source can then draw its own favorable conclusion about you. This can have an impact on whether you receive funds. It is important to remember, of course, that the process is designed to work to your advantage without the risk of your direct criticism of a competitor.

Gathering information on other organizations is essential to establishing that:

- You are unique as an agency, that is that you have no competitors within your marketing area.
- If you are not unique, there is a pressing need for what you do, that there is a reason requiring multiple agencies in your marketing area.
- Where there is an overlap of similar services, you are more cost-efficient, broader-based, &c.
- If you are not unique generally, yet there are essential aspects of your program which are and which must therefore be preserved.

If you fail either to prove that you are unique in whole or significant part or have failed to prove the need for several competing agencies within the same marketing area, you are on the road to extinction. Remember: given the current funding climate (which will continue to exist for years), hard-pressed institutional funders and individuals will use any excuse, no matter how slight, to disqualify your agency from consideration.

As the Competition Folder is being completed, the Needs Assessment and Planning Committee, with its staff liaison and the assistance of the executive director as in-house consultant, should be completing the same kind of in-depth scrutiny of its own programs. This is the Self Portrait. As you review each aspect of your organization, bear the items of this chapter in mind. Imagine presenting each program or project to a funding source which needs to be convinced about the good work of your agency which you know very well.

The Needs Assessment and Development Planning Committee has completed the first stage of its work when the Competition Folder and Self Portrait are completed. Now your agency has examined its marketing area, identified and analyzed competitors, and defined its own unique or essential community role or service.

Setting A Fundraising Goal For The Next Fiscal Year

In the first phase of the work of the Needs Assessment and Development Planning Committee, the value of your service was clearly established both absolutely and in relation to possible competitors. Now you know what you have. But what do you need?

The second phase of the Committee's work addresses this question. To begin, all your certain revenues must be calculated, program by program. Do not include one-time-only revenues such as gifts from estates which may have been used for current income needs. Only certain revenues should be calculated here.

Next, each program of your agency must be assessed. Needs assessment by program proceeds like a series of congressional hearings. Each program head is brought before the Committee to present his or her case. A three to four page synopsis of this information should be prepared in advance and given to the Committee (or staff liaison) for general distribution. This synopsis should answer the following questions:

- What is the projected need for this program/service?
- How do we know?
- How many people have we served in the last year?
- What success did our program have in reaching its announced goal?
- What success did our program have organizationally?
- What success did our program have from a programmatic standpoint?
- Was there outside support for what we did? Who or what kind?
- Was any evaluation (internal or external) done which could help us validate our success?
- Were testimonials made to this program?
- What about media mention?
- Was there a secure funding base for all or part of this program?
- Has any part of the program reached a natural end?
- Is there a need for cancellation of any portion?
- Are there capital needs for the next year? Specify both dollar amounts and reasons.
- Do you intend to begin a new project? If so, what is the justification and the budget?
- Are there operating expenses that do not fit into either existing programs or new projects? Do these exceed the secure funding base?
- Is there anything special to be noted about the people in your program? Has anyone won an award, published an article, &c.?
- Does your program play a critical role in the community? Can you summarize its importance in a few lines?

• Can the program coordinator suggest an amount to be a reasonable fund raising goal for this program for the next fiscal year?

In addition to these questions, each of which should be answered as concretely and specifically as possible (preferably the program coordinator will have statistics or significant examples to cite in support of any answers given), the coordinator should also have a copy of his current operating budget available for the Committee to review.

After each program head has presented this information to the committee hearing and the total "wish list" has been added up, the Committee returns to the agency's certain revenue figure. The first, tentative fund raising goal for the next fiscal year will usually be the shortfall — that is, the difference — between what the agency needs and what it can expect to take in before the fund raising effort.

Often times the shortfall, if taken for the fund raising goal, might be unrealistically high, especially if your organization has not undertaken a full-scale fund raising effort in the terms of this book.

But how can this Committee determine whether its fund raising goal is in fact realistic?

Here it is important to understand something about the overall world of private sector fund raising. Of the approximately $104.5 billion donated to nonprofit organizations and charities in 1988, about 89% came from private citizens, about 5.4% came each from corporations and from foundations. All things being equal, an organization approaching the private funding market should be raising its funds in the same way.

For many organizations, however, particularly those that sprang into being in the 1960's and after with the assistance of federal funds, this is a prescription for oblivion. This is because these organizations all too often lack constituencies which could provide 89% of any outside fund raising effort. Realizing this difficult fact, these — and many other organizations — rush headlong into fund raising seeking to raise funds from corporations and foundations and all too often failing miserably in the process.

A large part of the problem stems from the misuse by these agencies of corporate and foundation funding sources, their failure to understand how they should be used, and a failure to divide their fund raising goal into capital, program (or project) and operating objectives.

It is the job of the Needs Assessment and Development Planning Committee first to draw up three lists of fund raising objectives: capital, program and operating.

8

Capital Fund Raising Objectives

Capital objectives are those that tangibly increase the value of the organization in one way or another. They include the development or acquisition of land, the construction and renovation of buildings (called "bricks and mortar"), and the acquisition and rehabilitation of equipment. Capital grants may be made by corporations, foundations, and individuals, and are by far the most popular and least misunderstood kinds of grants. This is at least largely because once the capital item has been purchased it will have long-term usefulness, thereby suggesting that the donor will not immediately be asked for another, similar gift.

Program Objectives

Program (or project) objectives are the second most popular funding category. The key concept here is one of investment. Funding sources, particularly foundations and corporations, like to think of their grants as having a multiplier effect, of one of their dollars being leveraged to produce many times the value of the original grant. Such funding sources, having distinctly limited resources, generally seek projects offering "the most bang for the buck", projects, that is, which can provide regional and national models and offer real incentives for positive change, not just remediation.

The idea up until recently has been that such innovative projects would be started by the private sector and, once having proved their value, be adopted by the public sector and financed thereby. This model, it need hardly be said, worked well enough in the decades of the 1960's and 1970's. Its legacy, however, is distinctly unhappy.

Foundation and corporate officers all too often still prefer such projects even though nowadays the end result is likely to be a series of pilot projects which necessarily have abbreviated lifespans. Nonetheless, the fact remains that such institutional philanthropists prefer special projects because they imply a limited involvement and a measurable result.

Because it is relatively easy (the stress here is on the adverb) to market good programs, particularly those seen to be innovative community investments, to private sector funding sources, it is incumbent on the Needs Assessment and Development Planning Committee to package as many of the agency's expenses as possible into such special projects. Needless to say such packaging can be an important means of covering a significant percentage of basic operating costs which are otherwise difficult to raise. In this packaging process an outside consultant can often play a significant role.

Operating Fund Raising Objective

All that can neither be defined as a capital objective nor a special program remains in the category of operating money. This is the most difficult money to raise from corporations, foundations, and significant individual donors. First, as far as institutional givers are concerned, a grant to your agency's operating budget implies a long term commitment of the kind most wish strenuously to avoid. After all, so the reasoning goes, you will be back next year for more money (never the same, or less). Thus if such a grant is given, it limits the discretionary possibilities of the donor (and hence the prospects for creating the kinds of meaningful investment projects they prefer). If it is not given, your organization may collapse or have embarrassing public problems, thereby suggesting to the critical that any prior grant was a mistake.

As far as major donors are concerned, some of the same objections apply. Stability, continuity, permanence entice major donors, implicitly and explicitly. A grant to operating expenses, while no doubt laudable, is evanescent and fails to provide the kind of sustained satisfaction most major donors seek.

As a result of these facts, the Needs Assessment and Development Planning Committee must do two things and do them very well: 1) limit to the greatest extent possible the amount of outright operating money sought and work with the Budget Committee (or other relevant agency body) to redirect secure funds to operating expenses leaving the agency free to fund raise from corporations, foundations, and major donors for capital and project needs.

Prospect Evaluation

Once these capital, project and operating needs have been determined the Needs Assessment and Development Planning Committee must begin the difficult, artful process of evaluating the likely prospects for a gift from funding sources. This is a crucial process and one that many agencies disregard in their haste to write a proposal and approach (generally incorrect, apathetic) funding sources.

At this point the members of the Needs Assessment and Development Planning Committee (who are after all amateurs and not generally familiar with the often idiosyncratic personalities of private sector funding sources) must rely upon either a knowledgeable executive director and/or external development consultant. The process at this point is as follows:

To begin with, a list of the capital items needed by the agency is drawn up. Thereafter the executive director (assisted where available by development counsel) draws up a list of prospective corporate, foundation and (where applicable) individual donors. These sources, particularly the institutional ones, are known to be prospects, because of extensive agency research using:

- **The Foundation Directory** (see select bibliography for specifics)
- individual state foundation directories
- local reference libraries
- specialized publications such as **Foundation News**
- specific publications on corporate giving
- information gleaned from specialized seminars featuring corporate and foundation officers
- newspaper and periodical accounts of grants given to competing agencies
- foundation annual reports and tax returns
- informal conversation with peers
- information gathered through agency Facilitating Sessions.

Once it has been determined which (particularly) corporations and foundations are at least general prospects, the artful evaluation must be continued with answers to the following questions:

- Have we recently (within the last 3 years) approached this source?
- If the application was successful, have we maintained good relations? Was a thank-you note sent? A report of grant expenditure? Have we remained in regular, informal contact strengthening our relationship?
- If these things have not been accomplished, must we spend time re-cultivating and fence-mending?
- If we were rejected, was it for another capital item? If so, why do we feel an application for a capital item would at this time be successful? If we are uncertain, is there a way of finding out before an application is submitted?
- If we were rejected for an item in another category (program, operating) how did we leave matters? Can we go back now or in the near future without further cultivation or must we re-cultivate the source to indicate that we have learned how to deal with funding sources?
- What is the condition of the funding source? Remember, informational sources are *always* out of date even at the moment of publication. A company which may, because of a prosperous year, have given substantially may now have severely altered circumstances. It is your responsibility to know. A staff person should be assigned to watch the newspapers to collect relevant information which will later be needed by the Committee. This is an on-going responsibility.

Although the topic is discussed at length in a later chapter (see "The Facilitating Session"), clearly much relevant information can be obtained through informal contact with staff and directors of institutional funding sources. It is the responsibility of both the executive director and all trustees, not just those serving on the Needs Assessment and Development Planning Committee, to help gather this information. This process must be continued throughout the entire year.

Once this process is completed for capital items, it is repeated for project objectives and finally for operating needs. It is the job of the Committee to assess each supposed possibility with the utmost thoroughness and with deliberate caution. This is because the demands on available funding sources are intense and the Committee must try to spare the agency the embarrassment of announcing a fund raising goal and falling woefully short of it, as so many consistently do.

First Report To The Full Board

Once the Needs Assessment and Development Planning Committee has divided the agency's fund raising goal into the three objectives of capital, project and operating and has done a preliminary analysis of the likelihood of grants (preliminary for two reasons: further information will be collected and the prospects for operating support will be, at this moment, only imperfectly developed), it is time for an introductory report to the full board.

This report has two important aspects: 1) it contains an early indication of which corporations and foundations are good prospects and of the greater number where better links are necessary, thus allowing for board assistance in developing these links and in providing more detailed information about specific institutional targets. 2) It suggests the level of operating expense not covered by secure income sources and leads naturally to a discussion of both the board's own contribution towards this expense and of the fund raising effort which must be mounted later in the year to raise funds from individuals.

It is recommended that this preliminary presentation to the board occur in March so that the board feels fully cognizant of developments and so that the Needs Assessment and Development Planning Committee gets an early, complete sense of what still needs to be accomplished before its final report in May or June.

Unfortunately, many organizations either avoid the planning process or approach it with something resembling levity. It deserves the full attention of the board, its planning group and the agency's project directors. Organizations which do not undertake this process make a grave error which lessens board involvement and often leads to public embarrassment.

Once these steps are completed, the Needs Assessment and Development Planning Committee has two further tasks:
1) drafting of a Five Year Plan, and
2) setting the sum to be raised in the current fund raising effort for agency endowment.

The Five Year Plan

More and most institutional funding sources, particularly corporations, are requiring agencies requesting their support to make available for inspection a Five Year Plan. I have, however, never seen any guidelines for drafting such a plan, and it is not, therefore, surprising that there should be some confusion and uncertainty about how to create one.

To begin with, all documents written for the private sector must be concise and pungent. Lengthy documentation is frowned upon as inappropriate. A Five Year Plan in this context, therefore, bears no similarity to documents of the same name which grace the bookcases of Soviet commissars.

A good Five Year Plan begins with the current operating budget and grows naturally from it. It presents in synopsis format the following information:

- name of program (project)
- individuals served, current fiscal (or calendar) year
- cost of service
- projection for growth, stability or decline
- basis on which such projections were reached
- capital needs next year (land, buildings, equipment, &c.)
- project plans next year (including personnel and project operating expenses)
- certain revenues
- anticipated surplus or deficit.

If possible each year of the Five Year Plan beyond the current operating budget (which will ordinarily be the most long and detailed) should be entirely contained on the two sides of one 8½″ x 11″ sheet of paper. Smaller agencies may very well be able to synopsize their activities on a single side and should be encouraged to do so if this presentation gives a complete picture of the agency.

It may be that the Needs Assessment and Development Planning Committee will wish to deputize the executive director or a suitable staff person to draft the Five Year Plan for its membership. This is done for the convenience of Committee members who remain, however, entirely responsible for the final result.

The document once completed and presented to the board (which, of course, reserves the right to debate and alter any portion of it prior to public use) has several valuable uses. It forces the agency to deal with vital questions involving the organization as organism. Do we know where our programs are going and have we considered what must be done either in terms of growth or in terms of merger, consolidation, or liquidation of programs? Forcing board members to make conscious choices about each aspect of the organization is of immense significance in moving them not only to full participation but to the ownership which is inherent in the role of trustee. Moreover, this planning document is most valuable in developing proper relationships with the professional staff of corporate contributions programs and foundations.

These staff people are, it must be remembered, faced with a severe difficulty. On the one hand, the call upon their dollars is relentless. Beyond this fact, however, at any given moment the overwhelming majority of their dollars is not available for discretionary distribution having been committed elsewhere or marked for commitment. This statement deserves elaboration.

While in theory a corporation or foundation may say that the dollars in its annual distribution budget are entirely discretionary, such a statement needs clarification. The following situations may limit an institutional donor's ability to make you a gift no matter how worthy you are, or how willing they are to do so:

- prior commitments to other organizations such as multi-year pledges being paid annually
- expected reapplication of agencies which have already received support but to which no explicit or formal commitment has been made
- the need to maintain a percentage of funds unallocated so as to be available for the needs of senior officers; this is particularly true in corporations, though by no means unknown in the foundation world.

These and other constraints on institutional donors mean that upwards of 90% of corporate and foundation monies are actually committed at any given moment, no matter how discretionary they may in fact appear. Thus even if a funding source wishes to make you a grant, it may have to factor you in for a later date. Your Five Year Plan allows philanthropic officials to enter into a constructive dialogue with you, know when and for what you need the money, and to plan accordingly.

In practical terms it may take several months beyond the determination of fund raising objectives to produce the Five Year Plan. This is acceptable, so long as the document is available for use in the fall or so that interested funding sources get a precise idea of when this document can be made available to them. Remember that the production of the first Five Year Plan will be the most difficult. Thereafter the Needs Assessment and

Development Planning Committee is simply updating the work of its predecessors and adding in its own right the final, fifth year of the document.

The Savings Account

Once the capital, project and operating fund raising objectives have been set, the Needs Assessment and Planning Committee must deal with the question of how much the agency should put away in its endowment fund. Now the very word "endowment" conjures up images of mighty universities and prestigious hospitals, organizations which may bear little resemblance in form or level of wealth to your own. That is why I have chosen instead to call this concept the "Savings Account," a notion with which we are all familiar.

The concept here is a simple, powerful one best understood along the lines of the ubiquitous commercials for Individual Retirement Accounts and All-Savers Certificates, namely that small amounts of money, regularly added to over a long span of years, produce with the considerable assistance of compound interest quite healthy sums of capital.

For example, an agency saving $3000 per year and compounding at 10% over the course of 30 years will have an endowment fund of well over half a million dollars. I have not chosen the sum of $3000 without thought. This is, I think, the lowest acceptable amount that *any* organization should save annually. Organizations of over $100,000 per year in operating expenses should deposit at least $5000.

It should be understood that this sum, whether $3000 or $5000 or more, cannot ordinarily be raised either from corporations (other than small businesses which give unrestricted, operating grants) or foundations (except for small, family-run foundations which operate, for all intents and purposes, as individuals). Many such organizations explicitly prohibit gifts to endowment funds. This means that the funds you seek for your savings account must come, on the whole, from individuals and must be added to the amount you seek for operating expenses.

Thus if your fund raising objective for operating expenses is $20,000 and you decide to raise $5000 for the savings account, your overall operating goal would be $25,000. The raising of this sum is discussed in detail in the chapter on the Coordinating Committee, but it needs to be said here that at least 20% of the total sought for operating expenses *must* come from the board directly. This figure will undoubtedly come as a shock to a board which is not contributing either anything or anywhere near this total, but if this percentage is not pledged and raised by the board it will be very, very difficult to raise the remaining funds outside.

Many agencies, while recognizing the sense of establishing a savings account which will ultimately carry a significant percentage of operating expenses and allow them to go to corporations and foundations periodically and appropriately, complain that their immediate cash needs are such that this sound fiduciary course is impractical. There is, unfortunately, no easy solution to a problem which is admittedly perplexing. The firmness and resolution of both board and Needs Assessment and Planning Committee are essential to its solution, however. What has happened in recent years is a glaring illustration of what occurs when such a provident course is not followed.

Believing that federal and state assistance would be unending (and with it, too, the prosperity of the 1960's), agencies which had such funds all too often neglected to begin savings accounts. Had they done so throughout the years of their fiscal stability, the severe cutbacks would not have had the devastating impact they quite evidently have. Now, however, when the immediate needs are very real and very pressing, it will take all the more effort to inaugurate and sustain the savings process. Such savings accounts, however, are critical for the long term stability of organizations. Any board failing to recognize this fact is failing in its responsibility to the organization whose interests it is duty bound to protect.

The question of preserving and superintending this account goes beyond this book. However, organizations with endowment accounts of under $50,000 usually find it satisfactory to invest their money through the organization's Finance Committee, in such high yield instruments as money market funds, long term savings certificates or government bonds. Portfolios of over $50,000 generally need professional assistance. One encouraging development in this field is the recent emergence of professional investment firms catering to nonprofit organizations. A good development consultant can provide leads to these kinds of firms.

CHAPTER 2

THE DOCUMENTS

During your development effort, your organization will produce voluminous written communications. In addition to conveying information, these papers must speak for your organization as persuasively as any human advocate would.

If you have done your planning properly, the documents you must generate should follow quite easily from the planning process. All of the necessary documents present information about your agency, its staff, and its place in the community which is readily available to you. Each one listed below uses information which is likely to be part of another document. The key to creating these documents quickly and efficiently is keeping and using the files mentioned later in this chapter.

A word of warning: many organizations devote far too much time and energy to writing documents. Bear in mind that your main task is planning and pursuing your goals. Documents, created by means of peer production, are more of an essential offshoot of the larger planning process. Keep them in perspective. My rule of thumb is that no more than a day should be spent on any one document. And that you should keep them available on computer. (See Appendix II.)

The documents you will need are:

- a précis
- a proposal
- cover letters
- materials for a public relations package.

Gathering Information

The easiest way to begin producing development documents is to open the files or folders containing the information you will eventually need. Keep these files updated as new information develops. They will save time and enable you to produce future documents with relative ease.

The necessary files are:

- Your organization's successes. It is necessary to log information about your organization's successes in two distinct areas: 1) as an organization; that is, how it has been strengthened to insure long-term stability and continuity, and 2) programatically, that is in terms of program delivery. All information collected in this file should be as detailed and specific as possible and lend itself to being packed in short, fact-packed "bullets" of information showing that, from year to year, things have been steadily improving. Funding sources like to see documented progress, and this file allows you to demonstrate this kind of positive movement. In assembling this information, try to answer such questions as:

- What have we done over the last three years to make the organization stronger as an organization.
- How to we know, specifically, that we have been successful?
- Is life in our community better because of what we've been doing?
- How do we know?
- How many people have been served?
- What are the comparative service figures in each of our programs over the past three years?
- Have we received any outside recognition for what we're doing?

- Problem your organization addresses. This file has two purposes: it allows you to show as pungently as possible the dimensions of the problem you are in business to solve and also gives you the opportunity, within your own marketing area, to stand forth as the acknowledged expert in the field, thus underscoring the continuing need for your existence. You must collect information about the nature and extent of your problem in:

  - the nation
  - your state or region
  - your direct marketing area

Here are some of the kinds of materials you will wish to collect:

- legislative documents
- expert studies
- client comments
- periodical and newspaper features and reports
- all materials produced by your own agency

- History of your organization. Essential information about:

  - when your organization was started
  - by whom
  - for what reasons
  - agency developments and elaborations upon original idea

- Actual programs of the agency. Each program or project of the agency should be named in full. This file should include the following kinds of information:

  - objective of each program
  - people served in each program for the previous three years
  - staff involved in each program
  - cost

- "People File". Collect résumés, biographical information, copies of articles written, books published, citations, &c. about:

  - the executive director
  - the chairman of the board
  - all board members
  - members of advisory boards
  - expert staff members, especially program coordinators and project leaders

- Past Support. List the full name of each institutional contributor, the amount given, and dates of contributions within the last three years for:

  - public support: local, state and federal grants
  - corporations
  - foundations

Also keep on file the number of individual contributors over the past three years. Information from newspapers, magazines, &c about prominent organizations and individuals which have contributed to your agency should be clipped and maintained in this file.

- Audited financial statements. This file should contain audited financial reports for your organization for at least the last three years, preferably the last five.

- Past Proposals. Keep everything. This file should contain copies of all proposals you have previously developed and sent.

- Bibliography. Clip and save citations and information about current publications and information sources about your field of endeavor. This will be helpful in writing your problem statement and for citations you may wish to include in your proposal.

- Public relations materials. Include all brochures and other public relations devices including citations, fliers, advertisements for special events, tickets, &c.

To maintain these files, appoint a member of your staff. Also make sure that minutes are taken at meetings where information may be presented which can supplement these files; these minutes may simply be filed in the relevant folder.

The Précis

The précis is a versatile document that tells, briefly and inexpensively, who you are and what you are in business to do. It has the elements of a brochure and is the basic solicitation document you will use when approaching:

- individuals
- small foundations
- corporations

The précis is also useful for public relations purposes.

The précis lists all your fund raising goals for one year, and it is the only document you will need in many situations. The précis is all most people will want to read about your organization. Make it short, crisp, and convincing. Have it typeset on two sides of one–two pages of your stationery. The front page should list all the members of your board on it as well as the name of your organization.

The cost of producing the précis should be minimal. Typesetting is inexpensive, and you should be able to get a small printer to donate it. Do not turn to a large corporation for this donation, since many corporations which do offer such services as typesetting and printing do so in lieu of cash contributions. Getting a corporation that is capable of donating a substantial sum to donate a relatively minor one is a misuse of your contacts. Find a local business instead.

Plan to spend a day producing the précis, but plan to give the printer at least two weeks to print it. Allow more if you can. Remember that the précis must be ready by your kick-off date. Following the time line at the end of this book, you will see that, with a kick-off date of October 1, you must have the précis ready by the middle of September.

Note: as you will see, the précis must include a line which states that every member of the board has contributed financially to the realization of your fund raising effort.

Therefore in order to produce the précis on time, the board must have been fully solicited by early September. This is the responsibility of the chairman.

The précis contains a series of paragraphs or sections. Each one presents certain information necessary to presenting your agency to best advantage. You may wish to alter the sequence of these sections in order to highlight information; it is important, however, that none of them be deleted. For ease of presentation, I have suggested the number of words for each section. It is important to keep your sections to these approximate lengths, largely because people who read documents are always short on time and generally short on patience.

The sections necessary to a complete précis are:

- A history of your organization. This paragraph introduces your agency, tells when and how and why it was started, and what problem it addresses. It uses material from both your history and problem files. 100-200 words.
- Your successes. Stress the successes, both organizational and programmatic, of the last three years and select about three "bullets" on each. These must concern events, programs, or people which can be documented and are specific. It is also useful if they show comparative progress from year to year. You may wish to conclude each bullet with an appropriate testimonial comment from a newspaper editorial, legislative testimony where your work was cited approvingly, evaluation study, &c. 25 words per success.
- Ongoing programs. Describe each program of the agency in 25 words or less. Tell what each program does, how many clients it serves, and anything else which would enable the casual reader to have some understanding of what your agency does program by program. The objective here is to provide this reader with a bird's eye view of your work.
- Support in the last three years. Divide your past institutional and individual supporters into the following categories. Give the full legal name of each supporter.

    - Government. Federal and state agencies or grants by their full name. If your grant had no proper title, then create a descriptive title which encapsulates its purpose. Don't use jargon here.
    - Foundations
    - Corporations. If you have received cash or in-kind support and services cite the full name of the company but do not say what the gift involved. Never cite cash amounts.
    - Civic organizations. If you have received the assistance of civic groups, cite their complete names.

- Religious organizations. Give the complete names of all religious groups having assisted you.
- Individuals. Do not list the names of individual supporters. This can become cumbersome. Instead, give the overall number of supporters for your last fiscal year and the range of their gifts ("$5 to $10,000"). If the comparative figures are better this year than last, say so. It is acceptable to cite the number of contributors by gift range: "200 contributions under $10; 50 under $100; 25 under $1000" &c.
- Other donors. Don't forget to cite United Way support, if you have it. All institutional and individual donors should appear on this list in some fashion.

- Organizational leadership. In this section you will give brief (50 word) biographies of the chairman of the board and executive director. That of the chairman answers two questions: why is the chairman a person of consequence in the community and why has this individual been made chairman of our board. This section (in about 25 words) tells about the chairman's previous work within the organization, number of years on the board, previous committee chairmanships, organizational accomplishments, &c. The biography of the chairman always precedes that of the executive director since the chairman is the head of your organization.
- The biography of the executive director puts forth the chief experience of this individual, prior accomplishments which are relevant to the current position and both years at the present organization and leading achievements.
- Other biographies may be added as needed, including chiefly project coordinators for crucial fund raising objectives. They suggest (in 25 words) why this person is right for the job.

- Fund raising objectives for the next year. This section begins with the following kind of line: "In order for the fine work of our organization to continue, the board of directors has established the following fund raising objectives for (year). *Each* member of the board has contributed financially to the realization of these objectives."

This section sets forth the fund raising objectives for the next year. It is usually a good idea not to use the headings of "capital", "program", and "operating", but rather to create more interesting headlines for each fund-raising objective. If, however, it would assist you, arrange matters as follows:

Capital Fund Raising Objectives
1. item i
2. item ii

> subtotal for capital: dollar amount

Program Fund Raising Objectives
1. item i
2. item ii   subtotal for program: dollar amount

Operating Fund Raising Objectives

Here you may either simply list a dollar subtotal for operating objectives, or you may suggest 1-3 particular operating expenses you will cover with funds raised.

Note: Select items which are likely to have broader interest. The salary of your executive director won't arouse this interest; neither will your telephone bill or rent.

- Our critical role. This paragraph tells, in no more than 150 words, what difference your agency makes in the world. It is consciously designed to touch the nerves and heart of whoever reads it. It should evoke emotion and enthusiasm about the issues in which you are interested and which the organization exists to promote. This is the place for your larger vision of a better world. Clearly, this is a difficult section for most people to write, but it is extremely important. It suggests the theme for the entire fund raising effort and as such will be indispensable for inspiring your volunteer solicitors.

Three notes on the précis:

- At the conclusion of the précis, make sure you have given your name and address and telephone number. Also indicate that contributions are fully tax deductible.
- Do not print the précis on high-gloss stock. Offset print it and add the following line as a fitting conclusion: "This document has been produced as inexpensively as possible so that your contributions can go directly to work for the causes you support." If any part of the production expenses has been donated, say so.
- Think about both the tone and readability of the précis. Like all development documents you produce, this one should be written by someone on your staff who understands how good newspaper feature stories are written. It must be direct, upbeat, fast-moving, well written and capable of hooking a reader. If

it fails on any of these scores, the précis itself, no matter how worthy in substance, is a failure, too.

(See sample, page 185)

The Proposal

The proposal grows naturally out of 1) the planning process (which determines its substance), 2) the information files of your organization, and 3) the précis, which is ordinarily written first. As with the précis, your development proposals should always be written by your best writer and should be easy to read and accessible. It is best understood as a compelling feature story about a problem and your proposed solution and the reasons why you feel adequate to tackle it.

The proposal is required by most staffed foundations and many corporations. It differs from the précis in that it is a more comprehensive document about your agency, its work and its objectives. Large organizations will often create a proposal for each project which they hope to market to a funding source. Smaller organizations, however, are well advised to create one development proposal which includes capital, program and operating needs. It is usually unnecessary to create a series of proposals, and it is certainly time consuming and expensive to do so.

Elements of the Proposal: Synopsis

A synopsis of your proposal may or may not be necessary. If you choose to have it, it should include in about 150 words:

- a description of your program
- a summary of its need
- a one-figure total cost estimate
- amount you are requesting from the donor prospect
- an indication of how you will evaluate the program's success
- a description of how the program connects with your agency's overall goal
- a specific indication of who will benefit from the program

The writing of a synopsis follows the writing of the proposal itself. The synopsis appears on a separate piece of paper at the introduction of the document.

The synopsis may not, however, be necessary, if you tailor your cover letter to the donor prospect (as you ought). (See cover letters). If you do so, the essential information contained in the synopsis will be dealt with thoroughly.

The Problem Statement

The problem statement consists of a narrative of between 250-500 words. It deals with the national, state or regional, and local dimensions of your problem. This section is intended to show the non-specialist reader how grave the problem is at each level by marshalling the information you have either collected or, within your marketing area, generated yourself. This material must demonstrate the compelling nature of the problem you exist to deal with.

While you may draw upon any information from any source for those areas of the country not in your marketing area, within your marketing area you must cite only your own information, studies generated by your agency, the experts on your staff, &c. This indicates to the reader that you are in command of the local information, establishes your position as expert, and underscores the need for your continuing existence. Within your own marketing area, cite information produced by others only as a last resort and only because you have nothing comparable available.

The longest portion of the problem statement should concern the problem as you find it within your marketing area.

History of the Organization

This section naturally follows the one above. In that you directed the reader's attention to a problem. In this section, you are in effect saying: "This problem is why we exist." In 100-150 words tell:

- who started your organization
- when it was founded
- why it was founded

This section of your proposal is standard and changes little from year to year, although you may wish to update it as your organization develops from its original goal.

Successes of the Organization

This section you may duplicate from the précis.

Ongoing Programs of the Organization

As in the section above, you may duplicate this portion of your development proposal from the précis. It is important to remember that this section gives you a chance, in a few words, to acquaint the reasonably interested reader with the totality of your work.

Past Supporters of your Organization

As in the précis, this section should indicate your institutional and individual supporters over the past three years.

The People

This section, like the précis, contains the names and biographies of both chairman of the board and executive director. It also includes a 25-word biography for each program coordinator for whose program you are raising funds in this effort.

Fund Raising Objectives

This section will be elaborated beyond the précis. As in the précis, however, it begins with a statement indicating that the fund raising objectives have been set by the board and that every member of the board has contributed to realizing the funds needed. *This is mandatory and must appear in each development document.*

As in the précis, this section begins by setting forth the various fund raising objectives for the year, item by item. It is not strictly necessary that they be listed under "capital," "program," and "operating,", but it is necessary that each have an appropriate, descriptive heading. As in the précis, this section finishes by giving the grand total sought.

What is different in a development proposal, however, is that following the listing, each item is given a 50-75 word defense. The purpose of this defense is to explain the pressing reasons for this item, anything which would, in a few well-chosen words, convince a reader that you have selected your fund raising objectives wisely and with careful forethought. Clearly, here is where the work of the Needs Assessment and Development Planning Committee is so important, since the reasons which are cited here are those probably already advanced by that body.

Critical Role

If this document is advancing only one project, then this paragraph gives the reasons why your agency is the best and most sensible one to undertake the assignment and what results may be anticipated. If this is a general document dealing with capital, program, and operating objectives, you can use the identical paragraph from the précis.

Line Item Budget

A line item budget must follow every development proposal. It should fit easily onto one or possibly two pages. Items appearing in the budget should follow the order of items listed in the "Fund raising objectives" section of the proposal. Capital items will generally come first, then program items, and finally operating needs. Each item is ordinarily divided into "Personnel" and "Non-Personnel" sections. "Personnel" expenditures include full and part-time staff, consultants and subcontractors. All other expenditures appear under the "Non-Personnel" heading.

In drafting your budget it is important that all your assumptions be made clear to the reader. Do not leave him to guess at your possible meaning. It is your responsibility to show the reader how you arrived at each budgetary item. For instance, instead of writing that you need to raise $21,500 for your executive director, write: "12 months x $1,500 per month + 17.5% fringe benefits = $21,500." Each non-personnel item should be made similarly clear.

When you present your program needs, make sure to build in all operating costs. Each program you undertake involves a certain percentage of your time, the time of key staff people, agency operating expenses, &c and these expenses must appear as part of each project. Costs you should consider include:

- staff
- space costs
- equipment
- travel
- utilities
- heat
- telephone
- public relations and promotion

If it is necessary to the clarity of your proposal to add a section clearly outlining your assumptions, do so. Either attach this page to your budget or indicate that it is available upon request.

Appendices

Funding sources like to know that other materials are available to them if they need them. This section should be headed so: "The following documents are available upon request":

- Your 501 (c) (3) tax-exempt letter from the Internal Revenue Service

- a complete list of your board of directors with an indication of who they are. For example, "Dr. Jeffrey L. Lant, president, Jeffrey Lant Associates, Inc., Cambridge, MA." If a board member previously held a prestigious position, cite it, as with: The Hon. Edward Brooke, former U.S. Senator.
- Current operating budget
- Audited financial statements, last three years
- Five Year Plan
- public relations materials, including your agency brochure and testimonials rendered to the organization
- précis

There is usually no need to send any of these materials in advance; if you feel the need to do so, send the first two items: IRS tax-exempt letter and list of the board of directors. These are the least expensive to reproduce. It is important that you not be seen as sending unnecessary documents and wasting agency money. It is, however, equally important that potential funding sources know that valuable materials are available should they want them.

Notes on Development Documents

- Too much time is spent writing documents. The key to producing successful documents is the planning process outlined in Chapter 1. The actual writing can be kept to a minimum. A new document should take, at most, a day or two to produce; updates can be done in two or three **hours.** Remember: the system as outlined in this book allows you to retain large portions of any document and put them to use in later documents.

- Documents are like glasses of water in a restaurant. They are expected, but they have no nutritional value. It is unfortunately true that a good, well-written document usually has limited impact; it is expected by potential funding sources. A poorly conceived document, however, definitely works against you. In the obstacle course of fund raising, where any reason is sufficient to reject you, you make it easy when you give the potential donor a badly-written and poorly-produced document.

- Documents should not be too long. In the private sector, documents must be kept short — often as short as two back-to-back pages (that is, about 1000 words). The documents outlined in this book are longer than 1000 words because I'm making the assumption your potential funding sources know nothing about you. Nonetheless they enable you to present all the necessary information in a format which is still very concise. If you find you need a shorter proposal, of course, you can either submit a synopsis or use the précis, which should be about 1000 words.

- Readability is important. If your documents do not read well, if they are boring, disjointed, or otherwise unintelligible, your agency will come across with a whiff of incompetence which will be difficult to eradicate. If no one in your agency writes sufficiently well (all too common nowadays), retain an external consultant to produce top-flight documents for you. It is money well spent.

- Proposals are not cast in cement. Implicit in every proposal is a potential donor's counter-proposal, and you should anticipate that it may be forthcoming. Many donors after all wish to do more than passively distribute funds. They want to have a hand in shaping a project or agency. Understand, then, that your proposal is not necessarily the last word. It may indeed only be the opening move. This does not mean, however, that you should attempt to tack with every wind from the funding source. Be firm on major points and do not give rise to the suspicion that you are changing the purpose of the organization merely to get money. This tactic doesn't work, not least because funding sources despise it.

(See sample, page 191)

The Cover Letters

In the past, much was written about the need to tailor every proposal for each funding source. This is nonsense. To attempt to re-write your proposal each time you need to send it leads to an excessive amount of time and energy being spent on what should be a secondary activity. This is not to say, however, that from time to time a tailored proposal is not necessary. Neither is it to suggest that you should not make an effort to convince the funding source that you have thought seriously about why you are submitting your proposal to them. This convincing should take place in the cover letter which can and should be tailored to each specific funding source.

A cover letter from the executive director or chairman of the board must accompany each proposal formally submitted to a funding source. It should adhere to the following format:

- Introduction. Remind the funding source of any past dealings you may have had, including past support, recent meetings and relevant contacts. This introduction is critical. Do not force the funding source to look back through its own files. Present a synopsis of your dealings in the opening paragraph.
- If you have had no prior dealings, suggest in the opening paragraph why you are approaching this particular funding source. Perhaps you have been referred by someone; perhaps the funding source guidelines have suggested this

course of action. Whatever the reason, state it clearly and in the opening paragraph. Remember: if this paragraph seems weak and unclear, your reader may not bother to read the rest, so take the time to make this opening gambit a good one.

- Second paragraph. In this section, describe in concise detail the project for which you are approaching the funding source and the leading reasons for it. Even if your development document suggests that you have several fund raising objectives for the year, don't leave the choice of funding object to the donor prospect. It is your responsibility to say which of your objectives is the most pressing or which might be the most pertinent, in your opinion, to this particular funding source. This paragraph should be no more than 100-150 words long.

- Third paragraph. First, consider specifying the amount of money you seek from this funding source. Remember: at this point this amount is exploratory. That does not mean, however, that you should ask for an unrealistically high figure. What it does mean is that any actual gift will be subject to several other factors besides your own desire. Second, specify how you will follow-up this letter. It is always better to be specific about your follow-up than to be general; note the day or time you will be calling in your date book and make sure you follow through. Follow through may include a telephone conversation, a meeting in the prospect's office with you and a board member, or the request for an on-site visit. It is up to you to schedule any or all of these possibilities.

Copies of all cover letters should be kept on file, both for the use of your successors (and in future planning) and for keeping track of follow-up plans. As your fund raising effort gets geared up, the Coordinating Committee will need to peruse these letters and be aware of such approaches. (See Sample, page 202)

Public Relations Materials

This is not a book on public relations for nonprofit organizations, but since public relations has a key role to play in fund raising an introduction of the subject seems pertinent. Those desiring detailed on the subject of exploiting the media for the betterment of your agency are referred to my book **THE UNABASHED SELF-PROMOTER'S GUIDE: WHAT EVERY MAN, WOMAN, CHILD AND ORGANIZATION IN AMERICA NEEDS TO KNOW ABOUT GETTING AHEAD BY EXPLOITING THE MEDIA.** This volume is available from JLA Publications. Like many other useful organizational development materials, it can be ordered through my Sure-Fire Business Success Catalog, which you'll find at the conclusion of this book.

A public relations plan will assist your fund raising effort by bringing you to the attention of your community, projecting the image of a strong organization performing a useful (perhaps unique) service with effective administration and professional staff. People want to be associated with this kind of effort.

Crafting this image begins with the creation of a basic public relations department within the organization. This department need not (at first) be superintended by a full-time staff member; a part-time employee or external consultant is usually quite sufficient to get things started. Basic public relations materials include:

- An agency brochure. This brochure answers the run of typical questions about the organization. For many organizations, the précis will suffice, particularly if a membership insert is designed. Usually there is insufficient space on the précis itself to handle membership information.

- Two feature stories. Every nonprofit organization in America has both news and feature potential. It is the job of the agency to suggest story possibilities and to help professional journalists by drafting two or more articles. Among the story possibilities are:

  - profile of the executive director and senior staff
  - descriptions of innovative projects
  - the effect of agency work on the community
  - articles on clients and how their lives have been improved by your work

- Audio Visual Aids. It is a good idea for an agency to have a 15-minute audio visual or slide and tape presentation. This can be written into your fund raising budget as a justifiable development expense. It can be used for presentations to funding sources or as a public relations tool.

- Photographs. You should develop a "morgue" of agency photographs, including key personnel, which can be used to accompany your stories.

My rule of thumb is that your organization should get media exposure at least once every two months. This is the minimum acceptable. To do so, you must look for media possibilities and both create and exploit openings. Here are some possibilities:

- Issue regular press releases when you develop a new program, appoint new staff or members of the board of directors. Issue them whenever you have successfully completed a project. You need to be perceived as a strong, effective agency making the community a better place to live.

- If you are a one-issue organization, issue a press release any time your issue is featured in the news. "Piggy back" on national, state or regional or local coverage of your issue. Get quoted as a knowledgeable source on this subject. Any time your issue appears in any publication, send information about your work to the writer of the article. Soon you will be known as the place to go for authoritative quotes and material on this subject.

- Encourage local media to interview clients and staff members. Never forget the human interest possibilities of your work.

- If your organization or a representative is mentioned in any article, get copies offset printed on your stationery. These are called "leave behinds" and may be sent from time to time to potential donors with a cover note, past donors, or used to attract future press attention. Remember this rule: the more media attention you get, the more you are likely to get. People want to read what they've already read; they want to hear what they've already heard.

- If you are going to appear on a local media show, notify both past and present donors. They may not take the trouble to tune in, but they will know that you are worthy of media attention.

- Frequently suggest stories about your organization to the relevant editors of newspapers and magazines. Seek out newsletter coverage and coverage in professional publications.

Here are some possibilities for consideration as you think about which stories to promote:

- All anniversaries. Consider founding dates, golden jubilees, annual presentations of gifts, awards or acclaim to a special employee. This category includes anything that celebrates the history of your agency and its activities.

- Business news. Release information about your annual reports, the growth and stability of your agency, fund raising drives (both when begun and successfully completed). Consider also new organizational techniques you have introduced which might make an interesting story.

- Distinctive agency staff activities. People who publish books and important articles should be noted. Awards, research projects and findings can all be highlighted. Steps taken by board and staff members to enhance the professionalism of the agency may also be news.

- Improved, altered or unusual products. When you do something new, chances are it can be written up as an interesting news or feature story. Don't miss the regional or national angle on your work.

- Interviews with organizational leadership. It is important that your executive director, board chairman and trustees be built up as community leaders. As such they need to be regularly interviewed about trends in the agency, the work of the organization, and their own distinctive contributions.

Most articles about nonprofit organizations are positive; generally, the media will be of the utmost assistance and lend themselves to promoting you and your organization. Not always, however. If your agency is about to receive poor publicity, do at least two things:

- Inform major donors in advance, so that they do not learn about bad news from the newspaper. Particularly inform a donor if the bad news involves a project they may have funded. Do not wait for them to call you.

- Always ask for equal time. The news media like to foment controversy; it sells papers. The wrong thing to do, therefore, when a bad piece of news appears is run for cover. The best thing is for the chairman of the board to convene an emergency meeting of the directors and discuss whether it is better to ignore what has happened or ask for equal media time to rebut the charges. The determination in each case depends on the significance of the original charge and the number of people who may have been made aware of it as well as your ability to respond quickly, accurately.

CHAPTER 3

THE PEOPLE

This chapter deals with most of the essential people your organization must have involved in the fund raising process. The chapter on the Coordinating Committee (Chapter 5) has additional information.

The Chairman of the Board

The chairman of the board is the head of the organization. He is the chosen representative of the board which is the body wherein legal power for the organization resides. Both board members and the executive director are responsible to him.

The chairman during his tenure must make the organization his primary nonprofit commitment. This is because there is a significant time commitment involved. The chairman, after all, is pivotal in creating an effective board, motivating its members, and insuring that they meet their commitment. He is also responsible for board vacancies and for finding an equally-committed successor to himself. This position is no sinecure.

As head of the organization, here are some of the things the chairman is responsible for in the fund raising effort:

- overseeing the planning process
- soliciting board members for contributions
- appointing members of the Coordinating Committee and attending its meetings
- conducting the Facilitation Session(s)
- making solicitation visits to major donors, corporations, and foundations
- selecting chairmen for all fund raising committees

The chairman of the board and the executive director must maintain a close working relationship. Any problems between them must be resolved before an organization undertakes a public fund raising effort. This is also true of the chairman's relationship to board members and with non-board members of fund raising committees.

The chairman's first responsibility is to motivate his board members and insure that they both understand the need for a fund raising effort and the mechanics involved. Board members are not always likely to be receptive to the idea of fund raising, particularly when they understand what their involvement might be. Here are some common complaints:

- We've never done this before. We'll fail.
- When I was elected to the board, I was never told I'd have fund raising responsibilities. I won't help.
- Our organization isn't well enough known to conduct a fund raising effort.
- I can't ask my friends for money.
- The executive director is too busy to do fund raising.
- Why don't we hire an outside professional to oversee the fund raising. Let's contract out the responsibility.

Here are some responses:

- We'll fail. In this instance the chairman must point out that the work done by the Needs Assessment and Development Planning Committee and the overall fund raising techniques advanced in this book will enhance the chances for success and work against failure if each member of the board does his part. It is the chairman's responsibility to point out in no uncertain terms that successful fund raising is a team effort and that no member is immune.

- I was never told about fund raising responsibilities. This is a common response to any introductory discussion of fund raising. The chairman must point out that fund raising is a responsibility of each board member, including a personal donation each year. Clearly it is easier if new board members are apprised of this responsibility when they are elected. If they weren't, however, it is the chairman's responsibility to make it clear that it is the job of the board to insure the general fiscal health of the agency and that this will, as a matter of course, involve fund raising. The more sophisticated a board member is, the less likely he is to cavil about this point.

- We aren't well enough known. It is the chairman's responsibility to inform board members of how public relations will play a part in the fund raising effort. It may be that the chairman will wish to appoint a specific public relations committee of the board so that this problem can be dealt with. If such a committee is appointed, it should report monthly to the full board.

- I can't ask my friends for money. It is the chairman's responsibility both at the beginning of any fund raising effort and periodically through it to help train board members about the techniques of successful solicitation. The chairman should point out at this time that such training will take place and should also stress, again, that soliciting is both a humane and necessary act, that the board members are advocates for causes and as such are not asking for themselves. Moreover, the chairman may say that donor prospects are usually less difficult about visits than solicitors. This theme can be elaborated at the Volunteer Solicitor Meeting.

- The executive director is too busy. If this is true, some of his tasks will have to be delegated. The chairman can appoint a committee of the board to evaluate the executive director's activities and see which of them can be delegated. The executive director must participate in the fund raising effort, and a time analysis may be of assistance in determining which other activities can be delegated.

- Why don't we hire an outside professional to raise funds for us? The chairman must point out that fund raising cannot be delegated to any outside source. Outside solicitors will never have the legitimacy and authority of board members and other agency volunteers and will, in fact, often be suspect. External development counsel may be retained to assist with both strategy and tactics, but the actual act of solicitation remains a board and volunteer responsibility.

It is not a good idea to proceed with any fund raising effort until all the legitimate concerns of board members have been dealt with. Do not, however, postpone or cancel fund raising because of unnecessary squeamishness on the part of certain recalcitrant board members. Instead attempt to win them over by:

- Answering their reasonable concerns. Consult them about the planning process. Keep them informed. Calm their fears.

- Assuring them that they will not be overburdened. Each member should have assigned tasks but the chairman needs to insure that no member is given too much at any one time. Should directors need staff assistance with the writing of their letters, gathering information, visits and follow up, it is the joint responsibility of the board chairman and executive director to provide it.

- If reason is not working, suggest resignation. It is better to deal with this problem at the start than have it loom up later to frustrate your development effort. There are, unfortunately, people now serving on boards who are there solely for their own aggrandizement. They do not understand what the job of a director is and what he may justly be called upon to do and contribute. If a gentle educational effort fails with such an individual, suggest resignation.

If the Problem Is the Chairman

What if the chairman himself is the individual who cannot or will not make the intense commitment to the organization he should? This problem must be dealt with as forthrightly as possible.

To begin with, in my experience weak chairmen often know they constitute obstacles to the effective development of an organization. They are often longing to resign. If this is your case, it will not prove difficult to remove the chairman. I shall discuss a little later what to do to find a suitable replacement.

If the chairman is not willing to step down, the problem intensifies. If there are no terms for chairmen and board members, introducing them will provide one solution to the problem. If terms will not solve the problem, there are at least two possible solutions:

1. A senior member of the board can be unofficially delegated by his colleagues to sound out the chairman about retirement. Under no circumstances should the executive director be the one to make this visit.

2. An external consultant can be brought in at the suggestion of the board. His report will undoubtedly suggest the tension and lack of cohesion among board members and can lead to suggestions for leadership change. In effect his report will say, "Unless there is a significant change in leadership, this organization will be rendered ineffective."

Let there be no mistake, however, that removing a recalcitrant, obstructive chairman is difficult and often leads to bad feelings. It is essential, however, if the organization is to progress.

Once the decision has been made to remove an obstructive chairman, it is important that the public portion of the removal be handled as diplomatically as possible. One of the best ways of insuring good will and a minimum of backbiting is to give the retiring chairman a public luncheon, dinner or some such event at which appropriate speeches can be delivered, recognition rendered and media attention assured. It is hard for someone who has been the recipient of such attention to gain credibility when and if he feels compelled to talk against his former colleagues.

Finding a Replacement

It is seldom a wise idea to go outside the organization for a chairman. Chairmen are usually recruited from within the ranks of the board, often through a selection process outlined in the by-laws of the organization and often after serving in a series of preliminary board offices.

If a competent chairman is proving difficult to find, however, ask either a leading board member, past member or chairman to assume the job for one year. During this time a sustained search can be made for a chairman willing to serve a full 2-3 year term.

The Executive Director

Even though the chairman of the board is the actual head of the organization, the executive director is the person most often associated with its work. As the organization's recognized "star" representative, the executive director must be actively involved in all aspects of the development effort right from the start.

As outlined in Chapter 1, the executive director serves as internal consultant to the planning process. After this process has been completed, the executive director oversees the production of all development documents. Thereafter the executive director becomes an active member of the Coordinating Committee with major responsibilities for prospect identification and gift solicitation.

Clearly the executive director, like the chairman, must be fully committed to the success of the fund raising effort. Any doubt, confusion or hesitation will immediately be communicated to the board and thence to the public. This must be avoided at all costs.

The first question executive directors have about the development process is: How much time will it take?

Development is a slow-moving, time-consuming process. A good rule of thumb is that an executive director can expect to spend 40% of his time on fund raising and related tasks, that is two days out of five. During this time the following tasks must be accomplished:

- Planning for future fund raising objectives
- Data collection bearing on planning and production of future development documents
- Drafting development documents
- Drafting other public relations documents such as brochures, &c.
- Identification of institutional and individual donor prospects
- Identification of leads to these prospects
- Crafting individual approaches to prospects
- Undertaking solicitation meetings

- Follow-up to solicitation meetings
- Implementing training sessions for agency fund raising volunteers
- Participation in Coordinating Committee and other agency fund raising committees

Clearly, fund raising for the executive director is a major task.

An executive director perusing this list for the first time might rightly be concerned about how such a variety of tasks can be successfully accomplished. In large measure, they can be by involving other, appropriate individuals in their completion, individuals ranging from the chairman of the board, to other directors and agency staff and volunteers. Fund raising is not a job which the executive director can do alone. He needs the sustained assistance of many other individuals who are also firmly committed to the long-term success of the organization.

An executive director failing to realize this situation will either: 1) become resentful about the added burdens he has been forced to assume, 2) neglect necessary agency work, 3) burn-out and resign, or 4) quarrel with a board he feels is neglecting its own fund raising responsibilities. None of these situations can be productive for the organization.

To avoid this kind of debilitating situation, an executive director should work with both the chairman of the board and the Needs Assessment and Planning Committee and ultimately the Coordinating Committee to insure that the fund raising plan which is adopted by the agency insures a rightful role for many individuals and a measured, appropriate role for the executive director.

If an executive director upon consideration feels that he is being asked to do more than his share or is being forced to undertake functions which are really the responsibility of the board chairman and the other directors, he is advised to recommend to the board retaining a development consultant. Such a consultant, working with both board and executive director, will produce a plan which recommends alloting to each a more balanced role.

By the same token, if the board feels the executive director is shirking fund raising responsibilities, it may retain an external consultant to evaluate the performance of the executive director and suggest how to implement a fund raising plan. If the executive director resists the implementation of a reasonable fund raising plan, the board will have to consider asking him to resign.

The Board of Directors

Members of the country's thousands of nonprofit boards of directors constitute the heart of our private philanthropy. Unfortunately there are many misconceptions about the role and function of these directors. In part this is because of recent historical developments.

Traditionally, members of nonprofit boards have been responsible for guaranteeing the fiscal integrity and long-term financial stability of their organizations. This responsibility necessarily involved fund raising. In the 1960's and 1970's, however, many new organizations sprang up. Sometimes these organizations, to qualify for state and federal funds, were mandated to place certain people on their boards who had hitherto not been part of the nation's "board culture." Often these were users of the particular service the agency provided. Because money to sustain the work of the agency came from public sources, these boards thought their work was limited to insuring that the funds which had been provided were well spent and that quality service was provided. Little thought was given to what would happen if these funds were stopped and to how the long-term financial security of the organization would be brought about. The minute public funds ceased to be so readily available, the essentially limited and vulnerable nature of this conception of a board become patently obvious. Thus boards must return to a more traditional pattern of behavior. Rather than simply overseeing the resources which are otherwise provided, all board members must realize that their job is both to raise and superintend resources.

In this regard, it bears repeating that **each** member of the board must give a direct financial contribution to the organization **each** year. Members who do not do so are delinquent. Chairmen who do not solicit members are failing in their responsibility. Consultants who do not advise such contributions and solicitations are behaving unprofessionally. Moreover, board members must participate directly in the solicitation of other gifts.

These direct, unequivocal statements may come as something of a shock to those individuals who (rather blithely) feel that their presence at board meetings and well-meant advice are sufficient to warrant their continuing membership. They aren't. Boards are not rest homes for the **illuminati.** No one is so eminent that he cannot fulfill the proper function of a board member, which is to work directly and to donate personally to sustain the work of the organization.

Crafting a Board

Clearly the importance of fund raising to nonprofit organizations and the role the board necessarily plays in fund raising means that considerable attention must be paid to strengthening the board. In this connection each board should strive to have (at least most of) the following categories represented:

- A local foundation
- The largest corporate employer in your marketing area
- A small businessman, preferably a printer
- A banker, possibly a trust officer
- A lawyer
- An accountant
- A media representative or public relations expert
- A civic group leader
- A religious leader
- A distinguished representative from your service area
- Leaders from local professional groups such as doctors, dentists, realtors, architects, &c
- The chairman of the organization's "Advisory" committee, **ex officio**
- Leader of a "Friends" group or Auxiliary, **ex officio**
- The executive director, **ex officio**

Here's why you want these people:

- Representative of a local foundation. The basic principal of a well-crafted board is that representatives from each area will know or can get access to their peers, in this case, representatives of other foundations. You want to have either a foundation donor, trustee or professional staff person on your board. This membership is not a conflict of interest, although individual donors, trustees, or staff may so regard it. Ordinarily a donation from the foundation in question precedes membership on your board by one of its representatives, though this is not always the case. It is important to remember that personnel associated with foundations can be your best advocates to other foundations.

- Representative of the largest corporate employer in your marketing area. Corporations are likely to assume an increasingly prominent role in American philanthropy. They have recently overtaken the number of dollars given by America's foundations, and it is unlikely this trend will be reversed. It is therefore of the utmost importance that there be corporate representation on your board. You need **at least** one representative of the largest corporate employer in your marketing area. It is perfectly permissible to add other major corporate representatives. You will certainly wish to do so in areas where there are several large corporate employers.

- A small businessman: Most organizations can benefit from small business representation, particularly if they wish to solicit contributions from the local business community. In this regard, a printer is usually a helpful representative since he can offer his product at reduced rate or without charge.

- A banker. A banker has a key role to play both in the determination of fund raising priorities and in gathering leads to the trusts and foundations administered by banks.

- A lawyer. No organization should be without a legal representative on the board. This lawyer usually handles the agency's legal work either **pro bono** or for a fee approved by his board colleagues. Note: It is not a conflict of interest for a board lawyer to be paid for the work he performs for the organization so long as the board has been fully apprised of developments.

- An accountant. Unlike a lawyer, an accountant may not undertake an agency's audit when he himself is a member of the board. Nor is it usually a good idea to have a member of his firm do so, thus suggesting possible conflict of interest charges. An accountant needs to be a part of your board, however, because of his business planning knowledge. He may also be in a position to suggest significant facts about your organization to his clients who need to donate money for tax purposes.

- A media representative or public relations expert. As above, the telephone calls of media representatives and public relations personnel get returned by their colleagues, where those made by a chairman of the board or executive director may not be. This individual usually heads the public relations committee of the board and is responsible for insuring a steady stream of good publicity about the organization.

- A civic group leader. This individual should be recognized for past and present leadership in the local civic community. He or she may be drawn from: the Kiwanis, Rotarians, Soroptimists, Junior League, Masons, &c or any of the thousand other civic associations which distinguish American life. If your organization plans to solicit contributions from the civic community, it is a very good idea to have this individual on the board.

- A religious leader. As above, soliciting from churches and other religious organizations is made easier by heading the fund raising committee with an eminent lay or clerical figure from your community.

- Distinguished representative from your service area. Whatever business your agency is in, whether children's services or environmental affairs, it has its own cadre of experts. One of these should be elected to the board. He can be of the utmost usefulness both in the planning process and in lending credence to the fund raising objectives certified by the board.

- Leaders from local professional groups. These individuals put your organization in touch with important community opinion and can lend weight and significance to your board.

- Chairman of the organization's "Advisory" Committee. The best way to link a committee of professional advisors and experts with the work of the full board is to place the chairman of the Advisory Committee on the board **ex officio** during his term of office.

- Leader of the "Friends" group or Auxiliary. As above, it is important that this group, which has a distinct fund raising function, be represented on the policy group which oversees the process which allocates funds.

- Executive Director, **ex officio.** The executive director can be a member of the board, but only **ex officio.** It is a conflict of interest for the director to serve in his own right as a board member. That course suggests that if he is removed as executive director, he can continue to sit as a full director. "I want to be in that position," one executive director told me, "so that I can harass my successor!" Exactly. And that is why having the executive director in his own person as a board member is a direct conflict of interest. It is, however, perfectly acceptable for the board to decide that it does not wish the executive director to be a member even **ex officio.** In this case the executive director can advise the board as an internal consultant.

The Nominating Process

It goes without saying that to craft a board of 15-20 members drawn from these categories takes a good deal of time. That is why the work of the Nominating Committee is of the utmost significance, both to the organization overall and to its fund raising efforts.

Selection of the chairman of the Nominating Committee is the prerogative of the board chairman. Serving with the Nominating Committee chairman are two or three other board members, not staff, not outsider volunteers.

It is the job of the Nominating Committee to meet at least 10 months of the year, once each month, and to canvass names as possible board members. Elections for the board are usually held once a year at which time an approved slate is put forward by the Nominating Committee. Between elections, the Committee explores new possibilities and attempts to get these individuals involved in the work of the organization and so allow other directors the opportunity of meeting them and seeing whether they would in fact be a real addition to the board. No one should be elected to the board who has not undergone some intense scrutiny and no one should ever be elected merely to fill a slot or because his name would look good on the organization's letterhead.

The Nominating Committee will get its names from several sources:

- Questionnaires completed at the Facilitating Session
- Referrals from past and present board members
- Individuals known to members of the Committee itself
- Interviews with prominent directors of other, perhaps analogous organizations
- Information clipped from newspapers, periodicals, &c which indicate the compatible interests of individuals as yet unknown to Committee members
- Consistent donors to the organization, both institutional and individual

It is perfectly acceptable, as part of the cultivation and scrutinizing process, to involve potential board members in the fund raising effort either as chairmen of committees set up by the Coordinating Committee or as committee members. In fact, involving potential board members in the fund raising activities makes eminent good sense, since it will continue to be part of their job once fully elected to the board.

At each meeting of the full board, the Nominating Committee should be asked by the board chairman for a full report on the individuals under consideration, what is being done to meet them and involve them in the agency's activities, and how the formation of next year's slate of directors is shaping up. All too often, these questions are left for a month or two before the annual meeting at which time it is too late to locate suitable new candidates, thus allowing board members who may be past their prime to fill another term.

The Advisory Committee

Much rubbish has been written recently about advisory committees and their role in an organization. This is unfortunate, as an advisory committee has a very real role to play within an organization, though not the one which is usually suggested for it.

The proper purpose of an Advisory Committee is to advise the executive director and Needs Assessment and Development Planning Committee about developments and trends in the field in which the agency is working. Thus, a child welfare agency would be well advised to have an Advisory Committee composed of child psychologists, state welfare workers, social work professors, &c., all people, in short, who should be aware of the trends in social work. All too often, however, these people, whose role as advisors is quite proper, are wrongly elected in large numbers to a board of directors, where they take spaces which would better go to the representatives of the categories mentioned above.

Since this unhappy situation all too often occurs, organizations then seek to construct an Advisory Committee which looks like my suggested board of directors. This doesn't work.

An Advisory Committee has functions which are purely informal and hortatory. It may urge but it cannot command, unlike a board which has full legal powers. This function is entirely appropriate when suggesting to an agency and its board which direction it should take in relation to critical program issues. It does not work as well when undertaking to provide the critical assistance which ought to be present on the board.

This is because the chairman of an Advisory Committee lacks the sticks and carrots which are necessary to insure that assigned tasks are carried out, not to mention the moral suasion which comes as the trustee of a public organization. Advisors cannot be made to work, directors can.

Many organizations have recently attempted to establish advisory committees for fund raising purposes. These rarely work. Individuals are pressed into duty on these committees with illusory promises about not having to attend meetings and only to lend their names. This has little to do with fund raising. However, if members did take their duties seriously the result would be worse: it is inconceivable that responsible committee members would help raise money only to turn it over to a board that oversees its distribution but allows the Advisory Committee no direct role in its disbursement.

Organizations which wish to establish advisory committees should therefore do so only if such committees will be composed of eminent representatives from the agency's service area. The chairman of this group can be tied into the work of the full board by serving as an **ex officio** board member during his tenure.

The Development Consultant

The development consultant (sometimes called "professional fund raising counsel") can play a significant role in your fund raising effort. But not every organization either needs counsel or should retain it. Before doing so you need to ask yourself three questions:

- Will the consultant provide immediate services that your organization cannot provide for itself?

- Are the services of the consultant more professional than those you can provide for yourself?

- Will using the consultant ultimately cost less than if you were to do it yourself?

Unless you can justify hiring a consultant on all three points, do not retain one.

Once you have decided to hire a consultant, begin by checking his references. Any good consultant will be happy to provide you with parallel references — references, that is, to organizations like yours. If you are a human services organization, it does not do you much good to talk to the executive director of a community-based arts organization. There are significant differences. Ask, instead, for the name of your counterpart in a similar organization. When calling to check this reference, try to get detailed, specific answers to the questions that you and your board members have. If you are having trouble getting them, beware.

In interviewing a consultant, get specific answers to the following questions:

- Do you work with us to set our development priorities?
- Do you draft and edit development documents?
- Do you hold training sessions with the board of directors, assisting them to understand their role in the development effort, facilitating leads to prospective individual and institutional donors, and helping train them as solicitors?
- How often will we be meeting with you?
- Will you handle our account? Or will it be someone else in your operation?
- Will you work with our organization whether or not the board contributes towards the fund raising effort?
- Do you provide us with leads to institutional fund raising sources?
- Will you assist us in crafting the approach to such funding sources?
- Will you make your own fund raising contacts available to us?

Here is what you should be hearing in response:

- Do you work with us to set development priorities? It is crucial that your consultant help you set your development objectives and advise you on whether the sums you are seeking are about right, too high, or, very rarely, too low. He should also help you divide your overall goal into capital, program and operating objectives.

- Do you draft and edit development documents? At the very least, your consultant should provide you with pattern documents and work with you as an editor to craft your documents. Do not expect your consultant, however, to locate the information for the various sections of your documents. Development consultants are not best utilized as document research consultants; they are too expensive to use for this service. Full-service consultants should be well equipped to draft your précis, development proposals, cover letters and ancillary public relations materials.

- Do you hold training sessions with the board of directors? Every good consultant is an educator. He recognizes that his time with your organization, no matter how long in actual days, is limited and that he has failed to perform adequately if you do not know enough about his methods to carry them on by yourself. Thus, it is absolutely necessary that the consultant hold a series of meetings with the board: 1) to set forth the need for their own financial and other involvement in the fund raising effort; 2) to assist in getting leads to prospective funding sources ("the Facilitating Session"); 3) to answer questions from board members on suitable approaches to individuals and institutional funding sources; and 4) to help train both board members and other agency volunteers in the techniques of successful solicitation.

- How often will we be meeting with you? It is not necessary that you see your consultant each day, although you may want to know whether you can freely telephone him as questions arise. I call this kind of telephone access the "telephone privilege." Many consultants make it available to their full-service clients, but not to everyone. It is, however, important that you schedule regular meetings with your consultant. One good rule of thumb is between one and two hours per week. In a capital campaign longer sessions will probably be necessary. Each of these sessions should have a clear agenda. At their conclusion the consultant should summarize what the meeting has accomplished and the tasks which need to be successfully completed before the next meeting. Both should be put into the minutes. A good consultant will insist upon regular meetings as important to realizing the objectives of the fund raising effort.

- Will you handle your account? Or will it be someone else in your operation? Often the head of the consultant firm functions more as marketing director than service provider. As a marketing impressario, he is no doubt adept at impressing you! If he is not going to be your account representative, however, make sure that you know in advance who will be handling your organization and get the opportunity before you sign any contract to ask this individual the questions to which you must have satisfactory answers before going on.

- Will you work with our organization whether or not the board contributes towards the fund raising effort? Unfortunately, there are many consultants who are willing to take an account and gamble that they can raise money with or without the cooperation of the board. Beware of these consultants. The ones who demand the full financial participation of the board realize that this kind of commitment is essential to the success of any fund raising effort. Without it, it will be difficult for your campaign to succeed, and any honest consultant will say so.

- Do you provide us with leads to institutional fund raising sources? Good consultants peruse the literature to keep alert to the changing priorities of institutional funding sources. They are thus in a position to inform you about foundation and corporate leads which may be pertinent for you. If you are not getting such leads from your consultant, you are not getting your money's worth.

- Will you assist us in crafting the approach to such fund raising sources? If you are not getting this kind of assistance, why did you bother to retain your consultant in the first place?

- Will you make your own fund raising contacts available to us? In select instances, it may be possible for the consultant himself to provide you with a link to an institutional funding source or even to an individual. Don't count on getting your connection this way, however. Consultants are hired guns and are, as such, suspect to these funding sources. Going in under their auspices may, therefore, not be in your best interest. Rely on the tact and advice of your consultant, however; he will advise you when and under what circumstances he can aid you in any particular case. As a matter of policy, though, beware of consultants who promise to make their contacts entirely available to you.

Perhaps because these questions are not always asked in the beginning of a client-consultant relationship, things often go seriously wrong. As a result, the client may condemn the consultant for one or more of the following reasons:

- Once the consultant signed the contract, we never saw him again.
- His services were overpriced.
- He only gave advice. We had to do the work.
- He didn't deliver what he promised.
- We wanted to pay him a percentage of what he raised; he wanted a fixed, flat fee.

A few words about each of these items may spare both you and any future consultant some anguish.

- Once he signed the contract, we never saw him again. A good consultant will make sure that meetings are regularly scheduled, but if you, as an organization, don't feel you are seeing enough of your consultant and that he is not handling enough of your business, say so. The matter should be dealt with in any pre-contract talks at which time the consultant should be in a position to tell you how many regular hours of consultation time you are getting and what results should emerge.

- His services were overpriced. Consulting fees for professional fund raising counselors can be astronomical — and often are far, far higher than an organization should pay. The best thing for an organization to do is shop around. Consultants, like many independent entrepreneurs, will charge what the traffic will bear. Make sure that you know where both your consultant's fees and his services fit on the spectrum of available possibilities.

- He only gave advice. We had to do the work. Professional fund raising counselors are advice givers. They must work through the professional staff and volunteers of your agency to achieve their ends. Their influence is considerable, but it is generally indirect. This is as it should be. Neither individual nor institutional donors wish to see consultants whose loyalties are for sale. They want to see you and yours, and you must anticipate that the best consultants play their important role backstage and through you.

- He didn't deliver what he promised. This line could have any one of several meanings. It if means that the consultant actually did promise certain services and didn't deliver them, either consider cancelling the contract or asking for a percentage of money back. Both are suitable options. Unless the matter is in writing, however, and in your contract, you should consider whether you really have any options. It may be that you just misunderstood what kinds of services you were buying. This, then, is something to be very clear about in advance of signature, not afterwards.

- We wanted to pay him a percentage of what he raised; he wanted a fixed, flat fee. Many organizations like the notion of paying their fund raiser by his results, by the amount of money he is able to bring in. They see it as less expensive to them and more likely to insure the interest of the fund raising consultant. The National Society of Fund Raising Executives, however, thinks it unethical for fund raisers to be paid through a percentage of funds raised. They prefer that development consultants and other fund raisers receive a fixed, flat fee so as to insure their objectivity and the return of maximum dollars to the client. There are also a couple of practical matters to consider. Usually organizations which are prepared to pay out a percentage of funds raised do not want their current funding sources touched; they only want the percentage to apply on "new" funds. Just what constitutes a new funding source is often a difficult problem to solve. It should be pointed out, however, that it is not illegal for persons to be paid through a percentage of funds raised. Those who do raise money in this way are called professional fund raising solicitors and the laws of each state lay down what percentage of funds (whether with or without expenses) they can accept as a fee. You should be aware nonetheless that professional fund raising counselors, those who give advice, largely disdain solicitors as unethical and unprofessional. Moreover, the fact that there are regularly scandals across the nation concerning the percentages professional solicitors take of funds raised should make you very, very cautious about retaining such a person. At the very least, check with the office of the Attorney General of your state and be sure to get parallel references. These will insure that you are dealing with a reputable solicitor, if, indeed, you choose to adopt such a course.

A good consultant should always be preparing you for the day you can do without him. He expects to move on to other assignments, perhaps to return to you another day, and so should you. But as a teacher, the consultant should be assisting you in laying the groundwork not only for the current but also for the next fund raising effort. This means adequately training you to deal with the voluminous correspondence and assorted documentation of fund raising, so that it can be available to the organization over the next several years.

All too often board changes and the resignation or retirement of executive directors mean the complete destruction of the organization's corporate memory, thus making the organization's next fund raising effort even more difficult to create. Your consultant can assist you in organizing systems which will not only make the current fund raising campaign more efficient, but also help mount future efforts with less difficulty.

In conclusion, it is important to remember that you are not paying a consultant to be a "nice guy." He is there to help you realize your goals and reach your specific fund raising objectives. It is his job to tell you, as directly as he can, in what way your fund raising effort is going astray and assist you in coming up with apt solutions. In fulfilling this assignment, you may often find your consultant brusque and overly candid. If this is the case, remember: he may appear this way because he is firmly in pursuit of your best interests and because it is mutually beneficial to both of you for your organization to reach its goals and even exceed them.

Note: If you are interested in the profession of consulting, either from the standpoint of someone seeking to enter or of someone who purchases the services of consultants, you may wish to peruse my books **THE CONSULTANT'S KIT: ESTABLISHING AND OPERATING YOUR SUCCESSFUL CONSULTING BUSINESS** and **HOW TO MAKE** *AT LEAST* **$100,000 EVERY YEAR AS A SUCCESSFUL CONSULTANT IN YOUR OWN FIELD.**

CHAPTER 4

THE FACILITATING SESSION

Successful fund raising involves connecting people to people. The means through which the initial connection is accomplished is called networking. It is not difficult, but it does involve a system at the heart of which is the Facilitating Session.

This session is so called because it facilitates the introduction of your organization to individuals who might under ordinary circumstances prove difficult, if not impossible, to meet. It is an essential part of successful fund raising.

Preparing for the Facilitating Session

Much staff work goes into planning a successful Facilitating Session. Several sets of documents must be prepared and a good deal of research work undertaken so that the actual session, which only lasts for two hours, can move briskly along, accomplishing the many tasks for which it is being held.

The preparation of the documents for the Facilitating Session is the responsibility of the executive director. In small organizations the executive director may actually complete all or most of the advance work himself; in larger organizations, he should appoint a staff person, perhaps the director of development, to assist.

Here are the documents which need to be prepared in advance of the meeting:

- Select Corporate List
- Bank List
- Unselect Corporate List
- Select Foundation List
- Past Board Membership, last ten years
- Significant Donor List
- Contacts Questionnaire

Here is how and why each of these documents should be prepared:

Select Corporate List: As its name suggests, this is a select list of corporations within your marketing area which might make contributions to your organization. How do you find these corporations and how do you evaluate whether or not they may actually be prospects for your organization?

Finding the corporations is easier than evaluating the possibility of a gift. To draw up the Select Corporate List you need to use the **Standard & Poor's Register of Corporations, Directors and Executives.** Published annually with regular supplements, this series of three volumes contains vital information on corporate America. You need both volumes 1 and 3 in the preparation of the Select Corporate List.

First, examine the geographical listing of volume 3. Here you will be able to find most of the significant corporations which do business in your state. If your organization is situated in an important urban area, your city will have its own listing of corporations. For the first Facilitating Session, you want to deal with the top twenty corporations, not more. At later meetings, you can expand your list.

How do you know these are the twenty largest corporations in your marketing area? Usually, you are familiar with them because they are the most prominent businesses in your area. If you are not sure, however, check volume 1 in the series where you will find information on the annual revenues and number of employees.

Just because a business is prominent in your community, however, does not necessarily make it a target for your organization. You must try and discover whether the company might have some particular interest in your work, or, more usually, whether it might not grant to you under any circumstances. How can you tell?

First, call the corporation and see whether it maintains a corporate giving program. If so, you will need to know the name of its administrator, his title and telephone number in any event, so note these down for future reference. Then ask to have a set of the corporation's giving guidelines mailed to you. If you live in a large urban area, it is likely that there is a local reference library or special collection on philanthropy which may also have this information on file. To see whether your city maintains such a collection, check the introduction to **The Foundation Directory.**

You should understand that many corporations which do give money do not maintain guidelines as to how they give their money away. This is by design. Thus you will have to gather the information you need in a variety of creative ways:

- Ask for the corporation's annual report. Grants are occasionally mentioned in this document, particularly significant ones. But don't expect too much from this source.
- Collect information from newspapers and magazines. Nonprofit organizations which are anxious to get public relations attention often release information about grants they have received. If a comparable organization to yours gets a grant from a corporation, clip this information.
- Collect programs, brochures, &c from your competition. They often list the places from which grants have been secured. These can become sources for you, too.

Even if you have been assiduous about gathering this kind of information, you still may not know whether a corporation is or is not a possibility for you. In this case, simply add it to your Select Corporate List. Corporate fund raising is largely dependent on knowing someone within the corporation. The Facilitating Session has as its goal the identification of significant links, so when unsure add the corporation.

Once you have gathered the names of the top twenty corporate possibilities within your marketing area and have done some preliminary analysis to discover whether they might indeed be prospects, you are ready to draft Select Corporate List #1. To do so you need the following information:

- name of corporation
- its address
- its telephone number
- the names of officers who are directors
- the names of the other directors
- the name of the corporate contributions officer
- his title
- his telephone number

How do you get this information? Again, you need **Standard & Poor's Register.** In volume 1 you will find, under the individual listing for the corporation, its name, address, telephone number, the names of the officers who are directors, and the names of the other directors. To get the name of the corporate contributions officer, his proper title (not all are so called) and his telephone number, you must ordinarily call the corporation directly. The switchboard operator when you call may not have the slightest idea what you're talking about when you ask for the name of the corporate contributions officer. In this case, ask for the president's office. They will be able to provide you with the information you seek.

Once you have gathered this information together, you are ready to type the Select Corporate list. Here's what a typical entry will look like:

The Foxboro Co.
33 Neponset Avenue
Foxboro, MA 02035

(617) 543-8750

> (*Indicates Director) *Chairman and Chief Exeuctive Officer, Earl W. Pitt
> *President and Chief Operating Officer, Colin I.W. Baxter *Executive Vice
> President, Charles A. McKay

*Senior Vice President, Earl M. Kelley
*Senior Vice President, Allen E. Parritt

Other Directors: Rexford A. Bristol
Robert F. Jenkins
Harry W. Knight
James R. Nichols
G. Richard Westin
Bristol B. Brocker
John Jeppson II
Paul W. Murrill
Ralph Z. Sorenson

Corporate giving is handled by: Dick Plummer, Manager of Employee Services
& Community Relations, 543-8750, x. 2453

The Bank List

The Select Bank List is handled in largely the same way as the Select Corporate List.
Most banks both give money directly to the communities in which they do business and
many maintain trust departments which often administer accounts which can also
donate to your organization.

The larger banks are often listed in **Standard & Poor's Directory**. Most banks, however,
are not listed in this directory. To get basic information about them, their officers and
directors, you need to get a copy of the bank's annual report. This report is available to
all depositors of the bank and may generally be acquired simply by stopping in and
asking for it. If you telephone for it, you may be asked by the switchboard operator
why you want it; suspicion, after all, flourishes in the lower reaches of any corporation. To avoid the question, either go to the bank yourself or ask a board member or
staffer who banks there to give you his copy.

Only the largest banks maintain precisely defined corporate giving programs staffed
by an administrator. In the smaller banks, the president himself is likely to function as
the corporate giving officer. A call to his office will provide you with the information
you need on the individual situation of that bank.

Finally, unless you live in a large urban area that has many banks, your Bank List is likely to be considerably shorter that your Select Corporate List. The important thing,
however, is that on this list no bank or credit union be omitted. Often the sums donated
are small, but they are generally given consistently to favored organizations.

Unselect Corporate List

As its name implies, this is simply a listing of corporations within your marketing area. This list can be very, very long and some initial effort must be made to prune it. Remember, at later Facilitating Sessions you can present the names of companies which have not previously been dealt with.

Organizations in many urban areas may construct their Unselect Corporate List in one of two ways: 1) either by photocopying the pages from the **Standard & Poor's Directory** which simply list the names of corporations doing business in your marketing area, or 2) by applying to the local Chamber of Commerce or other local business group for a comparable list.

Organizations outside large cities can also apply to the Chamber of Commerce, and they may wish to see whether their county administrative offices maintains a list of businesses in the county. In addition, they may simply use the Yellow Pages of the telephone book. This is cumbersome, but what you are looking for at this moment is simply a general list of prospects. It is the purpose of the Facilitating Session to let you know whether you have a lead at any one of these businesses which is worth pursuing.

A good rule of thumb is to limit the Unselect Corporate List on any given occasion to about 200 names of businesses.

Select Foundation List

There are many more sources of information on foundations than on either corporations or individuals. The plethora of material perhaps is one reason why so many organizations immediately think about securing foundation grants; unfortunately, much of what is available is of indifferent quality or misleading in content.

As with the Select Corporate List, with the Select Foundation List you are attempting to locate the top 20 foundations which will give to your organization. Most of them will be local foundations either with a specific interest in the area in which you do business or in the actual work you do. How do you find these foundations and get an indication of their interests?

Begin with two reference directories: 1) **The Foundation Directory** which lists basic information about the country's largest foundations, and 2) the individual foundation directory for your state. To get information on the most recent edition of this book either call the attorney general of your state (under the Division of Public Charities or some comparable name), contact your local philanthropic reference collection, or the Foundation Center in New York City which can tell you how to go about securing a copy.

By reviewing the general interests of the foundations in your area, you make a preliminary judgement about which ones might be interested in your project. To get more specific information either call the foundation directly and request a copy of its grantmaking guidelines or use the materials on file at the local philanthropic reference collection. Most foundations with professional staff (the biggest, richest and best known) have guidelines; most smaller foundations do not.

In addition to these sources of information, you can also get information about the giving habits of foundations by reviewing such specialized periodicals as:

- **Foundation News**
- **Nonprofit World**
- newsletters (see the **Directory of Newsletters** published by Oxbridge Communications, New York)

Clip articles from local newspapers when your competition gets a grant and collect any information which refers either to the work of foundations in your area or specific individuals associated with the foundations. Also, with a staffed foundation don't hesitate to call and ask the professional staff whether they think there might be interest in what you do. If there is, add that foundation to the list of prospects.

Once you have reviewed this material, you are ready to type your select foundation list. Include the following information with your entry:

- name of foundation
- its address
- telephone number
- names of officers and trustees
- names of professional staff

If you are having trouble getting up-to-date information of any of these points, it should be on file with your state's attorney general. Some states unfortunately require you to be physically present before giving you the information you need; they will not give it to you over the telephone. I have never understood the reason for this absurd bar to public information.

Board Membership, Past Ten Years

This is what I call the "Family List," because it consists of the names of individuals who have previously made a contribution to your agency either in terms of service and/or money. Surprisingly many organizations have lost touch with retired board members, which is most unfortunate. One of the several reasons for maintaining a limit to the number of years any individual may serve on the board is to increase the pool of family members from which to draw resources. Losing touch with them once they are off the board defeats this critical purpose.

Understand, then, that it may be somewhat time-consuming at first to produce up-to-date addresses and telephone numbers on past board members. Moreover, there may be very real doubt as to whether some still live in the area or are, indeed, even living. That is the purpose of the Facilitating Session: to advise you on the location and condition of past board members and see which of them can be reconstructed to the organization. As you construct this list, make every effort to insure that names are spelled correctly; I have noted that an inordinate amount of time is spent at Facilitating Sessions by board members clucking over spelling errors on this list.

Significant Contributor List

Just what constitutes a "significant" donor will vary from agency to agency. It may be that donors of $50 or over are significant for one small community-based agency. Most groups, however, will restrict this word to individuals who have given at least $100 or more. The purpose here is to 1) gather current information on these people — name, address, telephone number — and, 2) assign members of the board to make personal visits. The Facilitating Session is intended to elicit information about who may know these significant donors. If you are coming up with more than 150 names on this list, your definition of significant is probably too liberal. Raise the qualifying amount.

Contacts Questionnaire

The final document you need to prepare for the Facilitating Session is the Contacts Questionnaire. This document is intended to show the depth and variety of the board's contacts and the networks of which they are otherwise a part. What follows is an explanation of why various questions have been added:

Business affiliations of board members, spouse and adult children: Most people's contacts come through their business and professional affiliations. They may not think of these individuals as leads to personal and corporate gifts, but they are, of course. You need to know where board members and their families work and where each individual is located within the corporate structure. This piece of knowledge will often determine the highest level of their access, which is a fact you ought to know. Answers to these questions can also help you discern just where a board member's contacts may lead. Employment within a certain business may suggest contacts with comparable businesses elsewhere and hence new prospects which would otherwise be beyond your grasp.

Schools attended: By a judicious reading of alumni publications for both schools and colleges, you can gather information which will help you gain access to helpful individuals. Ideally, you would like board members to annotate all their alumni publications and inform you who they know directly, which influential people are classmates they might not actually know, and which others are merely people who went to the same school. Board members are rarely sufficiently organized to produce this information. Thus, it is the responsibility of the executive director 1) to get the basic class information on each board member and then 2) to collect members' alumni publications and do the annotation personally or in individual sessions with board members. Remember: the old boy network (and now the old girl network, too) is alive and well and is often based on the old school tie. It is your responsibility to make it work for your organization.

Insurance company information: Most American insurance companies give both money and in-kind donations. One way of securing access is through your insurance agent, who can assist you in maneuvering through the bureaucracy. Another means is by having a sympathetic policy holder (somehow connected to your organization) bring your good work to the attention of the home office. The information provided through this question will enable you to find out how many insurance company prospects you have and the variety of contacts which are available.

Bank information: As above, you are attempting to discover a series of bank connections. As with all other examples, you are aiming for high-level contacts, but using networking principles you can leap-frog within a company by skillfully handling lower-level contacts. Most people have a bank contact: a loan officer, home mortgage representative, trust officer, &c. If they don't have a contact with their own bank, perhaps they know a banker for other reasons. This question should elicit that information.

Lawyer information: These questions have several purposes. If you do not now have a lawyer on your board, these questions will advance names which the Nominating Committee ought to consider. Here, too, you may find names of individuals who can be suggested, because of their contact with board members, for membership on professional fund raising committees. Also, lawyers are often connected with firms which administer trust funds; if they are not connected, perhaps they have a friend who is in the relevant firm. The fact is, however, that lawyers have excellent networks of their own, and it is advantageous for your organization to be connected to them.

Accountant information: The same reasons apply as with lawyers, except that, in addition, accountants are often in a position to suggest to clients needing a tax deduction the facts about your organization and so lead to a donation that is mutually rewarding.

Membership in organizations: The purpose here is to get access to the membership lists of other organizations and have your board members annotate the lists for your benefit. If you are going to raise funds from other civic organizations, religious organizations, &c., it helps to have an introductory contact who can pave your way. Also, by having members annotate the membership lists of other organizations, telling you useful information about these people, you can get the leads you need for both institutional and individual contributions.

Local businesses frequented: This information can lead to cash and in-kind donations and is of use both to your small business fund raising committee and to the special events committee which will be looking for in-kind donations.

Professionals with whom you do business: This information gets distributed to the pertinent fund raising committee. In some fund raising efforts, there is a separate fund raising committee for dentists, doctors, &c.; in some, the professionals are all placed under one committee. In any event, the answers to these questions provide necessary leads and suggest who should handle the solicitation visit.

Trade union contacts: Union contacts can provide both cash and in-kind services and should not be neglected. All too often they are.

Ten friends you would ask for contributions of $100 or less: These should be individuals who do not fit into any other category. This is an opportunity to expand the existing contacts of the organization. The expectation here is that board members will contact these people using the "Offset Letter," discussed later, and will telephone those who have not yet responded. Remember: people give to people, and it is absolutely necessary that the board members cooperate with the fund raising process by suggesting which of their friends might be interested in your project or who might otherwise be induced to contribute to it.

Facilitating Session Specifics

Once you have completed the process of gathering information, it is time to produce the documents and schedule the Facilitating Session. The first such session should be held in either March or April, preferably the former. This will insure that the information discovered can be turned over to the Needs Assessment and Development Planning Committee which will need it in attempting to identify prospects and calculate the chances for a grant.

In setting the meeting time, it is important that all board members be free to attend. Indeed, the Facilitating Session is a command performance for the board. Failure to participate in this meeting, with very few exceptions, means that the board member has a limited commitment to the success of the fund raising effort. However, even then, it is expected that the absent board member will complete all the forms at home.

The Facilitating Session generally takes two hours to complete; it usually takes place in the evening between about 7 p.m. and 9 p.m. at the organization's headquarters.

In advance of the session, it is the job of the executive director to prepare a sufficient number of documents so that each board member or other participant has at least **two** complete sets. The reason for this number will be seen shortly. It is also the responsibility of the executive director to insure that pens and writing pads are also available in sufficient quantities for each member. Do not expect board members to come to this meeting prepared in any way.

It is the responsibility of the chairman of the board to schedule this meeting (as all other board meetings) and to annouce its purpose. He may simply say that a session will take place to elicit necessary development contact information. He need not be more specific than this. Generally, no documents are sent out in advance. This is because the process can often appear a daunting one and thus discourages some board members from attending.

To insure that all board members are in fact attending this meeting, it is a wise idea to telephone them. At that time some gentle persuasion can be exercised on those who usually are delinquent in attending.

Who Acts As Facilitator?

The last important decision to be made prior to the actual session is who will act as facilitator? The answer to this question deserves consideration. It depends upon several factors:

- Who is the most knowledgeable individual in the organization about the various names which appear on the contact lists?
- Who is good at running a productive meeting?
- Who is respected by the board and can motivate the board?

Obviously the best person to coordinate the Facilitating Session is the chairman of the board. This is, after all, a board activity and involves his board and its members. If, however, the chairman cannot or will not serve as facilitator, there are several alternatives:

- find a board member who is most familiar with the names on the contact lists
- use the executive director
- retain an outside consultant

Since the purpose of this meeting is to link up your organization with key decision makers in corporations and foundations and to identify prospective individual donors, it is important that the facilitator be adequately acquainted with the names (and ideally the actual individuals) appearing on the lists. This means the facilitator must know as much as possible about as many of the names as possible. Where does this information come from?

Obviously the best resource is personal knowledge — contacts built up over a lifetime. This kind of information, however, is relatively rare and may not yet be found within your organization. If this is the case, you will have to research the information you need so that are in a position to help facilitate the creation of a link between these people and your organization.

To get the information you need, you should refer to the following kinds of biographical aids:

- **Standard & Poor's Directory,** volume 2 listing biographical information about many of the directors of America's largest corporations
- **Trustees of Wealth,** published by the Taft Corporation, Washington, D.C., this book contains information both about corporate and foundation trustees
- **Who's Who** and specialized regional volumes (**Who's Who in the East,** &c.)
- **Directory of Directors** for certain major cities list the directors of corporations, partners in leading law firms, &c.
- city social registers
- university alumni publications

The task of accumulating biographical details about the 200-300 names which may appear on your contacts lists (particularly the Select Corporate List, Select Foundation List, and Bank List) may seem initially discouraging. But remember: the names don't change much from year to year. These are the powerful people in your community, and while there is glacial change over time, the powerful generally stay powerful and well connected. These are the individuals who will hold most of the powerful positions for the next years. Your job is to connect with them and you can best do so by knowing everything you can about them.

In addition to the specialized directories cited above, much useful information is commonly available. You will find it in social columns in newspapers, business news and in feature stories. As you become familiar with the names on your lists, you should collect this information which may suggest both the individual interests of these people and how to contact them.

The Facilitating Session

It is a good idea to have refreshments available the evening of the Facilitating Session and to begin with a quarter hour of social conversation. This should reduce the defenses of individuals who have reservations about the entire process. It is the job of the chairman of the board and executive director to put directors at ease and to give them confidence in the process.

A round table or semi-circular arrangement is preferable for seating. All papers should be stacked neatly beside the facilitator. He should also have pencils ready. Next to the facilitator should be a staff assistant designated to take notes of the meeting. Although all persons are advised to jot their thoughts down on the various lists before them, some people will not do so. There must, therefore, be a secretary available to write leads down on what constitutes something of a pre-master list.

Under no circumstances should all documents be distributed at once. This may prove intimidating. Instead, each individual set should be distributed singly beginning with the Select Corporate List. To begin with, the facilitator should make sure that the board member's name appears at the top of each page. If this point is not made, you will very likely find unmarked materials after the meeting. This can be infuriating.

Once these introductory matters have been accomplished, the meeting runs rather like a tobacco auction. The facilator, beginning with the Select Corporate List, runs through the names of the officers who are directors and the other directors attempting to discover links between the people present and those senior officials of the corporation. If no direct link immediately surfaces, he should begin to mention other information which may prove pertinent: the college the individual attended, graduation date, nonprofit organizations on whose boards he sits, clubs he belongs too, other corporations with which he is associated, all information, in short, which is usually available from the kinds of standard reference works cited above.

If there are no links to directors and officers of the corporation, the facilitator will encourage board members to think of what other links they may have to the source under discussion: is a member of the family employed there? Do they hold stock in the corporation? Is an employee of the corporation a next door neighbor? Is there any link, in short, which can be parlayed into a substantial connection? Once one or two such links have been established, the discussion moves on to the next potential source and so on throughout the entire twenty corporations which constitute the first Select Corporate List.

After the list has been completed, the facilitator should pause for about five minutes and give the board members the opportunity to review the corporations and attempt to come up with additional links. If it is apparent that there are corporations on the list where no links have as yet been identified, it is the responsibility of the facilitator to urge the members to concentrate on these places and do their best to come up with connections.

When the Select Corporate List has been completed, the Bank List is distributed and the same process is undertaken. In addition to director and senior officer connections, lesser links may include: being a depositor, holding a home mortgage through an individual bank, knowing a bank employee who is not at the management level, &c. Clearly the former contacts are the best, but using networking principles even the lesser connections can be utilized to gain access to people who can truly be helpful.

Following the Bank List, pass out the Unselect Corporate List. Give the group about ten minutes or so to peruse the names on the list. You are simply trying to find out which of these names may indeed become a prospect by virtue of a significant link. If you find that members are not really concentrating on the names, read them aloud. This focuses the group.

Take a five minute break about this point. It is important that you give the board members the opportunity to brainstorm among themselves and a break presents a good chance to do so. Make sure that any leads mentioned during this break are in fact written down on the list being maintained by the staff assistant.

After the break, take up the Select Foundation List. It is not at all uncommon to find that you cannot locate a link to most of the names of this list. However, you can provide a copy of this list to the personnel of foundations which have previously funded you or are otherwise interested in your cause. Foundation people are generally your best links to foundation people, certainly at the staff level.

After you have completed the Foundation List, pass out the list of board members for the past 10 years. All prior board members should be visited as part of the development effort. What you are trying to discover at the Facilitating Session is: 1) where they are located, 2) whether some may now be deceased, 3) who knows them well, and 4) any other pertinent information which may make the solicitation visit successful.

The same is true of the Significant Donor List which follows. You will not necessarily be visiting every significant donor. But you will be trying to discover enough information to enable you to make sure an intelligent decision about which of these donors should be visited and who should make the call.

Finally, approach the Contacts Questionnaire. If you feel the meeting has gone productively so far, the board members may be too tired to cope with this questionnaire at the present meeting. If this is the case, just get them to complete the section on "10 individuals known to you who could contribute under $100." Tell the members that if they don't complete this section now, someone from the organization will call for the names in the near future. The members may well have some reservations about contacting their friends, but if it is understood that it is a general obligation some of the opposition to the idea may be softened.

If you feel that the meeting has not been producing the kind and amount of information you will need, then make sure the members complete the questionnaire in as much detail as possible on the spot. Inform them that no question should elicit a "Not applicable" response. The facilitator should stress at all times that the full cooperation of the board in the development process is absolutely essential; without it, the agency's likelihood of a successful fund raising effort will be considerably reduced.

After about an hour and forty five minutes have elapsed, begin to bring the Facilitating Session to its conclusion. You will need a few minutes to wrap up.

At this point members of the board may well have some pointed questions about what you intend to do with the information you have gathered. It is a good idea to address their concerns forthrightly.

The main question will probably concern access to the information and future use. Assure board members that none of the information will be used without their consent — indeed it cannot be since they are critical parts of the networking process — and that no information will be shared without the complete consent of the board member. A strong statement in this regard should sustain the board's confidence in the process.

All papers must be handed in at the conclusion of the Facilitating Session. Nothing which has been written on by the members should be taken from the room. There may be a protest from one or two members at this point, who will suggest that their notes are incomplete and that they want to take their lists home. At this time, pass out the second **complete** set of lists and documents and announce that board members may find it convenient to continue their work at home. Note: once most members are safely out of the Facilitating Session, they won't bother to deal with these papers. But because they think they might do so, they have to be given a second complete set. It is a good idea to telephone all members of the board within 10 business days and collect these papers if possible. Don't expect the board members to get them back to you on their own volition. It would be nice, but it doesn't happen very often.

In conclusion, thank the board members for participating and inform them that after a preliminary review of the documents by both the chairman of the board, executive director and (if possible) chairman of the Needs Assessment and Development Planning Committee, specific instructions will be forthcoming.

The Sifting Process

In the two or three days following the Facilitating Session, it is a good idea for the chairman of the board and the executive director (with the chairman of the Needs Assessment and Development Planning Committee, if possible) to meet and begin the process of sifting through the information which has been collected. To do their work effectively, they need to know about the Pyramid of Contacts and how it works.

The best contacts are those where an individual (perhaps a board member) either is a grantsmaking decision maker or has direct access to one. This is the apex of the Pyramid of Contacts. Thereafter, the contacts decline in value until at the base of the pyramid an organization without a contact is left usually vainly attempting to get access to decision makers, hoping to be able to sell them on their good idea.

This is how the Pyramid of Contacts looks:

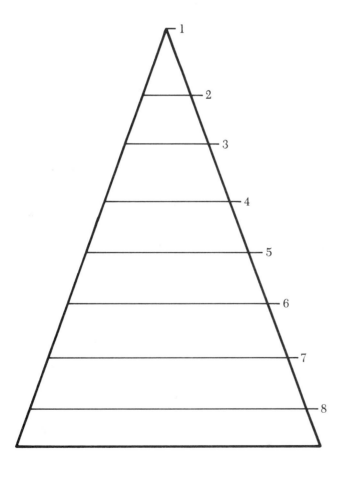

1. "I'll take care of it for you." (Either your contact is the decision maker or has direct access.)

2. "I know the decision maker; I'll schedule the meeting you need; I'll attend it with you; and if you need me to intervene later to expedite matters, I can and will."

3. "I know the decision maker, but I can't attend the meeting with you. But I can and will schedule it for you, and I'll call if necessary to expedite matters after you've met."

4. "I'll make your appointment, but that's it."

5. "I'll call after your meeting, when you tell me things have gone well, and when my call can expedite matters."

6. "I have a direct link, but won't use it for you. Call and use my name instead."

7. "Our organization has no direct link to the decision makers but we have a series of indirect links through shared associations, friends, relations, college roommates, and a wide range of business links. They may be parlayed into meaningful links with decision makers through networking."

8. "Even though we don't have any contact, we have a great idea. I'm sure we can sell it to the powers that be and get a donation."

A quick analysis of the Pyramid of Contacts reveals that at its apex, the emphasis is on process. Getting your agency into substantial contact with the decision makers in the right way, the way that maximizes the possibility of being accepted and minimizes the need for a hard sell, is your top priority.

At the foot of the pyramid, the emphasis is on selling yourself, your credentials, on proving the need for your services or on making sure that no one duplicates what you're doing. In short, it's jumping through the hoops when the donors say jump. At this level, an invidious process of comparison goes on: Is your day care center as worthwhile and important as the community arts organization? There is, of course, almost no way of really knowing. When you face the Pyramid of Contacts at the lowest level, however, it is most likely that the answer will be a resounding "No!" to almost every organization.

Thus when the chairman of the board and executive director meet following the Facilitating Session, their first task is to prioritize the leads that have been generated by attempting to discern which of them look promising in terms of future decisions.

The best way of handling this task is to draw up a work sheet corresponding to each list used at the Facilitating Session. The purpose is to list beside each possible funding source the various leads which have been gathered both from the specific list in question and from the various questions on the Contacts Questionnaire. These leads should be entered so that they correspond to the Pyramid of Contacts. This will enable you to determine which should be pursued first and how strong they may be. Thus the leads generated for the Foxboro Company, used earlier as an example on the Select Corporate List, might look like this:

> The Foxboro Company. Our board member X knows Foxboro Director Y moderately well. They went to school together. Board member Y knows an assistant vice president who lives in his neighborhood.
> Board member Z is a shareholder.

All the leads which have been generated should appear in one place, so that the entire situation may be considered before issuing any directions to board members. It may be that one lead, if located towards the top of the Pyramid of Contacts, may be worth any number of others you have discovered. If so, the others should be held in reserve until such time as they are needed.

Similar work sheets should be completed for the Bank List, the Unselect Corporate List, and the Select Foundation List.

The purpose here is not yet to issue directions to board members about how to pursue their leads. That cannot be done until the fund raising objectives have been settled. This task is handled by the Coordinating Committee (to be discussed later). Rather, the task now is to assist the work of the Needs Assessment and Development Planning Committee, giving its members as strong an indication as possible of what foundations, corporations and even individuals are relatively good prospects for the next fund raising effort. In this connection, it is important that the assessment process following the first Facilitating Session be hard-headed. Leads which appear to be insubstantial at first glance probably are. Moreover, leads which at this meeting appear to be promising, often evaporate. Your evaluation of what you have, therefore, should be very, very conservative.

Preliminary Facilitating Session Follow-Up

Most of the follow-up to the Facilitating Session is undertaken by the Coordinating Committee which oversees the distribution of information to the various fund raising committees and crafts the approaches to individual corporations and foundations. Some preliminary follow-up can be done by the executive director, however, shortly after the Facilitating Session. Within a week after the meeting the executive director should call:

- All board members who were present and took home duplicate sets of documents. They should be urged to return them with their comments.
- Board members who may have missed the Facilitating Session. They should be sent the relevant materials and pursued until they complete them.
- Board members who did not provide the names of "10 people known to you who could make gifts of under $100." They should be asked for the names and addresses of these people, and then asked again if this information is not immediately forthcoming.

The reason for this activity should be clear: the Needs Assessment and Development Planning Committee must have as much information as it can get so as to make the best decision possible about future funding prospects. The failure of board members fully to participate in the facilitating process means that such information cannot be available. This turns the planning process of the organization into a kind of blindman's bluff.

Assessing the Need for a Second Facilitating Session

If, after review, the material gathered looks thin, another Facilitating Session is in order. It should be held about six weeks after the first. Board members should be invited back and thought should be given to supplementing their numbers with: past board members, staff of the agency, agency "Friends" and members of the advisory committee. It is important that everything possible be done to collect the contacts of the agency. If this is done, it will make the later work of the Coordinating Committee much easier and help insure the success of the fund raising effort.

CHAPTER 5

THE COORDINATING COMMITTEE

The Coordinating Committee is the body of your organization which oversees the solicitation of funds from individuals. While the planning process is strategic, the work of the Coordinating Committee is tactical. Primarily the Coordinating Committee is responsible for producing the operating funds your agency needs, although as the next chapter demonstrates, it also has a role in raising funds from corporations and foundations.

Setting Up and Manning the Coordinating Committee

Once the board of directors has approved the fund raising objectives for the year, it is time for the Coordinating Committee to go to work. In practice, this means that the Coordinating Committee should be ready to function no later than July if you expect to kick-off your public fund raising effort October 1. Given the usual summer slow-down within agencies, it is a wise idea to hold at least the introductory meetings of the Committee in June, if at all possible.

Like any coordinating body, the membership of the Coordinating Committee should be limited. Its core group should include:

- the chairman of the board
- the executive director
- a staff liaison
- development counsel, if it has been retained

Other members may be added as necessary. These usually include the chairman of the various fund raising committees and the board liaison who is brought on to superintend various committees. It is usually not a good idea for the membership of the Coordinating Committee to exceed 8 or 9 people.

The chairman of the board, who functions as chairman of this committee, should make it clear to the members that their function is a critical one and that the success of this aspect of the fund raising effort rests on them. He needs to point out that the Committee will be meeting regularly, usually weekly, from July through December for about two hours each week. He should acknowledge that this is a major commitment from the members, but he should also point out that without this kind of commitment success will prove difficult to achieve.

The chairman also needs to point out that successful fund raising involves two key elements: 1) a thorough planning process and 2) a broad-based coordinated effort. He should remind the members that the agency has just completed the first step and that it is up to them to provide the second ingredient, the broad-based coordinated effort.

Document Preparation

It is the responsibility of the executive director and his staff to produce the wide range of documents which the fund raising effort requires. It is the job of the Coordinating Committee to suggest which documents it needs and to outline a production schedule which coordinates with other aspects of the fund raising effort. The following constitutes a list of the documents and written materials which most organizations are likely to need:

- development proposal(s)
- précis
- sample solicitation letter from individual committees to their prospects
- sample letter packet including a series of letters from board members to individuals connected with foundations and corporations
- letters from board members to friends seeking individual contributions ("The Offset Letter")
- log form
- pledge card
- check-list for Volunteer Solicitor Meeting
- letter to be sent out when fund raising effort is nearing its conclusion

Here's why you need these materials; (for a discussion of the development proposal and précis, see Chapter 2):

- Sample solicitation letter from individual committees to their prospects. This letter is used to introduce both the solicitor and the cause to prospective donors. The Coordinating Committee approves a draft letter. This is later sent to each individual committee chairman. He may either use it as is or adapt it to his own purposes, while making sure, of course, that its key points remain. (See sample, page 209)

- Sample letter packet includes a series of letters from board members and other friends of the organization to individuals connected with foundations and corporations directly or indirectly. This packet should contain the

72

following letter samples:

i. Letter from a Direct Link to a Foundation Trustee
ii. Letter to an Indirect Link connected to a Foundation Trustee
iii. Letter from this Indirect Link to the Foundation Trustee
iv. Letter from a Direct Link to Foundation Professional Staff
v. Letter to an Indirect Link connected to Foundation Professional Staff
vi. Letter from this Indirect Link to the Foundation Professional Staff
vii. Letter from a Direct Link to Corporate President
viii. Letter to an Indirect Link connected to a Corporate President
ix. Letter from this Indirect Link to the Corporate President
x. Letter from a Direct Link to Corporate Professional Staff
xi. Letter to an Indirect Link to Corporate Professional Staff
xii. Letter from this Indirect Link to Corporate Professional Staff

(See sample, page 211-217)

- Letter from board members to friends seeking individual contributions ("The Offset Letter"). This letter can either be produced with offset printing or on a word processor. It should be sent by each board member to ten individuals whom he knows who could give contributions of $100 or less. It should be followed up by a telephone call within two weeks if no contribution has been sent. Note: even though this letter is produced on agency letterhead and may be mailed in an agency envelope, solicitors should ask that donations be sent back to them (and may include for this purpose a self-addressed stamped envelope). Donors like to let those who asked them know that they have given, and it is therefore better for the board members to collect the contributions directly.
(See sample, page 219)

- Log form. Top donor prospects and corporate and foundation prospects should each have a completed log form. All such forms needed to be maintained in a loose-leaf binder for easy access.
(See sample, page 220)

- Pledge cards. Try to have a neighborhood printer donate the pledge cards to you. They need not be elaborate.
(See sample, page 221)

- Check-list for Volunteer Solicitor Meeting. It is a good idea to write down what you expect for each volunteer solicitor. This form can either be distributed at the Volunteer Solicitor-Motivator Meeting (discussed later) or can be mailed to each volunteer solicitor individually.

- Letter to be sent when fund raising effort is nearing its successful conclusion. This letter is sent about three weeks to a month before the end of a fund raising effort or at such time as 75-80% of the fund raising objective has been raised. Its purpose is to let people see that the effort is in sight of its goal and that with a little added effort on the part of past contributors it will be a complete success.

(See sample, page 225)

Setting Up the Committees

Just how many individual fund raising committees you establish is a function both of your constituency and your ingenuity. Agencies offering a service clearly perceived as beneficial to an entire town or region (a YMCA, say) should work hard to create all or most of the following committees. Specialized organizations will have to work harder to raise the funds from their committed constituencies. Here is a list of possible committees:

- Board Committee
- Past Board Member Committee
- Friends of Board Members
- User Committee
- People Connected to User Committee
- Civic Group Committee
- Religious Organizations Committee
- Special Events Committee
- Marketing Area Professionals Committee
- Small Business Committee
- Friends Group Committee
- Corporate Committee
- Foundation Committee

Here's why you should have them and who should chair them:

- Board Committee. This committee is mandatory. A minimum of 20% of the operating objective should come from the board. If your board members won't give, don't expect anyone else to do so. Moreover, board members who won't give can scarcely make good solicitors. Remember: each board member must be involved in the fund raising effort both as a contributor and as a committee participant. This committee is headed by the chairman of the board.

- Past Board Members. This is what I called the "Family" committee. Past board members, after all, are people who once made an exceptional commitment to your organization. Many of them will have drifted away over the years; some will have had serious disagreements over policy and may remain disaffected. It is the job of this committee to begin the task of recultivating past board members and of soliciting them for current operating support. The chairman of this committee should be a widely respected past board member.

- Friends of Board Members. All members of the board are 'members' of this committee in that each board member is expected to send a letter ("The Offset Letter") to at least 10 individuals who could make contributions of $100 or less. It is the responsibility of the chairman of the board to insure that these letters have been sent and are being followed up. The executive director can assist this process by urging board members to send in their 10 names and addresses, but if a board member is reluctant to do so, it is the job of the chairman to persuade him.

- User Committee. Most organizations have developed over time a body of individuals who have benefitted from this service. As beneficiaries, they should need only minimal (if any) persuasion as to its usefulness. Properly handled, they should be willing to contribute to its continuing existence. This committee should be chaired by a user or former user.

- People Connected to User Committee. Often times users of the service are themselves unable to contribute for one reason or another. If your organization is a child welfare agency, for instance, the existing clientele may be too young to do so. However, in many instances a committee can be established to raise operating funds from people connected to the users, such as, parents of current students, or the adult children of elderly users. This committee should be chaired by someone connected to a user.

- Civic Group Committee. If you have decided to raise money from the civic groups in your marketing area, you will need to establish a civic group fund raising committee. This committee should be chaired by a prominent member of the local civic community. This committee may either be chaired by a board member or by someone being groomed for board membership.

- Religious Organizations Committee. As above, if you are going to raise money through religious organizations, you need a committee chaired by a prominent layman or local cleric. As with the civic groups committee, your chairman may either be a board member or someone you'd like to see on the board later.

- Special Events Committee. Each organization should consider the advisability of holding special events twice a year. The chairman should have the ability to inspire and organize large numbers of people, since special events involve a significant amount of planning. (See Chapter 8).

- Marketing Area Professionals Committee. This committee raises funds from doctors, lawyers, accountants, dentists, &c. In some fund raising efforts, each of these professional groups will have its own individual committee. Most groups, however, will find one professional committee sufficient, if its membership is diverse. If there is no suitable board member to chair this committee, again look to this as a means of involving a prospective board member.

- Small Business Committee. This commitee should be established where an organization has local prominence and is well known for providing an essential community service. Either a board member or board prospect should chair it.

- Friends Group Committee. This group of past donors should be solicited as part of the drive to raise operating funds. Significant donors should be sought out by those who know them. The Facilitating Session (See Chapter 4) can provide helpful information about who should make the visit. The chairman of this effort is the chairman of the organized Friends Group.

- Corporate Committees. A little over 6% of the money raised from the private sector in this country comes from corporations. You should therefore set up a committee which has as its goal raising something close to this amount from large businesses. The corporate committee is made up of the chairman of the board and the executive director. It uses board contacts (coming from the Facilitating Session) as needed.

- Foundation Committee. This functions in the same way as the corporate committee.

Determining the Committees' Fund Raising Objectives

Organizations which have previously raised money from the private sector and have used some or all of the above-mentioned committees will have some idea of how much each committee should be seeking. Past performance will be their guide. In determining their fund raising objectives for the year, they will need to consider such questions as:

- Were there any unusual circumstances which contributed to the fund raising results of each committee last year?

- Can we re-assemble comparable committees?

- Has our universe of donors grown? Has it shrunk?

- How much can we increase the amount we seek?

In general, organizations cannot dramatically increase the level of their contributions from year to year unless conditions have substantially changed. For example, dynamic new members may have been added to the board. Or perhaps the weak executive director has left and a powerhouse personality has come into the office. These changes may raise contribution levels. Ordinarily, however, an organization would be well advised not to attempt to raise more than 20% more operating money than it did in the previous year. It is unlikely that it will have the fund raising structure to sustain a larger objective.

Organizations which have not previously attempted to raise operating money from the private sector have a different problem. They must find "hard" answers to a series of open-ended, fluctuating questions so as to arrive at realistic fund raising objectives for each committee. Here's what they must consider:

- Can we find a chairman for the committee?
- If we have identified a prospective chairman, does he have the leadership capabilities to inspire and organize?
- What is the universe of prospects for the committee?
- Have any of these prospects given before?
- Is there any competing fund raising drive within the universe of prospects we'd like to solicit?
- Do the prospects know about us or is this our first approach to them?

Never having raised money in a sustained fashion from the private sector before, these organizations will find the answers to these questions elusive and often confusing. Lack of hard data is, however, a common problem. The solution is to set a reasonable objective for each committee — such as 10% of your operating goal. Here, then, is how one typical fund raising effort for operating money might be set up if the objective was $20,000.

Committee	Percentage of Total to be raised	Total Sought
Board	20%	$4,000
Past Board	10%	2,000
Friends of Board	10%	2,000
Users of Service	10%	2,000
Special Events	20% (fall & spring)	4,000
Small Business	10%	2,000
Corporate Contributions	10%	2,000
Foundation Contributions	10%	2,000
Total	100%	$20,000

Note: success with this process is a function of the level of board participation. If the board fails to reach its assigned figure of 20% of the operating goal (in the example above $4000), then the other figures are probably unrealistically high, too. Remember: the operating objective sought should be 5 times whatever the board itself is willing to give.

In practice, it is probably a good idea for the Coordinating Committee to work with the Needs Assessment and Development Planning Committee to determine the realistic fund raising objectives for each committee. At the very least, the chairman of the Coordinating Committee might take the advice of the chairman of Needs Assessment Committee in setting its fund raising objectives. The important thing is that the individual objectives be realistic, not excessive. Excessive objectives only lead to frustration on the part of committee members and often to unpleasant recriminations by the board (to say nothing of the need to cut back the organization's necessary services for lack of funds).

Dealing with Committee Members

Once the fund raising objectives have been set, it is time to appoint the chairman of the individual committees and work to assemble the members. To begin with, each member of the board must be accounted for either in terms of a committee chairmanship or membership on an individual committee. It is, after all, the responsibility of board members not only to give money but to help in raising it, also.

Just what role they perform depends on their own capabilities and on the needs of the organization. It is up to the board chairman, after conversation with each member, to make the appointments. It is his responsibility to persuade, cajole, and wheedle board members into full participation.

Where there is no obvious candidate for a committee chairmanship, several courses can be adopted. Here are some of them:

- the chairman of the board can ask for nominations of prospective chairmen from board members.
- he can ask for the assistance of the Nominating Committee which should have identified prospective board candidates.
- he can bring in his own friends and associates to head committees.

Clearly, it is always better to select as chairman someone who is familiar with the organization and has made a commitment to its goals. The success or failure of any particular committee depends to a significant extent on its chairman. It is therefore not a wise idea to bring in an unknown entity unless absolutely necessary.

After the chairmen are appointed, it is their responsibility to fill out their committees. The Coordinating Council should, however, help them by:

- soliciting board members for possible committee members
- passing along suggestions from the Nominating Committee
- reviewing the materials produced at the Facilitation Session to see whether there are committee prospects
- giving chairmen lists of past committee members.

Needless to say, individuals who have had the least prior association with your organization should be given the most assistance. But as with all chairmen, they should be encouraged to bring in their associates and turn them into new friends of the agency.

It is the job of the Coordinating Committee to advise its chairmen and their members as to when the task of completing the committees should be accomplished. Assuming that the Coordinating Committee begins its significant work about the first of July, the committees should be entirely manned and operational no later than Labor Day. August 15th would be a preferable target date. Chairmen should be advised of this date as soon as possible.

As the committee is being assembled, it is the job of the Coordinating Committee to train the chairmen in the basic techniques of solicitation. The Coordinating Committee may wish to have a small training session in July on this topic or it may simply wish to draft a training memorandum. In either case the following points need to be covered:

- Once a solicitor has been given a prospect's name, it is his responsibility to see the prospect.
- If he has questions about the prospect, he should ask the chairman. If the chairman has any questions, he can refer the matter to the Coordinating Committee.
- The solicitor should begin the process by sending an initial letter to the prospect asking for an appointment and giving basic information about the organization.
- The solicitor should call and schedule the appointment.
- If the initial telephone call is not returned within two or three days, a second should be placed and so on until contact has been made and the prospect meeting scheduled.
- Solicitors will often approach the solicitation meeting with nervousness. If they do, they should tell the prospect that they are nervous, that they don't like asking for money, but that the importance of the cause is such that they feel they must do so. Most donor prospects have been solicitors at one time or another and will respond generously to this admission of nervousness.
- At the meeting it is the solicitor's responsibility to mention the gift amount. The amount must not be left to the imagination of the prospect.
- Prior consideration must be given to the amount that will be requested.
- If the prospect makes a pledge, the solicitor should fill out the pledge card on the spot.
- If the prospect needs extra time to think things over, the solicitor should arrange an exact time when he can call again.
- If the prospect says he will not make a pledge, find out why. It may just be that the time is wrong now. Find out whether the prospect will help in another way: making referrals, helping in the fund raising effort, &c.
- The solicitor should draft a brief report of each meeting (about 100-150 words) describing what happened. Any pertinent information noted in the conversation (leads to other sources, for instance) should be written down.
- The task of solicitation is not completed until the solicitor has a definite response from each assigned prospect and has communicated the results to his chairman.

The Volunteer Solicitor-Motivator Meeting

Once all the various fund raising committees have been fully manned, it is a wise idea to hold a general meeting for all volunteer solicitors connected with the fund raising effort: board members, committee chairmen who are not board members and committee members. This meeting, generally scheduled for about September 15, two weeks before the fund raising kick-off, has three distinct purposes:

- It is a training session for all the volunteers associated with the forthcoming fund raising effort.
- It is an opportunity to set the tone for the fund raising effort, establish its purpose and reaffirm the essential nature of the organization's work and its place in the community.
- It presents an opportunity to answer all the technical questions about the fund raising effort beyond the actual solicitation visit.

The meeting itself will take about two hours. It should be held in the evening between approximately 7:30-9:30 p.m. or on a Sunday afternoon. If your headquarters has suitable space for the meeting it should be held there. If not, a convenient space can be rented in a hotel or other local facility. Since it is a good idea to begin the meeting with a half hour or so of refreshments to set the proper social tone, make sure your facility allows for such amenities.

To determine who should make the presentations, it is helpful to suggest what they should accomplish.

The Motivator: Each fund raising effort needs to be launched with an inspirational message. The purpose of this message is to confirm the overriding importance of the agency, its place in the community and its continuing significance. These are expressed in the précis' Critical Role section. Indeed, if this section has been properly handled, it presents an excellent synopsis of the evening's remarks. By virtue of his position, the chairman of the board is the proper person to make these remarks. If he is not a good speaker, however, the agency may wish to invite someone else to present the keynote. Suggestions include:

- another board member
- past board chairman or member
- eminent community leader
- user of the service or someone who has benefitted from the work of the agency

The Technician: Someone must explain how the fund raising effort will proceed technically. This role can be taken by the executive director, the development consultant or by the two of them working in tandem. It is their job to:

- explain what is expected of each solicitor
- show how the individual committees and their chairmen will function
- indicate what supplementary documents have been developed and are available to solicitors
- outline the significant dates in the fund raising process (its commencement, mid-term review, expected conclusion)
- explain how the fall special event will contribute to the success of the fund raising effort, and
- clarify the role of the Coordinating Committee.

The technician(s) may wish to hold role plays (dramatic "dialogues") on common situations which will face the solicitors such as: 1) making appointments, 2) handling solicitation meetings, 3) following up meetings successfully.

In both the remarks of the motivator and the technician(s), the importance of each individual solicitor must be stressed. **With** their cooperation a successful result can be anticipated; without the full participation of **each** volunteer, however, success must be considered doubtful.

The executive director should insure that this meeting is amply supplied with précis, brochures, pledge cards, public relations materials, &c. Development proposals need not be supplied to every solicitor, but you will probably want to have some on hand for those who are interested.

As a concluding item of business, the executive director should urge all solicitors to undertake their tasks promptly. If this is not made clear some solicitors actually wait until they receive an "official go ahead" from the agency. The executive director and/or development consultant then can take questions about the fund raising effort. The time period for these questions should be limited to no more than a quarter of an hour; otherwise, the audience may become bored and restless.

Finally, the motivator should offer one or two minutes of summary and final uplift. It is important to conclude the meeting on a strong upbeat which will spur the solicitors on.

Identifying the Universe of Prospects

It is the job of each fund raising committee to identify the Universe of Prospects — the people or organizations, that is, who might supply the necessary funds. This task can seem mind-boggling and it often defeats organizations. It should therefore be approached briskly and systematically, proceeding committee by committee to identify the prospects for each one. It is the job of the chairman of the committee to define the Universe of Prospects. Both his committee members and the Coordinating Committee work with him.

Here is a list of the most common fund raising committees and where their prospects come from:

- Board committee prospects. Each member of the board of directors is a prospect, and the chairman of this committee (the chairman of the board) works from a complete list of his members.

- Past board members. This list should have been completed for the Facilitating Session. It includes the names, addresses, and telephone number of all board members for the past ten years. These are all prospects.

- Friends of board members. Each board member should be asked at the Facilitating Session to supply the names of ten individuals to whom he would be willing to write for a contribution of $100 or less. These are prospects for smaller donations. These individuals should not come under the aegis of any other committee. It is important that these names be reviewed by the Coordinating Committee to insure 1) that there are no duplicates and 2) that no individuals are being solicited for small donations who should be asked for larger sums or for help with corporations and foundations.

- User prospects. If you have determined to solicit users of your service, draw up a list of prospects who have benefitted from your work for the past five years. You need their names, addresses, and, if possible, their telephone numbers.

- People connected to users. Same as above.

- Civic group prospects. The Yellow Pages is usually a good place to start to get the names and addresses of community civic groups. Check under such titles as: "associations," "fraternal organizations," "organizations," &c. Call each civic organization and get the name and proper title of its chief executive officer. Sometimes they have exotic titles so make sure and get them spelled correctly.

- Religious organization prospects. Again, the telephone directory is a good place to begin assembling your prospects. You need to make calls to get the names of pastors, priests or rabbis. Again, make sure you have the proper title. Ecclesiastical titles are quite precise.

- Professional prospects. Each distinct professional group in your community (physicians, dentists, lawyers, accountants, &c) may have its own professional listing including the name, address, and telephone number of colleagues. See if such a list exists. If it does not, again you will want to use the telephone directory for information.

- Small business prospects. Most communities have either a Chamber of Commerce or corresponding business booster organization. If your organization is not a member, it should consider joining. In any event, this kind of organization usually maintains an up-to-date listing of local businesses. Call them to confirm the correct name of the proprietor, his proper title, mailing address and telephone number. Big city organizations can often find neighborhood business associations.

- Friends prospects. Each Friends organization should maintain a current list of its members. All members are prospects, but be sure to solicit from them according to what they can give. The Facilitating Session should help determine appropriate requests.

- Corporate prospects. Use the Select Corporate List supplied in Chapter 4 and information from the Facilitating Session.

- Foundation prospects. Use the Select Foundation List supplied in Chapter 4 and information from the Facilitating Session.

Top Prospects: Determination and Importance

The success of most fund raising efforts depends on the ability of organizations to persuade a few substantial donors to make larger gifts rather than to organize many small donors. These substantial donors begin by being "Top Prospects."

The question immediately arises about how you can discover whether someone is a top prospect. There is no easy answer to this question and the result is inevitably a subjective evaluation. Although this may be frustrating to you, be glad it is so. Fortunately we live in a country where it is still fairly difficult to get detailed information about the personal finances of most citizens. Still, it make life as a fund raiser unquestionably challenging.

Each committee works out its own top prospects and the amount they might give. They begin by constructing a Pyramid of Gifts which suggests the number and size of gifts the committee will need if it is to reach its fund raising objective.

Constructing this pyramid is not difficult. The rule of thumb is that the top three gifts must equal 50% of the amount you seek. After the top gift is determined (it's usually called the Leadership Gift), the remaining amounts are set by doubling the number of gifts sought and halving their amounts. Here's what a Gift Pyramid would look like for a committee seeking $1,600.

1 Leadership Gift @ $400
2 Gifts @ $200 each
4 Gifts @ $100 each
8 Gifts @ $50 each

Pyramids of Gifts from individuals generally conclude with a line to this effect: "Many gifts under (the last named amount)."

Not all committees can produce this kind of pyramid. Committees which are soliciting gifts from civic organizations like churches produce what I call an Aztec Pyramid. This is a flattened structure with less room between top and bottom. It represents the fact that most gifts from churches and other civic organizations tend to fall into a narrower range that the gifts from individuals. If your objective is $1,600 from civic groups here's what your Aztec Pyramid might look like:

1 Leadership Gift @ $300
3 Gifts @ $200 each
4 Gifts @ $100 each
Many gifts under $100

Once your committee has identified its Universe of Prospects and drawn up a Pyramid of Gifts, it is ready to discuss solicitation.

The first thing that should be accomplished is the solicitation of 1) the chairman of the committee if he is not a board member and 2) the individual committee members. You will remember that each committee chairman who is a board member will probably have already been solicited by the chairman of the board in July or early August. Other committee chairmen who are not board members should also be solicited by the board chairman. No solicitation of individual committee members can take place until the committee chairman has himself pledged or donated, since it is a well-recognized fund raising rule that no solicitor should ever ask for money from others until he himself has given.

It is a very good idea, if possible, to get a pledge for one of the three leading gifts from the chairman of each committee. He is, after all, a leader and as such should be willing to assume the forward position. It is the job of the board chairman to make sure this is done.

Having made his own pledge or gift, the chairman of the committee may feel confident about approaching his members.

It is not at all inconceivable that an effective, enthusiastic, committed chairman, who gathers an equally vital group of committee members could reach his objective without ever soliciting anyone else in the Universe of Prospects. It is more likely, however, that somewhere between 40-50% of the committee's objective can be raised from its members. For instance, if the objective of the Small Business Committee is $1,600, between $600-$800 should come from committee members. Note: Board members who may be members of individual committees should not be solicited by the committee chairman but by the chairman of the board. Any sums they donate count towards the board total, not the committee objective.

Once the committee chairman and his members have all donated, it is time for them to meet as a group and review the Universe of Prospects. By this time they should already have raised a significant percentage of their objective. If they have not, it is fair to question the commitment of both chairman and members; the Coordinating Committee should note that it may have a potential problem on its hands.

At this meeting each individual name within the Universe of Prospects should be discussed. What members are looking for are significant links to potential donors on the list. Remember: to meet your objective you usually don't need a link to every name. You need a few good links and individuals committed enough to carry through on the solicitation assignment. These are the questions the committee should answer:

- Who knows this individual (or this organization)?
- How well?
- How much do you think he might give?
- Why?
- What is the best way of approaching him? By letter? Telephone?
- Is there a better link through another member of our organization? (Refer back to the information from the Facilitating Session.)
- Is there someone outside the organization who would be a better solicitor and who we can persuade to act on our behalf?
- Is a team the best way to make this approach?
- Is there any reason we know why an approach at this time might not be successful?

If the members of each committee approach their work conscientiously, it should be possible to identify prospects, set prospective donation amounts, and assign either one solicitor or a solicitation team without difficulty.

Since most initial approaches to prospects are made by letter, it will be necessary for the committee members to have a draft letter they can adopt to their purposes. It is the responsibility of the Coordinating Committee to make such draft letters available to the committees.

If this schedule is followed, a significant amount of the money for most committees can actually be pledged or in hand before the formal kick-off of the fund raising effort. Indeed, by October 1st, the inauguration of the fund raising effort, the following tasks should already be accomplished:

- Board chairman's gift made
- Board members successfully solicited
- Committee chairmen who are not board members successfully solicited
- Top prospects identified for each committee
- Determination made about who will give what size gift, who will make solicitation visit
- Donor prospect contact letter drafted

These things having been accomplished, all that remains to do during the actual fund raising season is to schedule visits with and solicit the donations of the other prospects.

Note: once you are close to reaching your objective (about 75% of the way towards your goal), you should discuss the possibility of sending a general letter to all prospects whom you do not intend to visit. These are members of the Universe of Prospects whom no one knows or with whom no good link is apparent. This is, of course, a "cold" letter, but it may elicit some gifts and help you identify future prospects for the next fund raising effort. The cost of producing this letter and mailing it will have to be added to the committee's fund raising objective. (See Samples, page 226). This letter in no way takes the place of individual solicitation visits but is a small way of supplementing them and identifying new supporters of the organization.

The Role of the Coordinating Committee

It is the job of the Coordinating Committee to make sure that all the tasks outlined in this chapter are successfully completed. It has the following obligations:

- To prepare necessary documents and sample letters
- To insure that each committee has a chairman and members

- To make sure the Universe of Prospects for appropriate committees is completed
- To urge committees to identify and solicit top prospects
- To insure that other prospects are solicited
- To keep regular records on funds collected
- To deal with all problems arising in the committees.

Each week between July and December the Coordinating Committee should meet for about two hours. Minutes are kept of these meetings which 1) indicate what took place and 2) point out the tasks to be completed by the next meeting. The Committee is responsible for securing answers to the following questions:

- Does each committee have a chairman?
- Is he fully committed to the fund raising effort?
- Has he been successfully solicited by the chairman of the board?
- Who are the members of his committee?
- Does the Coordinating Committee have their names, addresses, and telephone numbers?
- Has the chairman successfully solicited them?
- Has the committee identified its Top Prospects?
- Has a draft solicitation letter been drawn up for each committee?
- Do the committee volunteers understand the essentials of solicitation?
- If they don't, is the chairman scheduling a training session?
- How is the committee insuring that individual solicitors make their calls?
- How much money has been raised from each committee this week?
- How much in total?

To gather the answers to these questions, the Coordinating Committee should appoint a liaison to each committee. Generally, this is a board member and generally he can effectively superintend and report on the activities of no more than three committees. More than this is cumbersome and can lead to dissatisfaction and disorganization.

At each meeting of the Coordinating Committee, each liaison should report on the successes and problems of each of his committees. Where members of the Coordinating Committee feel that individual committees are failing in their task, they should invite the chairmen in for a review of the situation.

If this procedure is faithfully followed, small problems need not become troubles threatening to disrupt the smooth functioning of your fund raising effort.

The Mid-course Review

Towards the middle of November — that is, about six weeks after the fund raising effort has officially begun — the Coordinating Committee should hold a mid-course review. This meeting naturally follows the Volunteer Solicitor-Motivator Meeting in September. It is intended to inform the volunteers what point the fund raising effort has reached and what remains to be done to accomplish the goal.

This time the motivational and technical aspects can mostly be accomplished by individual board members and committee chairmen and members telling their peers which techniques have worked for them and which techniques have not.

The chairman of the board, who conducts this meeting, should hold up examples of committees which are well along on the road to success and members who have been particularly helpful in the process. He should be lavish with his praise. If the sums raised by each committee are cited, the chairman should avoid negative comment on lower sums. It is not the function of this meeting to hurt people's feelings or ridicule them but to show them how successful committees are functioning. It is the job of the Coordinating Committee to be strict with individual chairmen behind closed doors.

The chairman should point out that about four weeks remain of the fund raising season and that all remaining prospects should be solicited by about December 15th. If there is to be a concluding party for volunteers before Christmas the date should be announced at this meeting.

It is not necessary for this meeting to take more than an hour. It should be handled so that the volunteers are again made to feel that their individual work is indispensable to the success of the fund raising effort and that the objective is going to be reached, even if only half of the money is yet in hand.

The End of the Beginning

By December, the Coordinating Committee begins to determine one of two things: either the fund raising objective will be entirely or nearly reached, or it will not.

If it looks as if the goal will be reached (that is, about 75% of the goal is either pledged or in hand by December 1), the Committee should consider the advisability of sending a final letter to those who have already given. This letter, sent only to committed donors, basically says: "We're nearly finished. Please help us over the top." All donors, board members, committee chairmen, committee members and outside donors, should be sent this letter and given the chance to complete the fund raising effort. This letter should be sent out, however, no later than the first week of December, so that people have a chance to respond to it before Christmas. And it should never be sent bulk mail, only first class. (See sample, page 229)

If the fund raising effort is falling short of expectations, it is the responsibility of the Coordinating Committee, particularly the chairman of the board and the executive director, to pressure the individual committee chairmen and their members to make the solicitation visits and finish the job. December is perhaps the most important fund raising month of the year, partly because of the general joy of the holiday season, partly because it is the last opportunity to make tax deductible gifts for the year. In any event, it would be most unfortunate not to capitalize on it, and the Coordinating Committee should insure that everything is done that can be.

Whether the fund raising effort is exactly on target or not, the Coordinating Committee should plan to hold some kind of volunteer recognition party some time between December 10 and 15. At this time even if you are aware that some of them might have done a better job, it is important that all volunteers be publicly recognized for what they have done and their significance to the organization reaffirmed. If the fund raising effort has been successful, you should indeed be grateful for what your volunteers have done. If things yet remain to be done, a graceful recognition by you of volunteer importance may perhaps spur the recalcitrants to some last-minute effort.

Now What?

If you have successfully raised the sum you set out to raise, you can congratulate yourself. You have worked hard and should be proud of yourself and your organization. There are now only two things to accomplish to wind up this portion of your fund raising effort:

> 1. Have a final meeting of the Coordinating Committee and assign one of its members (probably the executive director) to draft a two-to-three page report (not longer) about what went right and, more importantly, what went wrong in the recent effort. Make this report as specific as possible, since you will have another fund raising effort to coordinate in just 9 months.
>
> 2. Plan to send out a letter to all donors in about March or April informing them to what use you have been putting their money. Be as specific as possible about the good work you are doing. Try to concentrate on direct service provision. On the whole most donors want their money to go into direct service provision rather than the necessary expense of running your central office. You should describe how the service they supported has directly helped someone. Consider using a particular case study of where the collected funds made a

crucial difference in a human life. (See Samples, page 229). **Do not** ask for any further donation in this letter. The primary purpose of this letter is to inform them and again to express your gratitude for their participation. However, you can insert an unstamped self-addressed envelope and pledge card with this letter. If people wish to make a further donation, you have made it easy for them to do so; however, you have not pestered them for another gift. Some money is always forthcoming when this subtle approach is used.

If you have not yet raised the money you need, there are two possibilities:

1. You can return to the Needs Assessment and Development Planning Committee and begin the process of cutting your budget and reducing programs.
2. You can decide to fall-back on the March-May fund raising season and then mount a smaller version of your fall effort. I recommend that you consider this course.

Organizations which follow the steps outlined in this book rigorously and systematically should be able to raise all or most of the funds they need for operating expenses during one fund raising season. But for one reason or another, you may need extra time provided by the March through May season.

If you decide to use this season, however, you must take time in January (when, remember, the Needs Assessment and Development Planning Committee is beginning its work for the next season) carefully to assess exactly what happened in the fall, why some things worked, and, significantly, why some things didn't. Perhaps the leadership of certain committees needs to be changed. Perhaps board members need to be talked to about adopting a more positive attitude and taking a larger leadership role. Perhaps your fund raising objectives were not set forth clearly enough. A thorough review of the situation should pinpoint what happened and what you can do to finish things successfully next time.

CHAPTER 6

FUND RAISING FROM CORPORATIONS AND FOUNDATIONS

Fund raising from corporations and foundations should be carried on year round. Because corporations and foundations make their giving decisions on widely differing schedules, it is not possible to set a fixed period for raising money from them. Rather, you should begin your approach after:

- your organization's planning process has been completed
- the Facilitating Session has been held
- your development documents have been drafted
- the board of directors has been solicited.

This means, in effect, that you should be ready to make your first approaches in July or August.

Identifying Prospects

The process of identifying serious corporate and foundation prospects involves both science and art. Several factors must be taken into consideration in determining whether it would be advisable for you to make an approach to a particular corporation or foundation. Here are the key factors:

- If the prospect has guidelines (some don't), do they specifically exclude organizations like yours?
- Are you in the right geographical location for consideration?
- Have you got a fund raising objective (capital, program, operating) which the source can fund or are your objectives unsuitable?
- Has the prospect given to you before?
- If so, did it indicate a receptivity to funding you again?
- If not, what were you told about possible interest? Did it suggest other sources.
- Can you approach this prospect without a contact?
- Why do you think so?
- If not, do you have a contact who will assiduously work with you in crafting the approach?
- Is there a specific reason why you think this funding source might be interested in your organization?

To come up with the best answers to these questions, you need to know something about the varieties of corporate and foundation giving. You will find introductory information below. But remember, what follows is general. Corporations and foundations pride themselves on their individual approaches to their work. What makes fund raising from corporations and foundations so tricky and time-consuming is that you must know as much as possible about each funding source so that you can craft a suitable approach to it.

Here are the basic kinds of foundations and corporate giving programs, including information on how they work and how you should approach them.

- **Staffed foundations.**

These are the largest and best known of the country's approximately 25,000 grants-making foundations. Most of them are listed in **The Foundation Directory.** These foundations generally have part-time or full-time professional staff and trustees which meet from time to time to vote on the grants. Each of them usually has specific areas of concern, both programmatic and geographic, (and guidelines which are available upon request) although trustees can and do make exceptions, thereby overriding the "rules."

It is generally not difficult to get an appointment with the professional staff of these foundations. It is their job to see you. Do not expect these people to be forthcoming, however. They see hundreds of grant seekers annually and, as a result, are wary and restrained. Nonetheless, it is generally important not to ignore them. They have the power of gatekeepers throughout the ages: the power to block you. They do not like "end runs" (as they term them). Most attempts to get consideration from the foundation through trustees and not through the professional staff will engender considerable animosity on their (the staff's) part towards your organization. Yet because these people do not themselves always (or even usually) possess substantial power, it would be wrong to place too much reliance on what they may do for you. The professional staff can maximally frustrate and only minimally facilitate your funding search. Since trustees are higher-level managers, where you have or can create a trustee connection, you should do so. At the same time, the executive director can deal with his professional counterpart on the staff of the foundation. Because it is the job of most professional staff to decline your application as politely but firmly as possible, you need to create trustee links so that it will be more difficult to dismiss you as just another grantseeker.

- **Family foundations.**

By far the majority of foundations in this country are small and dominated by the donors, their family members, their attorneys or other representatives. To be sure, these foundations do not control the majority of foundation assets, but they are the more numerous.

These foundations for all intents and purposes work like individuals. Most do not maintain grants guidelines, nor do they have even part-time professional staff. They give exclusively to the causes in which the donor and/or family members are interested. Oftentimes these causes receive their annual donations automatically; they don't apply for them. The rule of thumb here, therefore, is stark: if you don't know a member of the board or cannot get significant access to one, don't bother applying.

Organizations currently waste a good deal of money sending proposals to these foundations. This is completely pointless. Instead, spend your time networking your way to introductions with the trustees of these foundations. Then convince them about the worth of your cause. Clearly the best family foundations to aim at are those where you think there might be interest in your subject (because of grants previously made or knowledge about the trustees).

- **Corporate Contributions Programs.**

The philanthropy of major corporations is usually handled either by a corporate contributions department or through an in-house corporate foundation. There are more similarities between these approaches than differences.

In most cases, the corporate contributions program has three purposes: 1) to enhance the image of the corporation in the community, 2) to permit the chief executive officer to project the image of a statesman when he needs money to do so, and 3) to a lesser extent to support the charitable activities of employees.

Thus when approaching a corporation it is usually a good idea to be able to establish that there is a senior management interest or else at the very least that one of your active volunteers is a corporate employee. Once your organization is linked to the source by such "inside" interest or volunteer involvement, then the executive director can approach the corporate contributions officer or administrator of the corporate foundation and make direct application.

Note: some corporations now maintain committees manned by employees whose purpose is evaluating grant seekers. Even in these instances, senior management retains significant power over grants. The corporate hierarchy generally supercedes other arrangements.

Remember: if you ever decide to by-pass either the professional staff or these committees, make sure you have a firmly-committed senior management or director-level supporter who is prepared to assist you as an advocate. You'll need it.

Crafting the Approach

Virtually all approaches to a foundation or corporation fall within one of eleven possibilities. These possibilities are given below with specific instructions on how to handle them:

- **Direct Link to Foundation Trustee**

In this instance, after you have determined that this foundation could give to you, the executive director drafts a letter for the board member or other individual who has the link. If the link is so strong that the contact feels he can activitate the link between himself and the donor representative with a telephone call, a memorandum should be prepared instead of a letter. This lists such specific information as the correct name and title of the professional staff of the foundation. Either the letter or the memo document covers the following points:

- Basic information about your organization.
- Your (contact's) desire to approach the foundation - stated explicitly.
- Your hope that the foundation trustee will meet with your agency contact and executive director to learn about your organization.
- Your hope that a meeting between the executive director of your organization, organization contact and professional staff (if there is any) can be arranged. Be as specific as you can be about who you want to see.
- Indicate how this letter will be followed up and when.

If no meeting with the foundation trustee can be arranged, he should still be asked to set up a meeting between the agency contact, agency executive director and the foundation's professional staff. Thus the professional staff will know of trustee interest and no doubt give your organization every consideration. If the trustee fails to schedule such a meeting and leaves it to your organization, mention your trustee connection during the conversation. Do so in a non-threatening manner, however.

Remember: every attempt should be made fully to involve the professional staff in all discussions. If these discussions break down, however, either on personality or substantive grounds, it may be necessary for you to deal directly with the trustee. In any event, keep the trustee informed of all developments with the professional staff through letters from either the contact or the executive director. Be sure to copy these letters and log all other communications on the form.

- **Indirect Link to Foundation Trustee**

Here, someone who is connected to your organization knows someone who is connected to the trustee of a foundation that you feel would be a good donor prospect for your organization. The difference in this scenario is that the indirect connection must be transformed into an agent acting directly on your behalf. To do this, a letter should be drafted for the person with the contact. This letter should initially ask for a meeting between the indirect link (the person outside your agency), the executive director, and your contact (the one who knows the indirect link). If your agency's contact is most knowledgable about the organization (a committed board member, for instance), it may not be necessary for the executive director to participate in this meeting.

What you are looking for from this meeting is:

- an enthusiastic commitment to your organization by the person with the contact,
- a willingness on his part to approach his foundation contact on your behalf,
- his assistance in getting the trustee to meet with the original organization connection and executive director, and
- back-up assistance in case matters get bogged down at any point. This reiterates the commitment between the indirect link and the executive director to be mutually helpful. It further extends the contact network.

Note: once you have met with the foundation trustee, you follow the instructions outlined in "Direct Link to Foundation Trustee."

- **Direct Link to Foundation Professional Staff**

Your contact has a direct link to the professional staff of a foundation you think might be interested in your organization. Your contact should either call or write his contact and ask for specific advice on how to proceed, or he should arrange for the executive director and himself to meet with the professional staff representative to discern this information.

Note: the person with the contact, not the organization, should make the direct contact including the scheduling of meetings. That is because he has the entrée.

- **Indirect Link to Foundation Professional Staff**

As with all indirect links, time must be spent transforming the indirect contact into a well-informed, committed agent of your organization. Thus the first thing to do is for the individual connected to your organization to set up a meeting involving the link to the professional staff, the executive director, and himself. The outcome of this meeting should parallel that detailed in "Indirect Link to Foundation Trustee": you want the link to prepare your way either by calling and scheduling your meeting or by writing ahead on your behalf. If necessary, offer to draft the letter that might be sent on your behalf.

- **No Link to Foundation**

The determination must be made as to whether the foundation might be receptive to a cold approach. If it is a small family foundation without professional staff, there is ordinarily no point in your approaching it. Don't waste your time.

If it is a larger, staffed foundation and you have adequately researched the prospect and determined that there might be interest in your organization, the executive director or chairman of the board should send a query letter asking for an appointment. In this situation, you must sell your organization to the funding source. How you can do so will be covered in the next major section.

- **Direct Link to Corporate President**

In raising money from corporations, the best link to have is a direct link to the president or chief executive officer. If you are fortunate enough to have such a link, the person who has it should either call or write the president. He may either know enough to go without the chairman of the board or executive director, or, more likely, he will want to arrange an appointment and take one or both of these individuals with him. It is always the responsibility of the person who has the link either to send the letter (which, of course, may be drafted by the executive director) and schedule the meeting.

It is very likely that the president of the corporation will want to involve the corporate contributions officer in the proceedings at some point, either at the first meeting or thereafter. If the president makes no mention of how such involvement may take place, the executive director should broach the topic and ask whether it would be advantageous for him to meet with this officer. It is essential that this point be clarified right from the start, since it is unlikely that you will have further meetings with the chief executive officer and may thereafter have to deal with the corporate contributions officer. Always establish how your first contact with this person will be made.

- **Indirect Link to President**

It should now be clear that the person who has the link must be made into your committed agent. Once this occurs, he should be willing to make the necessary connection, take you in hand to the president and act on your behalf. You want him to say to you, "I'll take care of it for you!"

- **Direct Link to Professional Staff**

Pursue this as you would any other direct link. You want the person with the direct links to set up a meeting with either your executive director or chairman of the board, himself and the professional staff officer. At all times remember the value of the direct link: if your case gets sidetracked for whatever reason, you can ask the direct link to intervene on your behalf to get matters moving again.

- **Indirect Link to Professional Staff**

In this case you know someone who is committed to your agency who knows the professional staff officer of a local corporation. You must convince this individual to work on your behalf, arrange an appointment for you, and attend it (if possible). You want him to shed his legitimacy on you and vouch for your organization with his active intervention. His physical presence should impress the corporate contributions officer or professional corporate foundation staff. It also gives you a friend with access in case things don't move just as you'd like.

- **Employee Connection**

Whether or not an employee knows either the president of a corporation and/or the professional staff, he is useful to you. Corporations consistently say they want to see their employees actively involved in community service; some corporations make this service a pre-condition of job promotion. Many employees, however, feel queasy about recommending an agency for support. Particularly lower-echelon employees wonder whether their assistance will come back to haunt them. You have several options.

If an employee is actively willing to assist you, have him send an inter-office memorandum to either the president of the company or to the corporate contributions officer. Express your willingness to draft the memorandum for him and, of course, do the necessary staff work to insure that it is going to the right person. Or alternatively, give this willing volunteer a development proposal, précis, brochure and public relations material and ask him to present it to the relevant contributions officer. Make sure you have done your homework so that the employee is not embarrassed by giving it to the wrong person.

If the person is not willing to assist you in this fashion (and the lower down the corporate totem pole he is, the less likely he will be to want to do so), write a letter to either the president or corporate contributions officer telling them that you are approaching them in part because of the fact that several corporate employees (or only one) are active in your organization. Of course if you mention the names of the employees you will have to get their permission.

While this letter does have some use, it is always better to get the employee to assist you actively. Understand that they may be nervous about doing so. All too often the corporate bureaucracy has a way of penalizing initiative, so you will have to spend some time familiarizing the employee with exactly what you are doing, why you are doing it, and with what his role in the process will be.

- **No Link At All**

Links help. There is no question about it. But there are situations where you may not need them. There are, for instance, both foundations and corporations (almost always those with professional staff) which pride themselves on their receptivity to new ideas and on their hospitality to people who are otherwise helping the community. Such institutions and the people who man them make it a real point of honor to lay down the welcome mat. They want to see the people who are emerging with powerful new ideas, and they want to forge alliances with them to make a better world. The problem is: how do you know which institutions and which people these are?

Here is where your informal communications network can be of the utmost importance. The best way of determining the receptivity of foundations and corporations and the way they really work (as opposed to the glowing superlatives of their printed brochures) is to ask other agencies about their experiences. Seek out particularly agencies which you know have recently been funded by the prospect. Make it a point to ask executive directors, chairmen of boards, and board members what they know about the foundation or corporation in question. How did they handle their own approach? Did they have a link? Did they go in cold and make the sale? Did they feel a link would have helped? How long did it take to process the whole matter? Unfortunately, this information, crucial in the fund raising process, is not listed in any book. But it is readily available through people who are in the fund raising business day to day, including development consultants who, because of their wide exposure to agencies seeking funds from corporations and foundations, are likely to have more of it than most practitioners.

What you need to remember at all times is that there are organizations which are receptive to bold initiatives and which make every effort to keep the door open to them. Sadly, there are also increasing numbers of funding sources which are closed shops. They give to the causes which directly interest their own corporate chief executives and foundation trustees. And that's that.

Your task is to determine which is which, so that you don't waste your time approaching a closed shop with your good ideas and enthusiasm when you should really know that there isn't the slightest chance of your getting a grant from them. Remember: for most non-profit personnel, time is one of the greatest resources; in many instances, it is **the** greatest resource. Fund raising can eat it up, quickly, leaving you depleted, demoralized, and actually worse off than when you started. Avoid this unhappy state of affairs by doing your homework. Use links whenever you can and be certain that the funding source you approach without a link is a receptive institution.

Preparing for the Interview

In each of the above cases, you are left facing an interview. This interview will be either with a chief executive officer, trustee, professional staff officer, or person who has critical entrée. Now that you have the prospect of presenting your case in person, you need to prepare to make the best impression.

Clearly, you have already done a significant amount of preparation to arrive at this point. You have, for instance, made the determination that the funding source you are visiting is indeed a prospect. Now what?

Preparing for your funding source interview should include:

- being as clear as possible about what the foundation or corporation might wish to support,
- knowing the possible amount of their gift or the range which is appropriate for your organization, and
- gathering background information on the person(s) whom you are seeing.

As soon as the interview has been scheduled, two things should occur:

- If any letters have been sent to the funding source by persons other than the executive director, he should get copies. These must be logged and kept as part of the organization's permanent file. These files must be kept up to date.
- The executive director should send the individual with whom the meeting is scheduled basic information about the organization including: précis, development proposal, brochure, public relations materials, &c. In this letter the actual time and place of the upcoming meeting can also be confirmed.

The executive director should then meet with members of the visiting team (of which he either may or may not himself be a member) and plan the visit.

- Being as clear as possible about what the funding source might wish to support.

Many organizations ask the funding source for the wrong thing. These days, of course, that probably means they are asking for operating support from a source that never gives unrestricted funds. Other cases include: asking for capital when capital is explicitly ruled out of consideration or going for a project involving the elderly, when the source is this year funding mostly juvenile programs.

It is always your responsibility to know as much as possible about the possible interests of the funding source. If you have followed the suggestions of this book, you should not have arrived at this point without knowing the interests of your "target" in as much detail as is possible. If you are, in doubt, however, make one last telephone call to the personnel at the funding source and ask whether the item(s) you intend to bring up in the meeting are in fact appropriate. If they aren't, re-think your approach. If worst comes to worst, cancel the meeting rather than make a bad impression. Remember: a whiff of incompetence remains and can do incalculable harm, not least because funding source officers discuss prospects among themselves. Having been privy to many of their meetings, I can affirm that their discussions in private are very candid.

On the whole, remember that foundations and corporations are looking for projects which will have a multiplier effect. In short, they are looking for investments. What they favor least is giving operating money, since it implies the kind of long-term commitment they generally don't want to make.

Remember, too, foundations and corporations are understandably conservative. They often don't like to be the first into the water. They want to know that others are supporting your work and even that other funding sources are buying into a particular project. You are in an immeasurably stronger position if you can approach an interview where you are only asking for a portion of the money you need and can say that the rest has already been committed. If you can arrange matters in this way, do so.

- Know the possible amount of their gift or the range

It is always possible to ask the possible funding source what size grant you should be asking for. But before you ask this question, you should attempt to find out what organizations like yours usually get. How can you find out?

In preparing for the interview, you will wish to review the various annual reports, grant guidelines, and specialized publications which are available to you. In addition, in the case of foundations, you may wish to research their tax returns. These are public records. Finally, don't hesitate to ask your colleagues (especially those who have recently successfully applied for a grant from the source) how much they asked for and how much they eventually received. Having done so, you should have a good indication of the appropriate range for your organization.

Remember: most organizations ask for too much money. This is a clear indication to the funding source that you haven't done your homework and can definitely prejudice your application. My rule of thumb: ask for only a little more (perhaps 20%) than you realistically expect to receive.

In case you are still having trouble determining how much to request, remember this: any gift over $5000 is considered major. Ask yourself whether you have the importance in your community, the visibility, the level of contacts and the project significance to get a major gift. Be realistic in making this assessment. Organizations which have not previously applied to a funding source and which are neither well known to the source nor otherwise prominent in the community will usually receive a first donation of well under $5000. The major exception to this rule is when one of the large grantsmaking foundations is funding your project because it has a significant interest in it. This is likely to be a one-time-only situation.

- **Gather background information on the person you are seeing**

Grantsmakers are a distinct breed of humanity. In crafting your meeting it is good to know as much as possible about the person you are seeing. If you have a contact, get that person to fill you in on the person by asking such questions as:

- How well does your contact know the person?
- Does he know anything about his education? His background? His family?
- Can the contact suggest which of the organization's projects might be the most likely to appeal to the source?
- Why? Is there a personal connection between the source and the work of the organization which would facilitate the building of a relationship?

Clearly, if you have a contact, you are very likely to get the answers to these questions. Otherwise, they become difficult to get. Still, here are some means of gathering background material on the people you will be meeting:

- If it is a corporate officer or director, try **Standard & Poor's Register of Corporations, Directors and Executives.** Volume 2 has biographical information on many of the nation's leading corporate directors and executives.

- If it is a foundation trustee, check **Trustees of Wealth** published by the Taft Corporation, Washington, D.C.

- Use biographical materials such as the **Social Register, Directory of Directors, Who's Who,** &c. Remember: the books you need to review vary from town to town. In Boston and New York, for instance, it is usually a good idea to check the **Harvard Alumni Directory.**

Keep reading profiles from the business and social pages of the local newspapers and magazines. The leaders you will be meeting are just the kinds of people likely to turn up in these articles. It is in the nature of feature pieces to reveal the kind of information it is otherwise often difficult to get.

Once you have taken the trouble to gather this information, write it down. Nonprofit organizations too often seem to live solely for the moment. The leaders of your community today will very likely be the leaders of tomorrow (or their sons and daughters). Be thoughtful of your successors. Make their jobs easier by filing the information you have laboriously gathered.

The last thing you should do before leaving for the interview is gather a complete set of all the materials you have already sent ahead. Oftentimes the funding source will either have misplaced the ones you sent or will want a duplicate. Include copies of all letters previously sent. You may wish to have these materials available in a manila folder with the name of the prospect typed at the top. Note: If your material has failed to arrive in advance of the interview or if the host has misplaced it, wait until the end of the meeting to hand over your documents. During the meeting you want the full attention of the funding source concentrated on you, not flipping pages and only half listening to your presentation.

If your information search has not turned up much usable material, arrive at your interview early and examine the walls for evidence of the person you are visiting: usually offices have diplomas, awards, photographs, even art work which reveals background, taste, and interests.

Handling the Interview

If you have followed the steps outlined above, your interview is on its way to being the success you want it to be.

Ideally you are going to the interview accompanied by someone who knows the person you need to meet. If so, let the contact who has convened the meeting begin things. Initially the conversation should be social. These first few minutes are most important. They either establish you as someone worth knowing or as merely another tiresome person who has to be dealt with. Handle them carefully. Smile. Be cordial. Don't feel pressured into getting prematurely into the actual subject of the meeting. Contribute your part to getting the right tone: a meeting of peers who expect a positive outcome.

After a few minutes of general conversation, a moment usually arrives when it is evidently time to get down to business. Either your host will then ask you why you've come or the contact person will say so. Try to agree in advance. One of them should make this move, not you. It is the contact's responsibility to say how he is connected to the organization, why he is interested in it, and why he supports its work. He need not go into extensive detail unless it is pertinent to establishing his vital interest. The fact that he is with you speaks for itself. The contact should not be shy about saying he hopes that the person you are meeting will become a supporter.

Once the contact's interest has clearly been established, he should turn the meeting over to the organization's representative (chairman of the board or executive director) for discussion of the agency and its current work. It is the job of the agency's representative to make the case.

It is best for this representative to handle his assignment as matter-of-factly as possible. He should be saying, in effect: "We are accomplishing important work in this community, and we hope for your support in order to continue it." Nothing derogatory should be said; indeed, avoid all comparisons with other organizations. Spend your time talking about your own work, not someone else's.

If you are meeting with the decision maker, point out which of your objectives might be of the greatest interest. Don't hesitate, however, to put these in perspective by mentioning the other fund raising objectives you have for the year. You need not ordinarily go into great detail on these subjects. Remember: you have already sent basic information on your fund raising effort (the précis and development proposal) or you will leave it at the conclusion of the meeting.

Once you have completed your presentation on the organization's fund raising objectives and the rationale for them, say that you hope for the support of the funding source. Act as if this support will be forthcoming because of the nature of your organization and its importance in the community. Beware of confidence turning into presumption, however.

Don't be shy about asking the funding source which of your projects might be of the most interest. Your aim is to come out of this meeting with as much specific information as possible so that your follow-up letter can be tailored to the funding source. Understand that the funding source will ordinarily not wish to make a definite commitment to you on the spot; (fortunately, there are those happy occasions when they do!) Tell the funding source that you are not necessarily looking for an out-and-out committment today, but you would be grateful for as much assistance as he feels comfortable in giving by informing you what you should be asking for — and in what amount.

Bear in mind that you need to leave the meeting knowing the following:

- Which project is the most attractive to the funding source?
- How much should we be asking for, or within what range should our request fall?
- Are there any supplementary documents the funding source needs in addition to those he has already been given?
- Does the funding source want a formal letter of request to follow this meeting? If so, to whom should it be addressed?
- What happens next? Is there a formal review, an evaluatory committee meeting? If so, when will this occur?
- When should you expect to hear from the funding source?

If you have the answers to these questions, your subsequent course of action should be clear. If you are uncertain on any one of these points, ask for a clarification. All too often agency representatives leave these kinds of meetings unsure both about what was decided and what they should do next. This is a business meeting and as such mutual clarity is expected. To insure that you have it take a moment at the end of the meeting and summarize what both parties have agreed to do and the deadlines by which the appointed tasks are to be completed. Write these points down on the spot.

Once it is clear who is doing what and by when, the meeting should be concluded. Do so on an upbeat. Thank the host for his attention and time and assure him that you will be back in touch shortly. Take this opportunity to mention how much you value the dedication and service of committed individuals like the one who brought you all together. Always take the opportunity of making your volunteers look good.

The question always arises as to how long it should take to reach this point. You should be able to make your pitch and the right kind of impression within fifteen minutes. At the outside, however, you should plan on not spending more than one hour. You are better off with a tightly controlled, brief presentation of a quarter hour than one which ambles over sixty minutes.

Note: If you have a link to the prospective funding source, but he is unable to attend the meeting, ask him to telephone his contact in advance and urge his active consideration of your organization. If he is unwilling to do so (or it otherwise proves difficult to arrange), make sure you mention your mutual contact early in the meeting: "I'm sorry our mutual friend cannot be with us today, but I'm sure you're aware of his strong support for what we're doing." Tell your host at the conclusion of the meeting that you will be in touch with the contact shortly to inform him how the meeting turned out. Ask him whether he wants any messages passed on.

If you are forced to go to a prospective funding source without a contact, assemble a team. One good team is the chairman of the board and executive director. Other board members are also acceptable. The point is to indicate that your approach is the joint initiative of the board and executive director. Funding sources continually stress the importance of this kind of approach.

Two Final Notes on Arranging a Successful Interview

• Show Passion About Your Idea

All too often funding sources complain that organizational representatives applying to them for support seem merely to be going through the motions. Their presentations are devoid of vitality; they themselves seem enervated and even bored. The passionate enthusiasm which motivates others and convinces them that here before them are the representatives of a vital new idea, an idea that they themselves would like to be part of is crucial. Good fund raisers have the knack of generating empathy in potential funders. "Only connect," the English novelist E.M. Forster wrote. Only connect and there is no end to the creative partnerships that will develop. Be sure there is someone on your team who can enthuse others and get them to share your vision of a better world.

• Show What You Are Doing To Help Yourselves

Charity, as every schoolboy knows, begins at home. All too often, however, funding sources complain that they feel misused by organizations which seem to have done little or nothing to help themselves. Funding sources emphasize over and over that their resources are limited. What they want is to help organizations which have done what they could to help themselves.

It is your job, therefore, to tell a funding source exactly what you have done, are doing, and will do to help yourself. A responsible funding source will respond with enthusiasm to your own attempts at sustained self-help. Don't expect them to do more for you than you're doing for yourself. Do put your efforts into perspective for a funding source. If you have worked long and hard to achieve a result which without explanation might seem rather meagre, explain the situation. Perhaps in actual fact your constituency is giving most generously. It is the American way to want to help people who are vigorously working for their own betterment. But nobody wants to give a hand-out.

Immediate Interview Follow-Up

Within forty-eight hours of the meeting, several tasks should be completed:

- A synopsis of the meeting and list of next steps should be logged. This synopsis should be about 50 words in length and should include mention of all that you agreed to do, by what date, and anything that the prospective funding source may have promised. (See Sample, page 230)

- A more elaborate set of notes should be written for the confidential files of the executive director. This file should include the otherwise difficult-to-find personal information about the funding source as well as a candid assessment about the meeting and its dynamics. These minutes can be tremendously helpful in planning future approaches and for your successors. 200 words is usually sufficient.

- The contact convening the meeting should send a thank-you note to his host. This letter, between colleagues, presents a useful opportunity to stress points about the organization and to rectify any omission. It also indicates the continuing interest of the contact. It would be helpful if a copy of this letter went to the executive director for the agency's files.

- The executive director (or chairman of the board, if he was present) should send a formal letter to the funding source requesting support. This letter is based on information gathered during the interview. It should ask for a certain amount of money for a certain project or fund raising objective. If you intend further immediate follow-up say what and when it will be. This letter should include your complete understanding of how your request will be handled, who will handle it, and when you expect to have the result.

Further Follow-Up

If a funding source makes its grant decisions by committee, it is important to know when the meeting on your organization will occur. Two weeks (ten business days) before this meeting, a representative of your organization should call the funding source and find out whether:

- your file is complete,
- you are still on the agenda, and
- there is anything else that needs to be done concerning your request before the meeting.

One of several people can make this call: the original contact person who knows the funding source, the chairman of the board, or the executive director. This is an important call. All too often some hitch has occured on the other side. Perhaps organizations with greater influence than yours have used their clout to move ahead of you; perhaps the available funds have been dispersed; perhaps your file has been misplaced. In any event you find yourself left off the funding agenda. If this happens to you:

- Find out whether your organization can be replaced on the agenda for the upcoming meeting.
- If not, find out when your application will be considered.

If the answers to these questions are not satisfactory, consider returning to your original contact and requesting his assistance. If you do this, however, make sure that the contact has sufficient influence to be helpful and that, given the time constraints, he can follow through quickly.

Conclusion

If you are fortunate enough to get an interview with a prospective funding source, you have landed an advantage in the fund raising game. Don't waste it. You want to be perceived as an effective, worthwhile organization that has carefully prepared for this meeting by:

- Thinking through its fund raising objectives.
- Drafting precise documents.
- Getting the full support of the board.
- Doing as much as you can for yourself.
- Researching the prospective funding source so that you are asking for the right thing in the proper amount.
- Coming up with a helpful link.

Make your case briskly and **con amore.** One of the major objectives of this meeting is to break out of the pack and connect with the human being on the other side of the desk. If you can do so, the long term benefits of this meeting can be considerable and the likelihood of a donation will be substantially enhanced.

CHAPTER 7

NOTES ON A CAPITAL CAMPAIGN

Previous chapters have dealt with annual fund raising efforts — the kind of fund raising which organizations must undertake year in and year out to raise money for small capital improvements, projects, and operating costs. From time to time, however, an organization also has major capital needs — usually of the "bricks and mortar" or endowment fund variety. These needs are significantly greater than those reflected in an annual campaign, and they can only be met by the transfer to the organization of significant sums of capital. The result is the Capital Fund Raising Campaign, a fund raising effort of major proportions which usually takes place over several years and replaces, for the duration, the annual fund raising effort. (Note: if your organization needs to raise a percentage of its operating budget each year through outside fund raising you will have to add this sum as an objective in your capital campaign.) Properly handled, these campaigns are among the most enjoyable to run for these reasons:

- The goals are clear-cut and usually tangible.
- They have a beginning, middle and end, unlike annual fund raising, which necessarily takes place each year.
- By far the most significant work can be accomplished before the campaign goes public. This means that the actual public campaign follows as a matter of course from the advance work which has been done.
- The result enriches and stabilizes the organization and makes it more capable of performing its good work.

How Often Should An Organization Have A Capital Campaign?

Organizations should consider the advisability of mounting a capital campaign at least once every ten years. Otherwise, organizations should plan campaigns for their major anniversaries and milestones: centenaries, jubilees, dates marking the commencement of important community programs, or upon the retirement of a founder or popular board chairman or executive director. In many capital campaigns begun in connection with a key organization date, the beginning of the fund raising effort is actually two or three years before the actual date. This allows that year to culminate the fund raising effort in suitably grand fashion.

The Pre-Public Phase

Two basic questions dominate the early stages of a capital campaign:

- Can we make a compelling case for needing the money?
- Do we have a constituency which can give it?

Both questions must be forcefully answered in the affirmative during what I call the Pre-Public Phase of the campaign. If they are not, you must either significantly reduce your expectations or even abandon the idea of having the campaign at all.

Making A Compelling Case: The Role of the Capital Needs Assessment Committee

As with the annual fund raising effort, a significant amount of forethought must go into the planning process for a capital campaign. Specifically, once the board has discussed the advisability of mounting such a campaign, it is the responsibility of its chairman to appoint a special Capital Needs Assessment Committee to look into the matter.

This committee functions in the same way as the previously-discussed Needs Assessment and Development Planning Committee. It must:

- assess the need for a capital campaign
- determine the actual fund raising objective
- produce a line-item budget for the objective
- send a report of its recommendations to the full board
- work to gain the concurrence of the board for its recommendations

The composition of this committee parallels that of the Needs Assessment and Development Planning Committee. It begins its work, however, earlier than its counterpart. Here it is important to know something about the schedule of a campaign.

On the whole, it is wise to begin a capital fund raising campaign in the fall, preferably in early October. Most organizations should allow between six and nine months for the pre-public identification and solicitation of top prospects. They should allow for at least as much time for their own work. Thus a campaign to be publicly launched in October, 1993 would be well advised to begin its work in about April, 1992 fully 18 months beforehand.

Do You Need An Outside Feasibility Study?

Many organizations feel it necessary to hire an outside consulting firm to assess their ability to raise capital funds from their constituency. They feel such a firm will be:

- objective about whether the campaign is a good idea or not,
- likely to ascertain from potential donors the true nature of their feelings about the organization and the possibility of them making a (perhaps substantial) donation to the campaign,

- candid in determining both the full-time and volunteer leadership's ability to lead the campaign to success,
- experienced in positioning your organization for best results,
- able to follow-up their introductory study with technical assistance in the campaign itself.

The result of their work is generally called a "Feasibility Study".

A good feasibility study by a reputable firm can save an organization time, money, and the possibility of public embarrassment through a poorly-planned and badly-executed campaign. However, while all organizations need a thorough pre-public planning phase, not all need to spend the often-substantial sums that a feasibility study costs. Note: the cost of such studies ranges from about $5000 to $70,000 and beyond.

Sadly, organizations often throw their money away on studies which are too general to do them much good. The fault in such cases is probably divisible. Organizations can be faulted because they:

- don't bother to ask for parallel references from their consultants. You need to see what they have done for other agencies like yours.
- rely solely on the consultant to inform them of what they need. Instead, exercize some caution and foresight. Seek out other organizations which recently completed successful capital fund campaigns and see how they did it.

Consultants can be faulted because they:

- do not identify the top donor prospects.
- fail to ascertain whether these prospects would give to a campaign and, if so, how much.
- do not evaluate the willingness and capacity of both volunteer and executive leadership to manage a campaign.
- do not point out significant public relations problems which will adversely affect a campaign.
- won't risk an account by being candid in advising you not to pursue a campaign which has minimal chance of success.

The result is often most unfortunate. An organization, relying on a vague promise of success advanced by an unscrupulous or perhaps just slothful and uninformed consultant, "goes public" with its capital campaign. Because of poor preparation, it seeks an amount of money far in advance of what it can realistically expect to raise. With uncommitted, untrained leadership and a case which is not persuasive to its constituency, its failure is predictable.

What happens next? The consultants move on to a greener pastures while the hapless organization is left to face public embarrassment, recriminations within the board, and the realization that it has squandered precious time and resources.

I wish this scenario were just fiction, but I see it continually. Fortunately this unhappy result is entirely avoidable.

Organizing for Success

Once you have determined for what you want to raise the money and the board has agreed with both the fund raising objectives and the overall goal for the campaign, here's what you need to accomplish:

- Draft preliminary campaign budget.
- Solicit board of directors.
- Select Campaign Chairman.
- Establish Campaign Coordinating Committee.
- Designate fund raising committees and chairmen.
- Set amounts they must raise.
- Identify Naming Opportunities.
- Identify Top Prospects.
- Craft your approach to these prospects.
- Provide solicitation training.
- Draft campaign development documents.
- Undertake solicitation meetings.

Draft Preliminary Campaign Budget

Amazingly, many organizations enter a capital campaign without knowing how much it will cost them to raise the money, whether they can do so using existing resources, or whether they must (as is usually the case) add staff and overhead expense. This is irresponsible.

As soon as you can, prepare a preliminary budget showing how much you expect to spend for development-related personnel and non-personnel expenses. Update this budget towards the end of the Pre-Public Phase of the campaign when your figures will probably be more accurate. Here are the major budget items you should consider:

Personnel

- Director of Development
- Development Secretary
- Development Assistants
- Professional Fund Raising Counsel

Non-Personnel

- design of précis and other documents
- printing of précis
- printing of direct mail letters
- printing of special campaign stationery
- printing of outside business envelopes
- printing of inside return envelopes
- printing of pledge cards
- computer and word-processing time
- travel
- accommodation
- entertainment
- telephone
- copying
- postage

Note: Once you have arrived at the cost of raising the money, you will probably have to add the amount to the overall objective of your campaign. This is perfectly acceptable. No sensible person thinks it is costing you nothing to raise your goal. They just want to know that the amount it is costing you is reasonable. You should be able to reassure them on this print.

Solicit the Board of Directors

The rule of thumb is that your board of directors should contribute at least 20% of your overall fund raising goal. It is time to solicit the board members once they have agreed to this goal (which should include the cost of the campaign and any annual operating funds you must raise from your constituency.)

Ideally, at the meeting at which the board chairman suggests the figure the board will have to contribute to the capital campaign, he himself makes a suitable Leadership Gift to spur the generosity of his colleagues. Having announced his own gift (or pledge), the chairman should then make it clear that over the next thirty days he will be contacting each board member personally about their own gift. He may then distribute a Pyramid of Gifts based on the figure the board must contribute so that its members may see how many gifts are needed and in what amounts. The chairman will wish to use this Pyramid of Gifts in working out how much he feels each board member should contribute.

Note: Most capital campaigns are 3-4 years in duration. You may wish to consider a longer time span if your board members feel they cannot reach their 20% goal in that time.

Remember: If your board is unable to contribute 20% of the capital fund raising goal, it is probably too high. Unless you have some special reason for thinking that the deficiency can be made up elsewhere, you will have to lower your overall goal. Also don't forget: Each of your board members must contribute and the fact that all have done so needs to be prominently mentioned in your capital campaign documents.

Select A Campaign Chairman

No capital campaign should proceed without a campaign chairman. This chairman provides the necessary volunteer leadership for what is ordinarily a very demanding assignment. The campaign must accordingly be his primary volunteer commitment, and he must be willing to devote considerable time and energy to it. Also, in many instances the campaign chairman usually makes one of the leadership gifts to the campaign so his capacity to do so should be considered before the appointment is made.

If possible avoid making the chairman of your board the campaign chairman. One of the leading reasons for appointing an outside chairman is to supplement your existing leadership rather than give it additional tasks. Don't waste this opportunity to bring others into your leadership team.

Note: Never appoint the executive director the campaign chairman. This is a clear conflict of interest that will be detrimental to your organization. The campaign chairman must at least be at the level of your senior board members and must be able to deal with them as an equal. The executive director, as an employee of the board, can never do so.

The role of the campaign chairman is clear: as chairman of the Coordinating Committee he must oversee all aspects of the campaign. He has a significant role to play (along with the chairman of the board) in motivating and directing both board members and the other volunteer leadership and in identifying and soliciting major gift prospects.

The campaign chairmanship is no sinecure. Do not place at the head of your campaign an individual who is not fully prepared to make a significant commitment in both time and money. You can, of course, appoint an Honorary Chairman, but if you do so understand that you still need a working chairman to provide the campaign with suitable leadership. If such a chairman is not readily available, either consider appointing co-chairmen or else assess whether you can proceed without this pivotal figure.

Establish Campaign Coordinating Committee

As in an annual fund raising effort, it is necessary for a capital campaign to have a Coordinating Committee. The major difference between the two committees is that where the Coordinating Committee for an annual fund raising effort generally meets weekly for about six months, that for the capital campaign must meet weekly for the duration of the campaign. Its membership is, however, comparable:

- Campaign Chairman
- Chairman of the Board
- Executive Director
- Staff Assistant
- Development Counsel

As before, the chairmen of the individual committees can be called in as needed. Detailed minutes of meetings should be kept: 1) to record decisions, and 2) to note tasks to be accomplished. This committee can begin meeting as soon as the board has approved the capital campaign.

Designate Fund Raising Committees and Chairmen

The following constitute the major committees of a capital campaign:

- Board of Directors
- Past Board Members Committee
- Top Donor Prospects Committee
- Users Committee
- Employees Committee
- Past Users Committee
- Those Connected to Users Committee
- Foundation Support Committee
- Corporation Support Committee
- Civic Group Committee

117

- Religious Organizations Committee
- Friends Committee
- Special Events Committee

Not all these committees will necessarily be appropriate for your campaign, although you may be able to create others which do not appear on this list. As a rule, organizations which can clearly demonstrate that they are providing a useful community service (hospitals, YMCAs, Girl Scouts, &c) will be able to look for support beyond their own immediate membership into the broader community. On the other hand, private schools, churches, universities, and the wide array of sectarian and ideologically-committed organizations will draw most of their support from those who have directly benefitted from the organization.

In the case of the former organizations, their task is to create committees which can tap into the broadest base of community support while continuing to draw from their own membership. The task of the second group is to ensure that all those who have benefitted from the service are identified and solicited as well as those who are somehow connected to the beneficiaries.

While the role of most of these committees parallels their counterparts in an annual fund raising effort, two deserve some words of comment:

- **Top Donor Prospects Committee**

Identifying and successfully soliciting Top Donor Prospects is essential to the prosperous conclusion of your capital campaign. This committee, therefore, has a significant role to play. It should be composed of individuals of weight and stature equal to the Top Donor Prospects. They will be, therefore, suitable solicitors as well as being Top Prospects themselves.

- **Employees Committee**

Employees may, of course, be solicited as part of your annual fund raising effort. But they should surely be sought out as part of any capital fund raising campaign. Needless to say, employees benefit directly from the operation of any organization and as individuals with a vested interest in your continuing success should be asked to contribute towards it.

As in an annual effort, all members of the board of directors must take an active part in the fund raising committees both as chairmen (where appropriate) and as individual members. A capital campaign cannot succeed without the full, active support of board members both as donors and as workers. Other chairmen can be drawn from the ranks of the donor prospects. For instance, an outstanding, committed employee should be asked to head the Employee Committee.

Set Amounts Committees Must Raise

If the groups represented by the committees have histories of gift-giving, you can analyze several factors before assigning them a fund raising objective as part of the capital campaign. These factors include:

- total universe of prospects
- percentage of those having given each year for the last three years
- whether this percentage has been increasing annually
- what is known about potential Top Prospects within this universe
- what these prospects may know about the organization
- whether they have previously been cultivated
- if there is any reason for feeling that these prospects may have an interest in the organization
- how much effort has previously been made to solicit gifts
- what were the results?

The analysis of these answers should enable you to assign preliminary fund raising objectives to each committee. Remember: During the Pre-Public Phase of your capital campaign, these objectives must be considered tentative. It is not until you have actually sought out your Top Donor Prospects that any final determination can be made.

Note: In most capital campaigns a significant amount of the total comes from Top Prospects. As a rule of thumb, at least 25% of your overall goal should come from these Top Prospects beyond the board, which is, of course, contributing 20% in its own right. If you deviate substantially from this formula, be sure that the other constituencies of your organization have both sufficient numbers of committed top prospects and other donors to sustain the increased weight you are assigning them.

Identify Naming Opportunities

Most capital campaigns contain possibilities for top donors to name either for themselves or for individuals of their choice (living or deceased) various fund raising objectives. You may exercize your creativity in selecting suitable Naming Opportunities for your campaign. Keep the following points in mind, however:

- You will want to have a spread of Naming Opportunities from fairly small amounts (for individuals whom you may recognize on a permanent lobby plaque) to substantial donors.

- Link your Naming Opportunities to your Pyramid of Gifts. Thus if you need a top gift of $200,000, your best Naming Opportunities should be for this amount.
- Print a separate sheet listing your Naming Opportunities. This can be used as an insert in your précis and sent to selected individuals or made generally available.

The question of how much an individual should give to be able to designate the name deserves a few words. In general, if a project can be divided into several Naming Opportunities, then the individual giving the lead gift need not donate the entire cost of the project in order to name it. For instance, if you are constructing a building as part of your capital campaign, it would present a number of Naming Opportunities such as:

- overall name of building
- names for individual floors
- names for individual rooms or suites of rooms
- lobby plaque with contributor names

Each of these Naming Opportunities is assigned a contribution level; the overall name of the building might therefore be available for only a substantial fraction of the total cost.

On the other hand, if a project cannot easily be divided, the naming donor would need to give all or substantially all the money required.

Identify Top Donor Prospects

Many capital campaigns fail because too little time is spent identifying Top Donor Prospects. Your success in identifying and soliciting these prospects will, however, determine the outcome of your campaign. Here's how to identify them and what to do once you have done so:

- Determine the Universe of Prospects for each committee. How many people are there who could possibly contribute to the committee's fund raising objective?
- Be sure that each possible giver to your organization is accounted for.
- Draw up a complete list of all prospects including their names and addresses.
- Invite committee members (and any other individuals who are knowledgable about the names on the list) to a Screening Session.
- Distribute a Pyramid of Gifts so that each committee member knows how many gifts you need to reach your objective and in what amounts.

- Go through each name of the list with a view to identifying Top Donor Prospects.
- If there are too many names to consider at one session, schedule another meeting. In a two-hour meeting, you can screen about 100-150 names.
- Get answers to the following key questions:
  i.   Is this person a Top Donor Prospect?
  ii. Has he given to our organization before?
  iii. In what amounts has he given and how recently?
  iv. If he is a Top Donor Prospect, what size donation could he give?
  v.   What size should we ask from him?
  vi. Who is the best person to make the solicitation call?
       (Remember: the solicitor(s) need not be on the committee.)

Craft Your Approach

Top Donor Prospects must be considered and approached one at a time. Each approach should be carefully crafted for maximum success. It is better to work on a few carefully-tailored Top Prospect approaches than to have many outstanding without adequate supervision and guidance.

Here's how the approach should be handled:

- If only one person from your screening session has indicated that he knows the Top Prospect, he will probably be assigned as the solicitor.
- If the committee chairman and the Coordinating Committee concur with the solicitor's assessment of the Top Prospect's gift potential and the fact that this solicitor is the right one for the job, the assignment can be made.
- The assignment memorandum should include:
  i.   The name, address, and telephone number of the prospect
  ii. Information on his past giving record
  iii. Size of gift the solicitor is to request
  iv. Any other pertinent information about the prospect that the committee has
  v.   A date by which solicitation is to be accomplished.

Note: Because timing is of the essence in the Pre-Public Phase of the capital campaign, you cannot afford to leave a Top Prospect's name indefinitely in the hands of a solicitor who may prove slow or reluctant about handling the case. Target dates should be assigned for assignment completion. If the solicitor does not make this date (after being reminded that it is approaching), the prospect should be reassigned.

No approach to a Top Prospect should be contemplated without the knowledge and approval of the Coordinating Committee. It has the ultimate authority about determining who should approach the prospect and for what size gift.

Provide Solicitation Training

Just as in an annual fund raising effort, your solicitors will need training. This subject has been covered earlier in the book, but two points should be made again:

- It is the solicitor's responsibility to mention the amount which the organization expects the prospect to give. This is true of **every** solicitation visit but is especially important in the case of Top Prospects. In these cases, the initial interview usually goes like this:

  Solicitor: "Because of your well known interest in our work and long-demonstrated committment, we regard you as one of our Top Prospects."

  Donor Prospect: "What does that mean?"

  Solicitor (looking prospect squarely in the eye): "It is our hope that you would make us a gift of (amount)."

  Donor Prospect (probably pausing for a moment): "I'm flattered that you think I'm capable of making that size a gift. You'll understand, of course, that before I could even consider doing so, I must think it over."

  Solicitor: "I quite understand. Why don't I call you (at a specific time to be noted down)."

- If the solicitor feels nervous or awkward about making the approach he should say so. This nervousness is not an acceptable excuse for not making the solicitation call. Moreover it may actually assist the solicitor in the long run. Most Top Donor Prospects have themselves been solicitors for organizations at one time or another, and they know what you're going through. Very likely your admission of nervousness will assist you in establishing the kind of atmosphere and human contact which produce donations.

Draft Campaign Development Documents

Although the dollar amounts you are seeking may be altered after you assess the information gathered in the Pre-Public Phase of the capital campaign, you still need documents to communicate your case and set forth what you hope to do. It should be understood that both figures and documents are tentative until the assessment of them, which concludes the Pre-Public Phase, is completed.

Most capital campaigns spend far, far too much money in developing documents. I think they are mistaken in doing so. A well-reasoned case, concisely put and communicated through simple documents, is usually quite sufficient for most donors. The case rather than the elaborate documents is what proves persuasive.

In this regard, I feel a standard précis document is quite sufficient both for the Pre-Public Phase of your campaign and the actual campaign itself. This document usually contains about 2000 words and may be printed in one brochure of 2 pages (4 sides). This document is entirely sufficient even for multi-million dollar campaigns.
(See sample, page 233)

If you are approaching the large staffed foundations and corporations with aspects of your capital campaign, you may wish to supplement the précis with standard development proposals.

Undertake Solicitation Meetings

It is the solicitor's responsibility to schedule solicitation meetings. The purpose of these meetings is simple: to gain the adherence of a Top Prospect to the campaign and to discover as specifically as possible how much and when this individual will give to the campaign.

At the meeting itself the solicitor should explain to the donor prospect that the organization would like to begin a capital campaign in the fall. The précis document (which may either have been sent in advance of the meeting or may be given to the prospect in person) explains the fund raising objectives the board has set and to which they themselves have contributed.

It is the solicitor's responsibility to explain that at the present time these are just tentative objectives. They cannot and will not be finalized until and unless certain key supporters of the organization give their explicit support to the project. The solicitor must make it clear that the organization regards the individual whom he is now addressing as such a key supporter. The donor prospect must be made to feel that the success of this undertaking depends to a considerable extent on his willingness to support it.

The solicitor should explain why the organization has chosen this prudent course of pre-public solicitation: it does not want to go public with a campaign without having previously ascertained that it enjoys broad support from the organization's important supporters. This essential support will ensure success.

Having said this much, the solicitor should be ready to inform the Top Donor Prospect that his support is vital and that as a committed supporter of the organization, it is hoped he will make a Leadership Gift.

Readers should understand that this gift need not be immediately forthcoming. What is important now is that the organization have a firm indication of the extent of the prospect's support so that this information can be considered in the assessment process. Actual payment may take place in installments over several years. All that matters now is to know that a certain sum of money will be forthcoming at some point during the campaign.

The solicitor should now write this information down in a memorandum which can be transmitted both to his committee chairman and to the Coordinating Committee. (See sample, page 239)

The Assessment Process

Two to three months before a capital campaign is scheduled to go public, the members of the Coordinating Committee must make a final determination on whether the amount of money being sought is realistic or not. The results of this meeting are communicated to the board which has the final responsibility for setting the actual goal of the campaign.

The rule of thumb is that at least 25% of your goal should be pledged or in hand at the public announcement of your capital campaign. This money comes solely from two sources:

- the board
- your Top Prospects

Whether this amount is sufficient to ensure success depends on several factors:

- How many Top Prospects are there?
- How many have been solicited?
- How many have made pledges to the campaign?
- Are these pledges at the level of our expectation, or are they less than we need?
- Do we have a realistic idea of how much our other, smaller donors will contribute?

The shape your fund raising effort is in depends on the answers to these questions. For instance, if you had counted on your Top Donors and board for 45% of your total but had, after soliciting them, received hard pledges for only 25%, you probably have a problem. You must then determine whether:

- The board can give more
- The contributions of those Top Donors who have already pledged can be raised during the duration of the campaign
- The minds of the other Top Prospects can be changed in your favor through cultivation
- Your smaller donors will be able to make up the difference.

In answering these questions, you must be very hard headed. It is always better to reduce the amount of your capital fund raising goal, dropping one or more of your objectives, than to set an overly-ambitious goal you probably cannot reach. It is the job first of the Coordinating Committee and ultimately of the board to evaluate the information gathered during the Pre-Public Phase.

If You Decide To Reduce Your Goal

Don't despair if you find, following the assessment process, that you must reduce your fund raising goal. You are actually protecting yourself from much later difficulty and the organization from the public embarrassment that inevitably accompanies defeat. The whole purpose of the Pre-Public Phase of your campaign is to make a realistic assessment of how much money your organization can expect to raise during a capital fund drive. As with any planning process, you must always keep open the possibility that your final goal may change. Depending on the interest and tangible support of your board and top prospects and on a realistic analysis of what your other constituencies may give, you may have to lower your expectations.

Reducing a goal you cannot realistically expect to meet is sound policy. After having carried through the stages of the Pre-Public Phase without gathering the money or pledges you need, don't behave irresponsibly by assuming the money is "out there" for you. It probably isn't.

If you decide to reduce your goal, don't make any public announcement that you are doing so. Just proceed with the actual goal that the Coordinating Committee recommends and that the board adopts. If at a later date some of your Top Prospects ask about why the goal publicly announced is less than the one mentioned during their solicitation visit, explain that the revised goal is the one the board finally deemed consonant with the giving potential of the organization's supporters. Nothing else need ever be said.

If You Decide Not To Hold A Campaign

In rare instances, you may discover that your organization cannot sustain any kind of capital fund raising drive at this time. Perhaps:

- The board will not contribute substantially.
- Top prospects are disaffected with the organization and will not contribute.
- There is confusion in your constituency about the work of the organization and hence a reluctance to contribute.
- The organization has public relations and image problems which reduce the likelihood of campaign success.

For whatever reason, the money cannot be raised at this time.

Two things should be done:

1. A letter should be sent to those making pledges saying that at this time a capital campaign has been deemed unrealistic. This letter should be brief and should not dwell on the reasons why a campaign is not possible just now. It should conclude by thanking the individual for his pledge and hoping he will make it instead to the general support of the organization.

2. The board should turn its attention to what caused your fund raising problems. Adopting suitable measures to insure that such problems are solved make a later campaign date feasible.

The Public Phase

Once the final fund raising goal has been set, you are ready to move into the Public Phase of your capital campaign. In its first year, the following tasks need to be accomplished:

- Develop campaign documents.
- Develop, print and post first direct mail piece.
- Make public announcement of the campaign.
- Establish personal contact with donor prospects.
- Develop, print and post second direct mail piece.
- Develop, print and post third direct mail piece.
- Undertake year-end review of progress.

Develop Campaign Documents

The documents used during the Pre-Public Phase of the campaign are draft documents. While very few (or even no) changes may have to be made in the copy you will now have to print up the final documents you will use during the capital drive. Remember: Many items can be printed once for the duration of the campaign. They include: campaign stationary, outside business envelopes, pledge cards, return envelopes , &c. It is more economical if you can do your printing in large runs.

Develop, Print, and Post First Direct Mail Piece

Your first direct mail piece is an important one. It is the first opportunity you have to explain to all your potential donors the purpose and goal of the capital fund campaign. Much care and attention should be given to making it persuasive and appealing. This piece should arrive at your donors' homes at the same time the public announcement of your campaign is being made. If you are using bulk mail, check with the post office to see how long it takes for it to be delivered in your area. Don't be surprised if it only arrives in two or three weeks.

Generally the first packet sent out includes:

- A cover letter from the chairman of the board. This letter should set forth the most pungent and cogent reasons for the campaign, should announce the goal and should indicate the amount of contributions already received. Note: You may not wish to announce just now all the money which has already been pledged or received. Hold back some for later mailings and for periodic news announcements.
- Campaign précis
- Pledge card
- Return envelope

Make Public Announcement of the Campaign

Do not neglect the public relations possibilities of a campaign or the need to publicize what you are doing to the broadest constituency. If yours is an organization serving the local community, use newspapers and radio and television if available. Consider holding a press conference or at the very least mailing a press release with basic information about the campaign. If possible you should get publicity for your campaign at least once a month.

Many organizations couple a public announcement of their campaign with a special event designed as a fund raiser. This is an excellent way both of drawing attention to your cause, familiarizing your constituency with what you are doing, why it is necessary and with what you expect from them, and raising some of your goal.

Establish Personal Contact With Donor Prospects

The best way of soliciting money is face to face. The more potential donors your solicitors can call on personally, the better for your organization. Arranging these face-to-face solicitation meetings is the job of the individual fund raising committees and their members. Once they have finished soliciting their top prospects (which should take place in the Pre-Public Phase), they should decide which of their other prospects they will visit. A good rule of thumb: try to visit all prospects capable of making either a lead gift or one in the middle range of your Pyramid of Gifts.

The remaining donor prospects should get telephone calls. Telephoning is not usually as good as a personal meeting. But it is preferable to just a letter. Do not overburden your solicitors by giving them too many calls to make. Five donor prospects are quite sufficient at any time. The Coordinating Committee should help the solicitors by drafting a sample script which can be used when they call their prospects.

Fund raising is a people activity. The more people who can personally be involved in it, the better. It is a very good idea to make contact with your donors as early in your campaign as possible when support, enthusiasm and motivation are all high and when you are able to project momentum and inevitable success. Try to follow up your first direct mail piece by either a personal visit or telephone within a month of its receipt.

Develop, Print and Post Second Direct Mail Piece

Your first direct mail piece should coincide with the public announcement of the campaign. Your second should be timed to arrive in late November or early December. This is the peak fund raising season, and your organization should be ready to take advantage of it.

By this time, a good many people should already have contributed to your organization. They include:

- board members
- top donors
- respondants to first direct mail piece
- individuals solicited by personal visits and telephone calls

The people who gave so recently do not want to receive another solicitation letter. At the same time there are many potential contributors who have not yet made their donation. How can you handle both?

It is a wise idea to produce a newsletter report which can be sent both to those who have already given and to those who have not yet done so. This report should be both upbeat and informative. It should highlight:

- the amount of money already given,
- the strenuous work of the fund raising committees and selected volunteers
- various aspects of the fund raising campaign, reconfirming their need, and it should
- indicate which special event and other campaign activities are forthcoming.

Two different cover letters should be developed to accompany this informative report. The first should be sent to those who have already given. Basically it is a thank-you note. It should:

- thank them for their support,
- dwell on the progress the campaign is making, and
- indicate when the first campaign objective will be accomplished (for instance, when ground will be broken for a new building).

The second letter basically says: "We're surprised you haven't contributed to our campaign yet. We know you're supportive of what we're doing. Surely you know we can only succeed if we have your support." This letter applies a little gentle pressure to donors who are assumed to be interested and committed supporters.

Both letters include a pledge card and a return envelope, although they are handled differently. In the first letter to those who have already given, no mention of the pledge card is made. This is not a solicitation letter **per se**; it is a report of progress. Nonetheless some people will give again when they receive it if a return envelope is provided.

The pledge card is explicitly mentioned in the second letter. "You'll find a convenient pledge card and return envelope with this letter. We hope you'll return them as soon as you can."

Develop, Print and Post Third Direct Mail Piece

The third direct mail piece should arrive in mid- to late March. It follows the format of the second piece. Individuals who have already made a pledge or contribution should not be asked outright for another. They should be sent instead:

- a cover letter indicating the current state of the campaign
- an informative newsletter about campaign developments
- a pledge card and envelope (unmentioned in letter text)

The third letter sent to those who have not yet contributed should apply more pressure to these recalcitrant supporters of the organization. It should say: "We're frankly surprised we haven't heard from you yet. We know you support us. We know you know the need for this campaign. You know its objectives are critical. Won't you please, therefore, make every effort to join the family?"

Undertake Year-End Review of Progress

It is the job of the Coordinating Committee to undertake a year-end review. If you began your campaign in October, this review should take place in June. The review principally involves evaluating the performance of each committee. If a committee has not met its goal for the year, was it because its leadership and solicitors were unproductive, or was its goal too high? In many cases, a committee will have substantially exceeded its goal, in which case the Coordinating Committee should consider raising its target for the next year.

Once this evaluation has occured, the Coordinating Committee should set the fund raising objectives for each committee for the next year. In doing so, it will wish to consider whether:

- selected donors can be asked to increase their contributions,
- Top Donor Prospects who have not yet given may be ready to do so, or
- more strenuous outreach can be made to smaller donors.

By the end of the first year of your capital campaign, you should have raised (in cash or pledges) **at least** 50% of your goal. Many successful campaigns will have raised substantially more by this point. This is as it should be. The first year of any campaign is crucial. Energy and commitment are probably at their highest, and you must take advantage of this fact and work diligently to raise as much of your goal as you can.

Succeeding Years Of A Capital Campaign

What helps maintain the enthusiasm of your donors and their interest in your campaign is the realization of your campaign objectives. Donors want to see their money being put to work for the cause. This encourages them to give more. Also, some of those who have not yet given may be waiting to see whether your campaign will succeed before they jump on board. They, too, need to be shown tangible achievement.

This is why you should begin to accomplish your objectives as soon as you can. If you are in a "bricks and mortar" campaign, for instance, try to break ground in year two of the campaign. Otherwise, try to show people tangible results for the money they've given. Publicize these results in the newsletter you send both to donors and potential donors.

Technically, the succeeding years of a multi-year capital campaign mirror the first, and there is, therefore, no reason to discuss them in detail here. Each year three (occasionally four) letters should be sent out; every attempt should be made to differentiate the letters sent to donors from the ones sent to those who have not yet contributed. You should continue to try to make personal contact with as many donors and potential donors as you can, using the techniques already discussed.

Final Note

A well run capital campaign should comfortably exceed its original goal. A classic case in point is the recent Harvard University capital campaign. Originally Harvard's goal was $250 million. But the campaign proved so successful (despite the fact that the $15 million Leadership Gift did not materialize) that the objective was raised towards the conclusion of the original campaign to $350 million, then the largest fund raising goal for any college in America's history. So it should be with you.

By following the suggestions outlined in the Pre-Public Phase of this chapter, you will start your campaign not only with a realistic goal but also with a major percentage of what you seek either pledged or in hand. You should have another sizable percentage by the end of the first year.

At that point your organization should be fully in place and entirely seasoned. Your constituency should be fully acquainted with what you want to do with their money and should actually be beginning to see tangible achievements from the funds already donated. There is therefore absolutely no reason why you should not be able to **exceed** your original goal and, at the commencement of your third or fourth year, announce a substantially higher objective for yourself.

CHAPTER 8

ORGANIZING SUCCESSFUL SPECIAL EVENTS

Virtually all nonprofit organizations should hold special events regularly. There are several very good reasons to do so. Special events:

- help raise unrestricted revenues which can be used to meet operating expenses and increase your endowment fund.
- boost the image of your organization in the community.
- attract new friends and supporters.
- allow you to cultivate individuals and institutional donor prospects.
- present a perfect opportunity to say "thank-you" to volunteers.

How Often Should You Have Special Events?

You should hold special events at least twice each year: in the fall and spring. Some organizations will want to have many more events. If they have the manpower to arrange them, they should be encouraged to do so.

Your biggest special event should coincide with your primary fund raising season. Thus, if you expect to do most of your individual fund raising in the fall, your autumn event should get the most sustained attention.

Organizations should use this major special event either to kick-off their fund raising drive or else to close it. Both are acceptable.

Making Your Event An Annual Feature

Wise organizations seek to create a fund raising event for themselves which can be mounted every year at the same time. This kind of special event is attractive for several reasons:

- the lessons learned in organizing it can be applied to make the next one better.
- you preempt competition from organizing something similar.
- you build a committed following which looks forward to what you're doing, and
- press coverage is easier to obtain because reporters are familiar with the event.

Before you consider establishing such a tradition, however, investigate your marketing area. What are other organizations doing? If someone else is already doing something similar, adopt another idea. File all information about neighborhood agencies and their events in your Competition Folder.

Select A Special Events Chairman

The first step towards creating a successful special event is appointing a dedicated, enthusiastic chairman. Such people, with their knack for organizing enticing, popular events, are rare. Perhaps, however, your organization is already lucky enough to have one. If so, consider inviting this individual to join your board with specific responsibility for your two main special events.

Your special events chairman may wish to limit his commitment to a specific time period. That's fine. It's no different, in fact, from any other member of the board. It is a very good idea to work out in advance just how long this individual will serve and what he'll do. Because of the importance of special events to most organizations, you may wish to exchange letters on the subject to avoid future misunderstandings.

If your organization does not now have within its constituency someone who can organize your special events, it is time to launch a search. Make finding a special events chairman the responsibility of the Nominating Committee of the board. They should search for this chairman (and potential board member) just as they would search for an accountant, lawyer, or foundation representative.

Here's something they should know about special events people: they're addicted to the process of special events organization. As certified "groupies," they have a hard time saying "No!" to an event which challenges their imagination and talent.

To find out about these people, check your local newspaper to see who is organizing the events for other organizations. The chairman of the board or chairman of the Nominating Committee should call on individuals who have successfully completed special events or are known for their skills in doing so and ask for leads.

Beware of asking the person you are visiting to come work for you. First, the organization he is already assisting won't like it. Second, you need to cultivate this person so that he knows something about you and your organization. Therefore, paint an exciting picture about the kind of special event you want. If you can excite this person with your vision, he may recruit himself. Finally, do ask for the names and telephone numbers of people known to the special events enthusiaste. Aim to recruit them. Note: Don't make your visit for at least a month after this person has finished an event. Special events groupies are consistently known, at the conclusion of their production, to swear off any further activity. Humor them. A few weeks after their latest success, however, most are ready to try and top themselves. That's the moment to strike.

Choosing the Right Event

Don't select an event and then attempt to recruit a chairman. The enthusiasm of most special events chairmen is tied to realizing their own vision. Let the chairman have a major role in determining what kind of event to produce. But don't necessarily give him a free hand.

Organizations should develop special events which are consistent with their public image. If your event is somehow inconsistent with the main message of your organization, it may result in bad press. Churches organizing gambling events, for instance, constantly face criticism for sponsoring an activity which seems to conflict with their religious message. The kind of event you sponsor should ultimately be decided by the board. If they wish to have an event which may produce unsavory press, that's their decision. They had better be sure, however, that it will produce such a good return that the press won't matter.

These days the most successful special events are those which return something tangible to the participant. That is, in return for a contribution to your organization, the donor gets some kind of property. Keep this fact in mind: you want to sponsor a special event with the broadest popular appeal. This is a very good way to attract dollars to your organization from people who might otherwise have no interest in the cause. As you think about what kind of special event to hold, think both about what will interest your constituency and what will attract the outside public. You may have to hold significantly different events for each. Here are a few suggestions you may wish to consider:

- **Travel Auction**

All items must deal in some way with travel. Individuals are encouraged to donate: a week at their vacation property, a day of sailing on a boat, or even a taxi ride to the airport. Businesses might consider: air travel passes, luggage, train tickets, or even a set of tires for the family car. All are items which it would cost money to purchase but which the donor can either give without direct cost or as a business deduction.

Once a large variety of travel items has been lined up, the special events committee produces a booklet with complete descriptions of what is available. This booklet can be sent out in advance or left in popular locations around town.

Admission tickets may be sold to the auction (at around $5-$10). A cash bar (also revenue-producing) should be provided. The organization should make sure they have found a good auctioneer who can stimulate the crowd.

A successful travel auction can easily produce $75,000 for your organization.

• **Liquor Auction**

Americans spend a fortune on liquor. You may therefore wish to consider tapping into this multi-billion dollar market by holding a liquor auction. The principle is the same as the travel auction: get local liquor stores to donate bottles and cases of various kinds of liquor and liquor accessories (glasses, &c) which you can auction. You may be able to persuade a service club (such as the Jaycees) to sponsor this kind of event for you or else a fraternal organization such as the Elks or Moose which maintain bars in their headquarters. A successful liquor auction can be produced virtually without direct cost and will provide your organization with thousands of dollars of operating revenue.

• **Celebrity Auction**

The aim here is to auction off a block of time and perhaps an interesting event with a celebrity: lunch, say, with Jackie Onassis. Aim to produce an interesting list of about 50 celebrities. To attract them, use contacts (remember the links generated by the Facilitating Session) and try to suggest a possibility which will interest the celebrity.

Recently a Boston organization persuaded Joan Kennedy to participate in a celebrity auction by giving a piano lesson. The fact that Mrs. Kennedy is known for her interest in the arts and has a degree in teaching music to elementary school youngsters probably helped the cause.

Use the Celebrity Auction to get access to people you need for your various networks. There are some people who would find it difficult to turn down your invitation and who can provide you with access to the influential. They include:

- the mayor of your town
- your state representative
- your state senator
- your congressman
- the governor of your state
- your senator
- the editor of your local newspaper
- local talk show hosts
- the president of your local college

Also, keep alert for other individuals who can derive some publicity value through participating. Authors promoting books are good candidates for consideration; so are athletes.

- **House Raffle**

One of the good things to emerge from the sagging national home market has been the house raffle. Under this plan, an organization usually gets a builder to donate a house outright. The agency then raffles it off by selling tickets for around $100 apiece. Another alternative is for the householder to set a reserve price and for the organization to sell a sufficient number of tickets at a price which will result in profit for both owner and organization.

Several states have now banned the house raffle, but if your state still allows it, it can be an excellent way of raising funds. Note: it usually takes more time than you think to dispose of the tickets. If you can, check with an organization which has already run a house raffle and see how they did it.

- **Percentage of Big-Name Group Ticket Sales**

Most groups should avoid trying to produce big name groups on their own. Whether you are promoting Henri Mancini or the Rolling Stones, the promotion business is best left to the professionals. This doesn't mean, however, that you can't benefit.

Approach any local promoter with the idea of having a co-sponsored event between your organization and his. What you want is to derive a certain percentage of ticket sales, say $1 for each one sold. You might also like to have a block of seats reserved for your organization so that you can sell them directly.

Why would the promoter be interested? Either he maintains a personal interest in the cause, or he can see the public relations benefits to be gained through associating himself and the group of your choice with your organization.

Don't be put into the position, however, of guaranteeing any portion of the expense.

As you see, the possibilities for special events are limitless. Here are some others:

- celebrity roast
- telethon
- art raffle
- dance
- road race

- walkathon
- fashion show
- festival
- lecture series

Whenever possible, produce a special event which will have the widest popular appeal but does not work against your public image. Where an event involves an individual getting something tangible in return for a donation, check with your attorney. These gifts often have tax consequences which you will probably want to spell out in any materials you produce promoting the event. As a rule of thumb: An individual is only able to take as a tax deduction the portion of his gift which exceeds the commercial value of the item he has received.

Note: Beware of gambling events and those who promote them. Recent media stories have focused on the connection of organized crime and the Las Vegas Nights which have become popular around the country. In deciding whether to sponsor such an activity, always check with the office of your state's Attorney General. If you are proposing to hire an outside group to handle this event, ask for references. Check them out. Also, check to see whether there are any complaints on file against the group at the Attorney General's office.

Selecting A Date

Give due consideration to selecting an appropriate date. This is not an inconsequential matter.

In large cities particularly many events occur on a single evening. The presence of a competing event may both limit your audience and diminish your press coverage. For this reason, most major cities maintain an official calendar of events. Before scheduling anything check with your city's convention bureau, the office of the mayor, or the chamber of commerce.

Once you're sure you are not competing against anything of importance, select the date which gives you the most time to organize your event. Most organizations allow insufficient time to produce their event. At the very least, it takes organizations about six months to produce a substantial event. Eight to nine months may be needed if your organization has not produced something similar to your current project.

To gauge how much time you'll need, answer the following questions:

- Has our chairman organized something similar before?
- Is the chairman a good organizer?

- Will there be difficulty assembling a dedicated committee?
- If we are trying to get services and materials donated, how long will it take us to make contact with those who can give them?
- Are we doing something in which there is wide interest?
- Or do we have to spend extra time stimulating enthusiasm?
- Do we have sufficient ticket salesmen if we need them?

Note: As a rule of thumb, each ticket salesman can sell five tickets: one to himself and four to others.

Draw Up Your Budget

All too often an organization proceeds with a special event without knowing how much it will cost it to do so. The results are predictable: cost overruns and diminished profits. Establishing a sound, thorough budget enables you to decide how much you need to charge people to attend. It also gives you an idea of what volume of business you must stimulate to make money. You can plan accordingly.
Your budget is divided into two parts: Personnel and Nonpersonnel.

Under Personnel consider:

- cost of agency staff (including secretarial and clerical assistance)
- outside special events consultant
- other personnel retained especially for event.

Your Nonpersonnel items may include:

- graphic design
- typesetting and printing of promotional flyers
- typesetting and printing of tickets
- printing of press releases
- special events stationary and envelopes
- space rental
- licenses and permits
- refreshments
- rental of silverware and plates
- band or other entertainment
- postage
- telephone
- copying
- decorations

It is the responsibility of the Special Events Chairman to draft the budget and present it to the board for final approval. No special events chairman should ever have independent authority to commit the agency to an expenditure of funds. This task remains the job of the board. On the other hand, the board may wish to allow the chairman to make certain discretionary expenses without board approval. The board should, therefore, establish a reasonable limit for the chairman. The budget should be approved by the board as soon as possible; any substantial deviation needs to be approved by its membership.

Appoint Subcommittees

If the planning of special events is to proceed expeditiously and pleasurably, the responsibility for organizing them must be divided. To obtain this result, the special events chairman should consider appointing the following committees:

- **Facility Committee**

It is the responsibility of this committee to select the best possible location, to insure that it is properly prepared for the event, and that everything which occurs at the facility is well arranged. It should:
  - Find a central location near where most guests live and work.
  - Locate or design maps and directions to the facility.
  - Meet with the manager of the facility to discuss the event. Note: if you feel unsure of yourself, ask him what you need to consider.
  - Detail everything that will happen from the time the guests arrive at the facility (parking) until the time they leave (coatroom and the validation of parking stickers).
  - Oversee the menu. Will your facility arrange for catering or can you? What is the difference in price?
  - Provide liquor. It is usually cheaper to bring your own liquor and sell it. Does your facility allow you to do so?
  - Set up the facility. Do you need to bring: chairs, tables, screens, artwork, speaker's podium, &c?
  - Provide special equipment. Does your facility provide you with: audio visual equipment, microphone, tape recorder, movie screen, &c, or do you have to bring them? If you are having an audio visual presentation make sure the ceiling is high enough. Ensure that poles and pillars will not block the guests' view. Note: This committee should always completely run through any audio visual program in advance at the site.
  - Research permits and licenses. Be sure you either have or don't need permits for your program. Ask the facility manager for his assistance. Call the local police department if necessary.

- Hire guards. You may well need guards or off-duty policemen to assist with security and crowd control. Consider how many people you will have in attendance and what crowd control measures your organization can comfortably handle.
- Look into insurance. If you are having a display of valuable objects, who is responsible if one is damaged, lost or stolen? Check with your insurance agency.
- Provide medical assistance. If your event will involve many people or people subject to medical problems, make suitable arrangements for a nurse or doctor. You may also need a retiring room.
- Arrange for parking. The good tempers of guests can be considerably frayed if there is insufficient parking or they have to pay alot for it. See about getting a facility where parking is included in the rental fee.
- Provide a coatroom. Most guests usually arrive at about the same time and depart at the same time. Make sure your facilities are suitably equipped to handle the demand.

- **Program Committee**

Many special events are ruined by a poor or ill-considered program. To make sure this doesn't happen to you, think carefully about what you are trying to achieve and whether each aspect of your program helps realize your goal. Also practice your timing. You want to leave people wishing for more rather than piqued that they didn't stay home. This committee's work includes the following:

- Write an agenda covering every item of your program from the introduction of the head table to a few notable last words.
- Arrange for speakers or entertainers. Confirm their appearances in writing and call three days in advance of your event to insure they are coming. Arrange for their transportation and accomodation, if necessary. Note: tell your speakers or entertainers *exactly* what you expect of them, how long you'd like them to perform, when you'd like them to stop, and whether there is anything special you want of them. Remember: If you are having amateurs provide your entertainment, you need to be especially clear in your instructions. An untutored speaker, suffering from a bad case of nerves, may ramble and carry on for too long, destroying the point of having him in the first place. Work with him in advance to insure the best result.
- Provide a Master of Ceremonies who is good at keeping things on schedule and can either improvise or (with good humor) stop an ambling speaker and put things back on course.
- Develop a backup program. Remember Murphy's Law.

If you intend to tape or otherwise record your program, make sure there is adequate coordination between the Facilities Committee and the Program Committee so that the equipment you need is available when you need it.

- **Printed Materials Committee**

Most special events need many kinds of printed materials: tickets, flyers, stationery, envelopes, name tags, signs, menus, programs, posters, &c. To insure a consistent design and thorough superintendence, all should be handled by one committee. This committee should:

- Set the design. You need not necessarily hire a graphic designer and produce a new logo. You can probably use the agency's logo properly embellished for the occasion.
- Develop a time-line showing when materials must be drafted and delivered to the print shop so that they can be printed and either posted or distributed in plenty of time. Work with your printer and mailing house so that you know how much time they need. Here are some rules of thumb:

    1. Allow at least six weeks for printed materials to be created, approved, and given to the printer.
    2. Allow two to three weeks for the materials to be printed.
    3. Allow an extra three weeks for color processing.

    Remember: printers are congenital optimists. You need to add 20% to their estimate of how long they need.
- Proofread documents. At least two people should proofread everything. Those working closest to the project can easily overlook errors. After all, they know what they mean. Have others review all materials.

- **Publicity Committee**

Special events are a good way of publicizing your organization to the community. As such you need a good Publicity Committee. This committee:

- Develops public relations angles. Every story needs a "hook" — the slant, that is, which makes it appealing to the editor of a particular newspaper section or the producer of a radio or television show. Committee members should brainstorm and come up with various angles: news, feature, interview, business &c. The more angles you can come up with, the better your chance.

142

- Drafts all necessary announcements and releases. These generally take two forms:

  1. A 50-word announcement covering: name of event, name of organization, place, date, time, cost, follow-up telephone number.

  2. Media release with background information on event and organization in no more than 500 words.

- Draws up media list:

  1. Of newspapers, radio and television stations which print public service and calendar announcements. Mails announcements about three weeks before event.

  2. Of appropriate editors of newspapers and producers of radio and television shows who might be interested in the special event and your organization because of the angles you've conceived. Begin making contact with these people about five weeks before the event.

- Plans a press conference. Don't automatically assume you need a press conference. If you have a genuine news angle to your event (you've snagged a reclusive celebrity, for instance) or a cause with unusually widespread interest, do consider a press conference. Otherwise, work with the media mainly by mail and telephone. If you do put on a press conference, however, prepare press kits containing: background information on your organization, background information on the event, a biographical sketch of leading participants, photos, basic media release, &c.

- Places telephone calls to all media sources contacted by mail. Don't wait for a return telephone call or letter. Media people, on the whole, tend to wait for you to contact them — unless your story is sizzling. Thus, if you are interested in getting a print story or a place on some electronic media show, systematically work through your list contacting every name. Again, you must be clear about what you want, what they can give, and who will be interested in your story and why. Assume that the media people you contact are sophisticated but not knowledgeable about your cause.

Remember: publicity doesn't stop before the event. Some of the most worthwhile press occurs as a result of the event. Therefore:

- Be sure to make arrangements for a photographer to attend. Newspapers (particularly smaller newspapers) like to feature their local readers. If you have an unusually sought-after guest, for instance, arrange for pictures to be taken of members of your board, other guests, &c with your celebrity. Make sure every newspaper in your marketing area is covered by this process. Send the newspaper a photograph of their local resident and a suitable 25-word caption.

- Invite media representatives to attend the program. Even if a media person is not doing an advance story on your organization, invite him as your guest to the actual function. If you invite him verbally, make sure to follow up with a written invitation. Special events provide a perfect opportunity to cultivate media people. Perhaps on this occasion they won't do a story, but by being nice to them you're developing a link which will prove helpful later.

- Issue a press release after the event. The more work you do for your media sources, the more likely they will run something about your event. Immediately after the program, draft a 500-word (maximum) story about what took place; highlight the most significant aspects of the evening. Send this to your print media outlets with appropriate photographs.

Remember: Always send thank-you notes to your media contacts. The more often you can contact them **without** asking for something, the better. And if they have assisted you in any way, do tell them.

Notes on Paid Advertising: Paid advertising is expensive but you may wish to consider promoting your special event in this fashion. If you do, make sure you do the following:

- Ensure that the vehicle you have chosen is the correct one for the audience you wish to hit.
- Include the cost of advertising in your budget.
- Allow sufficient time for the development of ad copy.
- Develop some means of demonstrating whether the ads have worked or not. If they don't, you need not do them again next time.

- **Ticket Sales Committee**

More than any other special events committee the Ticket Sales Committee must keep in mind the rest of the fund raising effort. There's a good reason for this: many people you want at your special event will be prospects for various fund raising committees. These prospects probably will make just one donation to your organization this year: if they make it for special events tickets, who gets credited for it? Special events and its fund raising objective? Or another fund raising committee? This is an important consideration.

Remember: The special event, like all the other fund raising mechanisms within your organization, has to raise a set dollar figure towards your unrestricted revenue. Thus, if your Small Business Committee sells fifty tickets for the special event and gets credit for this amount towards its goal, it may be diminishing the likelihood that the special event itself will raise its objective. How can you avoid this difficulty?

First, consider how much space is available and how many people you can realistically accommodate. In some cases the numbers are set: if you are renting a theater, there are only so many seats you can sell. In other instances, the numbers will be flexible.

Next, consider how many people you are inviting as guests of the organization. A special event is a prime opportunity to cultivate people who can be helpful to the organization in various ways, so a body of tickets should be set aside for the larger purposes of the Chairman of the Board and the Coordinating Committee which should handle this aspect of the event. They will want to include:

- representatives of corporations and foundations
- media personnel
- Top Donor Prospects
- individuals being cultivated for the board

Now, how many guests can you still accommodate? Set this against the dollar objective for your event. If, for instance, you are trying to raise $5000 from the special event and you can accommodate 250 people, each ticket must be sold for $20. In deciding whether you can affort to give credit to other fund raising committees if they sell tickets, you need to decide whether:

- The ticket price can be raised. Or will there be market resistance? Consider the attractiveness of your special event and how much your constituency can afford to pay.
- There is some way the number of tickets can be increased. If, for instance, you are holding an event in flexible space, you may sell about 10% more tickets than you expect people to attend.
- You should change the space to allow for more people.

Remember: People like getting something in return for their money. It may assist your various committees in their individual fund raising effort if they can make available tickets to your special event. You will probably want to make a set number of tickets available to each committee. You will have to decide right from the start, however, who gets credit for the tickets sold. Make sure that you structure matters so that your special event can make its own fund raising objective. You can best do so by selecting an event with broad popular appeal.

Once you have decided how many tickets each committee can have, turn your attention to the number of ticket sellers you'll need. As stated above, as a rule of thumb each ticket seller can sell five tickets: his own and four others. Where possible enforce this rule: if an individual takes tickets, he is responsible for either selling them or paying for them himself. This tends to engender the saleman's commitment to disposing of the tickets.

- **Hospitality Committee**

There will always be people at your events who come alone, who don't know many people, or who would simply like to meet new people and expand their circle of friends and contacts. It is the job of the Hospitality Committee to provide the introductions and to bring people together. All too often this genteel service is neglected, and the result is that many people simply don't return. It is your responsibility to make people feel truly welcome at your events.

This committee should provide:

- A table at the door of the event where guests may be met
- Name tags
- Someone connected with the organization to make appropriate introductions to the chairman of the board, executive director, &c
- A crew of hosts and hostesses who circulate throughout the event dealing with wallflowers and making sure that people are attended to.

The work this committee does is not just simply courtesy (though that would be enough!). It is also good business. If people feel warm and welcome at your events, they will tell their friends about them and will make a point of coming back themselves.

Always make sure your hosts and hostesses are well informed about the organization itself, so that they can answer basic questions. You may wish to hold a brief orientation meeting before any event to so instruct the crew. Make sure that they note any special requests from the guests. A good host always carries a piece of paper and a pencil so that any matters needing follow-up can be attended to.

- **Clean-Up Committee**

Your broom and bucket crew is **de rigeur,** especially in situations where you have been loaned a space. It should go without saying that you will want to return it in better condition that it was before your arrival.

Your organization may need other committees, too. Consider the following:

- **Mailing Committee**

If you are mailing invitations, you will need a crew to handle the work. They should:

- check mailing addresses
- type labels

- sort the bulk mail
- fulfill orders

Note: Here are some statistics on direct mail invitations:

- Ten percent of those invited will come if the special event is free and they know your organization.
- Five percent of those invited will come if the special event is free and they don't know your organization.
- Five to ten percent of those invited will come if the event is not free and they know your organization.
- Two percent of those invited will come if the event is free and they don't know your organization.
- In the last four days before your event, you will receive RSVPs amounting to ten percent of those you have already received.

- **Telephone Committee**

You have a better chance of selling your tickets and persuading people to come, if you call them. The Telephone Committee:

- recruits callers
- checks telephone numbers
- writes a sales script
- fulfills orders.

- **Related Promotions Committee**

Ticket sales are only one way of making money from a special event. You may also wish to consider:

- writing and selling a souvenir program
- assembling an ad book
- holding a lottery

The Special Events Coordinating Committee

No matter how many committees you need for your special event, their chairmen should meet regularly with the Special Events Chairman. This committee functions like the Coordinating Committee for the overall fund raising effort. It should:

- insure that each committee has a chairman.

- make sure each chairman has a committee.
- specify the tasks for each committee.
- set a time for completion of these tasks.
- keep minutes of all meetings.
- circulate these minutes to all committee members and to the Coordinating Committee.

The Special Event Committee's Facilitating Session

Once the special event has been determined, its budget drawn up and approved, and its committees appointed, it is time to see how many of the supplies and services that you need can be donated. One of the secrets to a successful special event is to have as many things donated as you possibly can, so that all the money which comes in can be used as unrestricted income for your organization. A Facilitating Session should assist you in getting the leads you need to those who can provide you with goods and services at low cost or without charge.

The chairman, working with special events committee members, should draw up a complete list of **everything** they will need including both personnel and nonpersonnel items. This list should be exhaustive.

Once it is drawn up, it should be submitted to two groups for consideration:

- the board of directors
- members of the special events committee itself

The purpose here is simple: to discover a link to a source which can easily provide you with the product or service you need. In attempting to gather these links, go back to the information supplied in the original Facilitating Session held by the board. The Contacts Questionnaire distributed at that meeting sought information about where board members shopped, did auto business, bought pharmaceutical supplies, &c. Information supplied in this portion of the questionnaire should prove helpful to the special events committee as it looks for donated goods and services.

If the Facilitating Session fails to turn up a lead, you have two options:

- get either a board member or member of the committee itself to donate what you need.
- approach the possible provider cold. Attempt to interest him in your cause to gain a discount because of the service you provide and your nonprofit status. If you get such a discount (or outright gift), see if you can't do something in return for the provider: give him tickets to the event, mention his name in the program, &c.

Following Up Your Successful Special Event

Once your special event has been successfully concluded, there remain a few final tasks. They tidy up matters nicely and position you for a reprise of the event next year.

As is clear from this chapter, many people contribute to a successful special event. You need to thank them at the event itself, and they need a written thank-you note and/or some momento afterward. The note that is sent may be jointly signed by the chairman of the board, executive director, and special events chairman. It should be as personal as possible. If you are going to produce your message by word processor, at least write a personal note at the foot of the letter.

The Special Events Committee should meet at least once after the event and discuss both what went right and why — and what went wrong and how it could be avoided. This discussion should be positive. Destructive criticism has no place in this post-mortem even though one or more of your committee members may have verged on the inept. The point of this exercise is not to point the accusing finger but to prepare things so that next year's version is better. Extensive minutes should be kept of this meeting.

In addition, a Special Events File should be opened. Place in it an example of all written communications, printed materials (including stationery and envelopes), the minutes of meetings, and the summary from the last committee meeting. Don't neglect the event's budget and the actual final accounting. It is also a good idea for the special events chairman to produce a one or two page report with recommendations for the future. These recommendations should be as specific as possible: perhaps you left too little time for the local printer. When would he recommend dropping off your copy?

Finally, add copies of all the press coverage you received. You will want to note, in future, both the angles the reporters (and photographers) took **and** the names of those who covered your event. While these people may not be available next year, you will at least know which department to deal with.

Final Notes on Special Events

Here are some final tips for your consideration:

- The executive director should meet regularly with the special events chairman throughout the planning stages. The executive director should not, however, get directly involved either in the planning or implementation of the special event. This is not a good use of his time.
- If you are booking space in either December or June, remember to do so well

in advance, since these are the most popular months for functions.

- Discuss a rain or snow date for your event and print it on the invitation and in all media announcements. This is necessary both for outdoor events and for winter events.
- Provide the names, addresses, and home and business telephone numbers of committee members to all individuals involved in the special event.

Special events should be fun. If they come across merely as fund raisers or with a touch of grim necessity, they defeat their purpose. **You** can be deadly serious about them during the planning phase — but keep smiling publicly!

CHAPTER 9

ESSENTIALS OF DIRECT MAIL FUND RAISING

This chapter is devoted to the essentials of direct mail fund raising. It is directed primarily to those organizations which do not now raise money through direct mail and are wondering whether they should try.

These days, with many nonprofit organizations making a serious effort to increase their independent sector contributions, direct mail is frequently seen as a panacea. At first glance it's no wonder. It is perhaps the one fund raising technique with which most individuals are familiar, since most of us have probably been the recipient of a postal solicitation. The temptation, therefore, often seems overwhelming to get into the business. For most organizations, however, direct mail can be a snare — a costly alternative which can actually leave you worse off than when you started. Any organization wishing to consider this option must do so with the utmost care.

What is Direct Mail Fund Raising?

There is no mystery as to what direct mail fund raising is. It is the process of connecting an organization by post to both donors and potential donors. It is a form of communication carried on solely by correspondence. Through direct mail, an organization attempts to market itself to donors by setting forth its need for funds and requesting a return gift.

Stages of Direct Mail Fund Raising

Direct mail fund raising is best approached through a series of stages. If you succeed at each (less involved, less costly) stage, you should consider going on to the next. Here are the stages:

- Identification and direct mail solicitation of organizational beneficiaries.
- Determination of whether organization is an optimum direct mail candidate.
- Acquisition of new names.
- Potential Donor Solicitation Pilot Project.

Identification and Direct Mail Solicitation of Organizational Beneficiaries

Most organizations can easily identify individuals who have benefitted from their service. These individuals should be solicited before any other effort is made to add to your donor base.

In selected cases, the individuals who benefit from your organization may themselves be unable to contribute. They may be, for example, children or incapacitated adults. In such cases, the organization should collect the names, addresses and telephone numbers of those connected to the direct beneficiaries who might be able to contribute: parents of children, relatives of incapacitated adults, &c.

Remember: Those who have in some way benefitted from the service you provide are the ones most likely to give so that your work can continue. If these people do not wish to give up to the level of their capacity, it is extremely unlikely you will be able to persuade others, who may not have benefitted directly, to contribute.

Once you have identified the beneficiaries and collected their addresses and telephone numbers, you must produce an influential direct mail appeal letter. This letter should:

- remind potential donors that they are beneficiaries of your organization. In effect, you are asking them what would have happened if your organization had not existed.
- stress that the good work of the organization cannot continue without funds.
- point out in detail exactly what use will be made of the funds when they are contributed.   (See Samples, pages 240-242)

This letter may either be signed by the chairman of the board, the executive director, or by someone who has benefitted from the organization. Enclose a return envelope and pledge card with this letter so that contributions can be mailed directly to your organization.

If you are using this letter in connection with your annual fund raising drive, it should arrive at the same time your drive is inaugurated. This will be either the first week of October or early in March.

It is advisable to follow this letter with a second communication timed to arrive either the last week of November or early in December. This will have to be a differentiated communication: those who have already given should not be re-solicited. They should instead be given either a progress report on the fund raising effort or information about some aspect of the organization's work. This will help solidify their connection to you.

Those who have not given, however, should be reminded of why their contribution is necessary. Return envelopes and pledge cards should be placed in both communications, although you should not refer to them in the letter you send to donors.

A third letter should be sent in March. This letter should again be different for those who have contributed and those who have not. The letter to those who have not given should contain a sense of urgency (**not** desperation) about the need for the prospective donor's gift. It should focus on the good works that the organization is accomplishing.

Handling the Mail

Organizations mailing fewer than 10,000 solicitation letters should be able to find a sufficient number of volunteers to handle the stuffing and sorting of the mail. Remember: to maximize your return, try whenever possible to utilize volunteers instead of contracting with a fulfillment house. In my experience, however, unless you have an unusually high number of committed volunteers, you should probably contract with a fulfillment house when you mail more than 10,000 pieces.

Telephone Follow-Up

For most organizations, those who have benefitted will prove the likeliest donors. Therefore it is a wise idea to institute a telephone follow-up to your direct mail solicitation. There are several ways of doing so.

If your list of direct mail prospects is relatively small (1000 or less), it should be possible to make direct contact with each of them by telephone. The best way of doing so is by appointing a Telephone Committee. The job of this committee is to:

- collect prospects' telephone numbers
- place numbers on a Prospect Information Card
- develop a good solicitation script
- send duplicate materials to all those who did not receive the original packet
- continue working until all prospects have been contacted.

The best place to do this work is in a business office after regular hours. Through your board or contact network you should be able to find a businessman who will allow you to use his telephones after work. If you will be making numerous calls beyond the local dialing area, try to find an office equipped with Wide Area Telephone Service (WATS) lines.

Note: As a rule of thumb, each member of your telephone team should be able to look up the telephone numbers and call at least five prospects per hour.

If your organization is soliciting by mail more than 1000 people, you may not be able to telephone them all at once. You should, however, attempt to make contact with some substantial fraction of them. One national organization I know with about 16,000 members attempts to call about one quarter of them each year in selected

153

states. Over a four-year period, therefore, most members of the organization get contacted and asked in person for their donation.

Remember: Whenever possible, try to make your calls no later than a month after the mail solicitation is timed to arrive. People have short memories; they also tend to dispose of materials quickly. If you can possibly arrange matters so that your solicitation calls are made within two weeks after the mail arrives, do so. Your response rate should be higher.

Assessing The Return

Your success rate will be determined by several factors:

- Have you previously kept in regular touch with your beneficiaries, or is this the first time you've contacted them?
- Do your beneficiaries clearly feel they have substantially benefitted from your service, or are they unsure?
- Have you made a good case for needing the money, or has your appeal been perfunctory?
- Have you made personal (telephone) contact with your donor prospects, or have you left the main burden of solicitation to the letter?

Assuming that you have followed the steps outlined in this chapter, you should have a profitable rate of return and the beginnings of a mail responsive list. The question now becomes, should you try and extend this list by sending solicitation letters to those who have not benefitted from your organization?

The Optimum Direct Mail Solicitation Organization

If your organization wishes to acquire by direct mail new donors who have not necessarily directly benefitted from its services, it must be in at least one of the following categories:

- it must represent an electric cause, or
- it must be generally perceived within its marketing area as providing an essential service.

- **The Electric Cause**

By "electric," I mean a cause which is capable of causing people to make an intense, almost visceral commitment. Very often such causes have an "us versus them" aspect. Sometimes they play on people's fears and anxieties. "Support us," they say, "or else something you have or believe in will be taken away." Very often, too, they play on explicit or latent guilt feelings.

These causes are often national in scope; often they center on a single issue. We are all familiar with such causes: pro-life, gun control, pro- and anti-ERA organizations, the Moral Majority, gay rights groups. There is no reason, however, why smaller organizations with a localized issue cannot successfully utilize direct mail.

- **The Essential Service**

Successful electric cause organizations generally appeal to the darker human emotions. Either explicitly or implicitly, they usually motivate through fear. This is the secret of their success. While this motivation is by no means absent in the appeals of those organizations providing essential services, they tend to approach donor prospects on the basis of their good work and the need for it to continue. In this sense it is both a more positive and a **weaker** appeal than that made by organizations with an electric cause at their command.

The secret to this kind of appeal is whether the organization is clearly and generally perceived as providing an essential service within its marketing area. Each donor who is solicited through direct mail ideally knows in advance about this service and understands that his life is more secure or somehow improved because of its existence. A classic case in point is a community hospital.

After you have used direct mail to solicit those who have benefitted from your organization ask yourself:

- Does our organization elicit an intense, emotional response from people who will, therefore, give generously to sustain it?
- Is our organization clearly perceived throughout our marketing area as providing a unique, essential service? Is there a way of marketing this service so that prospective donors can be made to realize what its loss would entail to them?

If you can answer these questions in the affirmative, you should consider a Potential Donor Solicitation Pilot Project.

The Potential Donor Solicitation Pilot Project

The purpose of this pilot project is to test your organization's ability to identify and successfully solicit new donors. Here's what you need to consider as you undertake this project:

- This pilot project is a capital expense to your organization.

To be able to do this project you must very likely purchase:

- the names of prospective donors
- graphic design and printing of solicitation letter
- outside business envelopes
- pledge cards
- inside business envelopes
- postage

You may also need:

- a copy writer
- direct mail consultant
- mailing house

You must consider:

- This pilot project may result in a net loss to your organization.
- Even with this loss, the project can be rated a success if you are near the break-even point.
- It will be rated a definite success if you recover your initial investment.

Prospective Donor Name Acquisition

One of the two key variables in direct mail fund raising is the list you use to solicit contributions. The other is the copy you develop.

For the pilot project you will need about 10,000 names. How can you find them? The answer lies to a significant extent on whether yours is an electric cause or essential service organization.

- **Electric Cause Name Acquisition**

There are three main ways this kind of organization can acquire the names it needs:

1. Ask for the mailing lists of ideologically compatible organizations. If organizations share similar goals, they will occasionally share lists and overcome a natural hesitancy to letting others see their proven givers. Often exchanges are possible on a name for name basis. For test purposes, try to get a

selection of names from several organizations. Your pledge cards or return envelopes can be coded to see which list draws best.

2. Ask for (or purchase) the subscription lists of publications sharing your views. You can either approach the publication directly or act through a list broker.

3. Contact a list broker for assistance.

- **Essential Service Organizations**

Essential service organizations draw their names from their marketing areas — the areas in which they provide services. When looking for names for a pilot project such organizations should:

1. Review the real estate tax lists for the communities they serve. The name of anyone paying over $2000 or $3000 in real estate tax annually should be considered a prospect. These lists are public information and are available at city halls.

2. Seek to use the membership lists of prominent service organizations and other groups where members will have discretionary funds.

3. Consult a list broker for assistance.

The Role of the List Broker

Organizations using direct mail fund raising must ordinarily consult a list broker for assistance since they may not be able to acquire the names they need through other means. Given the importance of the list you use to the result you will have, you will probably wish to consult one from the start.

Brokers exist to tell you what mailing lists are available and to advise you on which you should use given the objectives you have. In using a list broker, it helps to know as much as you can about the people you want to attract to your organization. Here are some things you should know:

- What are the demographics of the constituency you seek: age, income, education, place of residence, &c?
- What publications do you think they read?
- What organizations might they support?

If you give the list broker this kind of information, he can advise you on what lists to purchase. Remember: Your list broker wants you to succeed in realizing your goal. If you are happy with the result (i.e. you raise money), he knows you'll probably come back; if you aren't, he's lost a customer. Allow him to take the time to explain just what's available and why he feels a certain list might be preferable to another. If he doesn't take the time to advise you, beware.

Also, for your test, don't use just one list. You want a selection so that you can assess results. Note: For a 10,000 piece mailing you can probably use two or three lists since many have minimum orders of 3-5,000 names per list.

Before you purchase the use of any list, shop around. The rental cost of lists varies considerably. You want to make sure you are getting a good deal.

Finally, you must know before you place your order just how you will be handling it. If you are using your own volunteers, you will want pressure sensitive labels; if you are using a mailing house, you will need cheshire labels.

Developing Persuasive Copy

Developing persuasive direct mail copy is a craft which deserves more attention than can here be given. If yours is an electric cause organization, here's what you should consider in developing the copy:

- What is the greatest fear of people who support your cause? Address this fear directly and demonstrate that your organization is the best weapon against its realization.
- What is their greatest hope? You must persuade people that you share their vision of a better world and are working to bring it about.
- What are you going to use the money for? Show specifically how the money you request will go to preventing the realization of their fear. Promote their hope. Concentrate on program objectives and frame them in such a way that the donor will feel his life can and will be made better through his gift. **Never** ask for money to pay your direct mail costs and try to minimize requests for other operating expenses.

If yours is an essential service organization you should:

- Describe as specifically as possible what you intend to do with the money you are requesting. Make sure the items you choose are explained in such a way that the need for them is absolutely clear.

- Stress the variety and number of people who will benefit from the gift. You can often make your copy colorful and dramatic by including mini-case studies or individual examples.
- Bring home to the potential giver the possible effect of your organization on his own life and that of his loved ones. What might happen if this essential service did not exist?

In all cases direct mail copy should be simple, lucid, cogent, and compelling. It must:

- Impart a sense of urgency to the donor prospect so that he will act — **now.**
- Persuade the donor prospect that **his** gift is vital — whatever its size.
- Satisfy him that his money is needed and will be used wisely.
- Fulfill him by offering him the chance to shape a better world and demonstrate that he is a concerned, humane, responsible individual.

Note: Direct mail copy should never be very long. Although there is a raging debate within the profession about the best length for copy (some experts swear by shorter letters, others by longer ones), I advise you to produce about 1000 words. This copy can be comfortably typeset on the two sides of an 8½″ by 11″ sheet of your agency's stationery.

Production of Materials, Mailing

Here are the tasks you need to perform in getting your pilot project together with an indication of how long each task may take:

Task	Completion Time
Delivery of names from list broker	Allow at least four weeks
Delivery of names from other sources	Find out when you ask for them. Remember: unless it is their business to supply names, it will probably take longer than from a professional.
Drafting direct mail copy	Two weeks. Several people should review this copy. As Pascal, that elegant stylist, once noted: The shorter the letter, the more difficult to compose.
Design of letter	Two to four weeks if you are having it done by outside consultant.
Typesetting of letter	One week

Proof reading of letter	One week
Production of letter	One week
Design of outside envelopes	You can probably use your regular agency envelopes. Make sure, if you do, that you have an adequate supply — with bulk rate stamp if you intend to mail this way. Otherwise, allow two weeks for design and production of envelopes.
(Typesetting of outside envelopes)	
(Proof reading of outside envelopes)	
(Production of outside envelopes)	
Design of pledge card	Two days
Typesetting of pledge card	One week
Proof reading of pledge card	Two days
Production of pledge card	One week
Design of return envelope	Allow two weeks for design and production of return envelopes. Remember: make sure properly to code your return envelopes so you can check on which lists produce the best results.
(Typesetting of return envelope)	
(Proof reading of return envelope)	
(Production of return envelope)	
(N.B. Your pledge card and return envelope can be printed as one piece)	
Fulfillment from mailing house	Two weeks. Confirm in advance and reserve the time you need.

Fulfillment by your volunteers	This depends on you! Allow for 50% more time than a professional mailing house takes.
Delivery of bulk mail	Ask the post office. Even within a single city, delivery is often erratic.

Fortunately, many of these tasks can be undertaken simultaneously. Even so, if you wish to have your direct mail piece delivered by the first week of October, you must begin at least two months beforehand.

Remember: if you plan to include a copy of your organization's brochure in your direct mail package, be sure you have enough on hand for distribution. Allow sufficient time to print more if you don't.

Assessing Results

How do you know whether you've succeeded? Your test mailing has been worthwhile if:

- You have raised more money than it has cost you to produce and mail your direct mail package. This result, it must be stressed, is rare. If it happens to you, congratulate yourself. You have a very marketable organization and one which direct mail can probably assist. If you have used several lists, see which of them has drawn well, which less well. See if you can determine the reasons for the differing response. Your analysis will prove helpful as you plan future mailings. Ask your list broker for his opinion and advice.

- You have broken even. You should be able to break even if you have an average response rate of one to one-and-one half percent with an average gift of between $15-$20. If you do, your pilot project has proven successful: you have identified a group of mail responsive individuals and have turned them into proven givers for your organization. On your next mailing, you will transform them into an outright revenue source.

- You are within one half to three quarters of a percentage point of breaking even. If you figured that you needed a return of one and one half percent with gifts averaging $15 to break even and you fall short of this goal by as much as fifty percent, you may still reckon your pilot project a qualified success under certain circumstances:

- What amount of money did you new donors contribute?
- Is this sufficient to produce revenue in the event of a repeat mailing to them?

- Did certain of your lists draw better than others?
- Are there comparable lists available which could supplement your mail responsive names?

Ask your list broker to help you analyze the results of your pilot project. Such an analysis at this point is absolutely necessary and must be as thorough as possible. Depending on how these questions are answered, you will either risk further organizational resources in a second test mailing, or postpone your attempt to develop a direct mail fund raising plan.

You should seriously consider postponing any further direct mail effort if you have fallen more than fifty per cent short of your break even point. This, of course, does not mean that you should not add your new mail-responsive names to the list of others regularly contacted by you by mail. It does, however, suggest that any further test mailings would not be productive for you just now.

If you make the decision not to proceed with the acquisition of new names, make it as positive as possible. Try and determine why the organization is not ready now, why individuals did not respond as expected, and what must be accomplished before you can try again.

The Second Test

If, upon analysis, you have decided direct mail is a profitable medium for you, do a second test mailing to a new set of names. If your first piece was sent to arrive in early October, your second should be timed to arrive in late November or early December. To arrange matters in this fashion, however, you will probably have to attend to your labels and printing **before** you have the results of your first test mailing. If you feel confident about the result or if your organization can afford to do a second test mailing regardless of the outcome of the first, go ahead and make appropriate arrangements. If not, wait until the spring. This option is safer, but by adopting it you miss the best fund raising month of the year.

The purpose of the second test is to confirm the results of the first. Again, if you either recover your costs or come near to doing so, direct mail is a likely fund raising vehicle for your organization.

The only problem you will face with the second test is if it fails to confirm your initial pilot mailing. In this case you must work with your list broker to isolate the variables and to deduce why your different mailings produced significantly disparate results.

If your tests coincide in their results, you are in the direct mail business! This means that you should solicit your mail-responsive names on a regular basis. You should also continue to conduct test mailings to acquire new names and add them to your proven donor list. You will probably want to conduct at least one test mailing of 10,000 pieces a year to do so.

Analyzing Donors

After you have begun your direct mail program, you will have to stay alert to the three key factors that influence donor response to postal solicitation:

- How recently the gift was made,
- How frequently the donor makes gifts, and
- The size of gifts.

- **Recentness**

There is a direct relationship between an individual's response to a mail solicitation and the recentness of his last gift. Recent donors are likely to contribute again. After you have kept donor records for several years, two primary groups of contributors will emerge:

- Active Supporters are those who have supported you within the last 18 months, and
- Lapsed Supporters are those who have contributed to you but not within the last 18 months.

- **Frequency**

You need to know how many donors have contributed to your organization more than once. With these donors your communications should be regular. It is important to note that 70 to 80 percent of those who give more than twice to your organization will continue to do so. A surprisingly healthy percentage will even send in a contribution in response to your organization's thank you for their last donation.

- **Amount of Gift**

The amount a donor has previously given suggests both how large a gift you can expect and how you should craft your approach for the next gift.

Crafting Your Approach

After your direct mail program has been operational for two or more years, you are ready to develop different letters corresponding to the recentness, frequency and amount of donor gifts. Here are the major categories you need to consider:

- Active contributors of $100 or more
- Lapsed contributors of $100 or more
- Active contributors of $10 to $99
- Lapsed contributors of $10 to $99
- Active contributors of $9 or less
- Lapsed contributors of $9 or less

Obviously your approach to each category will vary considerably.

- **Active contributor of $100 or more**

  Stress the importance of this level of sustaining support. This individual wants your organization to succeed. Treat him with care. Explain in dramatic detail the work that his money is financing. Point out what plans are in the works. The individual wants evidence of progress and achievement, and he wants to know how he is contributing to it.

- **Lapsed contributor of $100 or more**

  You need to reactivate this important link. Show this former contributor just how much has been done in the last year. But also let him know how much more could have been done if he'd been with you and how much still remains to be accomplished. Ask him to tell you why he's stopped giving. Suggest that the organization's critical work cannot move forward without him.

- **Active contributor of $10 to $99**

  Often these people feel that their donations are too small to make a difference. You must show that this donor's involvement is critical to the good work you do. You could, for instance, point to an accomplished or advanced project solely financed by moderate givers and the effect it will have. The key here is that moderate contributors must be made to feel that their gifts matter significantly.

- **Lapsed contributor of $10 to $99**

  As above, these people need to be shown to what use you put their money. You must point out what the organization has been unable to accomplish without their support and why you need them now. Moderate contributors are likely to feel overwhelmed with the enormity of tasks set against the size of their possible donation. You must convince them they are vital to your success.

- **Active contributor of $9 or less**

  Your job here is to upgrade the level of contribution without in any sense denigrating the help already given. This letter should point out in detail your immediate fund raising needs and the significant results you expect — results which can improve the contributor's life. Ask the contributor to give as much as he can and suggest a level higher than his last gift.

- **Lapsed contributor of $9 or less**

  More than in any other category this donor is probably unconvinced about the utility of his gift. Persuade him. But if he still does not respond, drop this person from your list. Don't continue spending your money on small former donors who may have entirely lost interest.

In all cases, your copy should focus on the work you are doing and the importance of the individual contributor to it. These letters should focus on programmatic aspects of your organization, rarely on the money you need for operating expenses.

Record Keeping

Good record keeping is essential to productive direct mail fund raising.

Not too many years ago all organizations maintained their donor information on individual three by five inch cards. Now most advanced organizations use some kind of computer to help them record donors and keep track of the recentness, frequency, and size of gifts.

How do you know when to switch over?

At the beginning of your direct mail effort, use cards. After all, you are uncertain about whether you will continue with this kind of fund raising. When you have assembled a donor base of over 1000 individuals giving an average of $100 or more, you are ready to seek computer assistance.

When you do so, consult with several firms on the types of systems they have available and exactly what they can and cannot do. Sadly, these days there is widespread confusion about computer systems. Most organizations are not equipped to analyze on their own just what they need and what alternatives are available to them. If you are in this position, retain an outside consultant to assist you. Tell him what you want to achieve and let him advise you on the various systems available and on their relative strengths, weaknesses, and cost. Here is an excellent example of where a small outlay of money for a consultant can save you years of frustration and needless expense. Alternatively check with other organizations which use direct mail and see how they arrange their records.

The Direct Mail Fund Raising Consultant

Consultants can assist you with direct mail fund raising in several ways. They can:

- write copy
- design layout for letters and accessory pieces
- advise on mailing list acquisition
- interpret test mailings
- analyze a donor list and advance strategies for target groups
- devise an entire direct mail campaign

In choosing the right consultant for you:

- Select the person who has worked with comparably-sized organizations and agencies with a mission similar to yours. His experience will prove helpful.
- Ask for references to similar organizations to yours. Be sure to follow-up these references. If you are uncertain of what you need and what the consultant can provide, ask his references what they learned by working with him.
- Be cautious about signing a yearlong contract, particularly if this is your first direct mail effort. You should explore bringing on someone on a project basis. After you evaluate the success of this effort, you can decide whether you wish to continue.
- Avoid firms that promise or guarantee results. Direct mail is necessarily a fairly capricious business. A consultant can tell you in detail what he has already accomplished, but he can only suggest what he might be able to produce for you.

Remember: Whatever an individual consultant or full-service firm does for you, you still have the responsibility for the final result. Direct mail fund raising necessarily involves and affects the image of your organization and as such you should be both conscious and chary about what is done in your name. Make sure your board gets briefed about your direct mail efforts and is given the opportunity to review copy and hear the thrust of your campaign. Whatever a consultant may want or advise, it is the board of the organization which, as the governing body, must feel comfortable with what is being done.

CHAPTER 10

A FEW WORDS ABOUT FEDERAL FUND RAISING

This is basically a book about fund raising in the private sector. It has concentrated on how to raise funds from individuals, corporations, and foundations. However, because participants in my fund raising workshops are usually interested in federal grants and contracts, I have decided to include a few words on this subject.

If You're Eligible, Apply!

If you are eligible for federal funds, you should explore the possibility of getting them. Through its various agencies, the federal government distributes between $20 and $40 billion each year to several hundred congressionally-created programs. The two basic mechanisms by which these funds are dispersed are:

- Grants in which the government gives money in advance for services later provided by the organization, and
- Contracts in which the organization provides services and is later reimbursed by the government

Keeping Informed About Available Money

By law, federal grants and contracts must be publicized. Three federal government publications provide basic information about available federal funds and the officers who administer them:

- **The Federal Register** lists all available federal grants and supplies information about general program guidelines and contact people. It also gives advance notice of pending grants so that when funds finally become available, you can apply.
- The **Commerce Business Daily,** a publication of the Department of Commerce, gives notice of all federal contracts and serves as a bidding journal. The CBD is published each business day. A one-year subscription costs approximately $245 if mailed first class.
- The **Catalog of Federal and Domestic Assistance** provides information about categories of federal funding and programs the government wants to fund, and lists names and telephone numbers of funding officers. The CFDA is published yearly; although it is updated regularly, much of its information becomes quickly out-dated.

In addition to these publications, keep abreast of funding at the federal level through contacts. If you are eligible for federal (or state funds), invite program officers, administrators and other officials to your functions. Also, cultivate congressional assistants. These people are in a position to provide you with valuable information and technical assistance, if you need it.

Information Packages

When you write to request information about a particular contract or grant, you will receive in return either a Request for Quotation (RFQ) or a Request for Proposal (RFP).

An RFQ is simply a contract memorandum and usually pertains to contracts of under $10,000. It may either be a request for a brief narrative on your organization, or it may ask for a bid. An RFQ is not a request for a lengthy proposal.

The package you receive with an RFP will vary according to the funding agency. In general, however, it will include the following materials:

- Standard application form
- Instruction sheet on filling out the application
- Fact sheet, which is usually filled out after you get the grant and is signed by the administrator in the organization taking responsibility for the proposal
- Budget information, including charts for breaking down your budget on a quarterly and a yearly basis
- Assurances. You must assure the federal government that you are in compliance with all relevant federal laws. The assurances may include Equal Employment provisions pertaining to the handicapped, special qualifications required under the grant or contract, or a statement ensuring that none of the people in the organization is related to the people in the funding agency. You need file these papers only once. After that, you can check a box on the form indicating that you have already filed them.
- Program specifics. This section, in the form of an extended narrative, is the critical part of the package. Read it to determine if you are eligible for funding; there may be requirements that disqualify you. For example, there may be geographical constraints, procedural limitations, or service-population requirements. This section should clearly delineate what the funding agency wants in a program. It should also include evaluation criteria.

Do You Want To Apply?

When you have scanned the program requirements and determined your eligibility, decide if you want to submit a proposal.

- Is your organization providing services that fall within the program guidelines?

- Can the organization provide these services and comply with the guidelines without overextending itself?
- What are the implications of this program for the agency?
- What does the board say?

Crafting The Proposal

If you are eligible and have decided to apply for funding, you must craft a proposal. To do so, concisely and precisely relate what you are doing, or what you want to do, in a way that exactly conforms to the guidelines set forth for the contract or grant. Begin to conceptualize your program when you see the notice in **The Federal Register** or **Commerce Business Daily**. Once the information package and program guidelines arrive:

- Refine your concept of the program. Meld your ideas with what you think the government can provide you. Get specific answers to the following questions:

- What will you do?
- Who will do it
- Who will the program serve?
- How will you implement it?
- What will it cost for the program?
- What personnel are necessary?
- What will your overhead be to run the program?

Remember: All those who will be involved in implementing the proposal should be involved in this planning process. Moreover, if the program has implications for your agency's future, all the principal decisions makers (including board representatives) must cooperate in developing it.

Once you have answered these questions, outline the proposal production process. This must be written down and circulated to all concerned:

- Designate the proposal writer and the production manager. These need not be the same person.
- Arrange for good secretarial help. There will be many drafts before you arrive at the final proposal. You won't have time to write, type, rewrite and retype the entire proposal yourself. If a word processor is involved, make sure to reserve enough time in advance.
- Develop a proposal outline.
- Assign sections of the proposal outline to different individuals for drafting. Although it is better for one person to write and edit the final proposal, several people can research and draft sections.

- Tell each individual how many words he should write for his section and in what format, if possible.
- Arrange a time chart so that you can monitor progress. On this calendar, specify who will do what and by when. Allow extra time, because it will probably take longer to write the proposal than you think. Always allow sufficient time for a final copy edit.

The Proposal

There are two basic parts to any proposal: the Problem Statement and the Technical Approach.

- The Problem Statement should describe the problem, its importance, why it is of national scope, the people who will benefit, &c. It shows the funding agency that you know your service area and that you propose to address a great need. You should already have this information on file and available, since it is also used in private sector proposals.
- The Technical Approach section details how you plan to effect what you propose. There are several parts to this section:
  - Management structure. This section should include charts that briefly describe tasks against the time frame in which they must be accomplished, charts indicating the manpower this project requires (how many hours per year for each individual and the cost in terms of hours multiplied by the hourly rates), descriptions of the personnel structure for the project, and an outline of responsibilities.
  - Personnel qualifications. Include two résumés for each person: a standard one in outline form and a narrative one that indicates qualifications and experience.
  - Corporate capabilities. This section outlines your organization's credentials. Describe your demonstrated successes even if they are not specific to the proposal.
  - Evaluation. This section describes how you will evaluate the program and whether an outside consultant or someone in the organization will evaluate it.

Some Hints

- Writing a proposal is a production process. You must produce both the narrative and the proposal itself. Allow time for typing, binding, printing a cover, &c.
- Feel free to contact the individuals whose names are listed in the information packet. It is their job to assist you and to clarify matters of concern and confusion.

170

- The person responsible for the final proposal should collect the sections from the people assigned to write them; he must organize the sections and rewrite and edit them.
- Editing is a crucial part of proposal writing. Several drafts may be necessary before the proposal is final. No one should feel offended if what he writes is edited or omitted altogether.
- Apply for a federally-negotiated Indirect Cost Rate. Once you have established an Indirect Cost Rate, it is easier to determine federal proposal budgets.
- The budget should reflect two elements: what it is going to cost to run a project and what other ongoing expenses will be relevant. The person responsible for planning the project must work with the organization's fiscal officer.
- When you submit a contract bid or a proposal, you must get it in on time or it will not be considered.
- Schedule a meeting with your congressman or his administrative aide to inform him that you have submitted a proposal. Send him a copy. If you later have a problem you can follow up this meeting and ask for assistance.

Note: Negotiation is part of the proposal process. If you initial budget figure is higher than the funding agency expected, you can alter your proposal accordingly.

Project Management

Here are some suggestions for good project management:

- Establish rapport with your project officer, the individual assigned by the government to manage a grant or group of grants. He is in charge of your project and is the one to whom you will speak if you want to make budget changes, &c.
- Be prepared for occasional site visits by the project officer. Project officers will inform you that they are coming; they do not usually make surprise visits. Have your program well-organized for the visit:
  - Know what the agency is doing
  - Have materials ready
  - Be honest, but don't focus on your weak points
  - Anticipate questions and be prepared to answer them.
- Depending on the conditions of your grant, you may like to hire a consultant to evaluate your program. The government may like to hire a consultant to evaluate your program. The government may conduct its own evaluation or hire someone to do it. Provide the evaluator with information and performance data. Cooperate and make his job easy so that you will get a good evaluation.
- Regardless of whether it is an audit, a site visit, or an evaluation, don't worry

about minor criticisms. An outside person has to justify his existence, too; if he doesn't find something that could be improved, he'll probably feel he's falling down on the job.

- Submit reports on time. Provide the project officer with more information than he requests. Your file should give a complete picture of the agency.
- To prepare for audits:
  - Hire an accountant who is well-acquainted with your books and familiar with government regulations pertaining to nonprofit organizations.
  - Cooperate. If a minor mistake is discovered, ask what can be done to correct it.

The Federal Funding Consultant

A consultant can be most helpful in providing you with technical assistance as you seek federal funding. He can:

- Help you conceptualize your project, gather information, and write the grant.
- Work with a committee of knowledgeable agency personnel to clarify the project; organize, plan and oversee progress; handle technical aspects, and write and edit the final proposal
- Function as a task-group leader to oversee the proposal production process and ensure progress. In this instance, he will not necessarily gather information or write the document.

You may not write the consultant into the grant proposal unless it is for future services. Pay the consultant on a *per diem* or per project basis. He may not receive a percentage of the grant in return for assisting you to get it.

Conclusion

FIFTEEN FATAL FLAWS FRUSTRATING FRUITFUL FUND RAISING

Fund raising is not magic. It essentially involves just two things: motivating and organizing people. Still, many organizations fail to raise the funds they need. This is, I think, because they make one or more of the following Fifteen Fatal Flaws which doom them to frustrated fund raising efforts:

I. Incomplete Planning

A thorough planning process is imperative to successful fund raising. All too often a harried executive director will, by fiat, decide what the organization will raise money for. The board usually approves the choice but refuses to work together to raise the necessary money. A board planning process of the kind outlined in this book will insure that the directors both understand what is needed and take responsibility for providing it. It also enables you to present a united front to the community in which you are seeking funds: it is not just the executive director of the agency requesting assistance; it is the combined governing structure of the organization.

II. Minimal Board Commitment

I am constantly amazed by the number of boards which refuse to make financial contributions to their own organizations. Fund raising is like a pyramid: at the apex stand the board members of an organization. If they fail to give to their agency, it seems doubtful that any one else would give either. Boards which are now minimally committed to the success of their organizations must be trained to accept their proper responsibilities. This training can be accomplished by a committed director from a comparable organization or by an outside consultant. Don't wait. More often than not fund raising fails because a board will not give its own support both as donors and as members of fund raising and planning committees.

III. A Lackadaisical Executive

For whatever reason, executive directors often doom their fund raising efforts to failure. Sometimes it's because of their distaste for the job; sometimes it's outright sloth. Whatever the reason, no fund raising effort can succeed unless the executive director is entirely committed to it. If he isn't, there remain three courses: board persuasion of the executive to adopt the task, postponement of the fund raising, or removal of the executive.

IV. Setting a Goal Too High

All too often organizations set goals which are dramatically higher than their capacity to raise them. If the planning process has been careful, however, and due attention has been paid to the track record of the organization and its ability to mount a fund raising effort, this problem will be averted. It is always better to set a goal which is too low — and can, therefore, be exceeded — than to set one which is too high and cannot be met.

V. Involving Too Few People

Successful fund raising needs many committed volunteers. You will need chairmen for many committees and members drawn both from the board and outside. It is a mistake to try to raise money with only a few people. They will get frustrated and you will not reach your objective. Plan ahead: fund raising is a people-intensive business.

VI. Improper Use of Corporations and Foundations

There is much, much confusion about corporation and foundation fund raising. The best use of these philanthropic sources is for capital and project needs. On the whole they are not best utilized for raising your basic operating expenses. Remember: of the money raised in the private sector in this country, only about 12% (in roughly equal amounts) comes from corporations and foundations. The rest comes from committed individuals. Don't seek a great percentage of your goal from corporations and foundations. Remember, too: each corporation and foundation has a distinct personality. It is up to you to discover what it is and to plan your approach accordingly.

VII. No Attempt To Gather Links

Successful fund raising means linking people to people: the people who are already committed to you with those who still need to be persuaded. A Facilitating Session can assist you. The process of gathering links to both institutional and individual funding sources is ongoing. You must be prepared to keep working to gather the leads you need.

VIII. Failing To Cultivate Potential Givers

It constantly astounds me how many organizations feel they can approach an individual cold or on scant acquaintance and simply ask for money, and are affronted when they get a negative response or cool reception. Potential givers of every size need stroking. Cultivating prospects is a long-term endeavor, not one to be accomplished swiftly. No organization should be cultivating and soliciting simultaneously. You need to cultivate your prospect in advance; the more valuable the potential gift, the longer ahead you need to work. Don't expect people who scarcely know you either to value your organization as you do or to have your intensity of commitment.

IX. Going Public With a Capital Campaign Prematurely; Inadequate Pre-Public Campaign

Much of the important work of a capital campaign takes place long before any public announcement is made. All too often organizations, through a process best known to themselves, set a capital campaign goal and go public with it — never knowing whether this goal is realistic or not. Don't assume the money is "out there" for you; undertake a pre-public assessment of your chances for campaign success before you make any public declaration, including the availability of leadership gifts.

X. Failure to Solicit Leadership Gifts

Most successful fund raising efforts need to locate a series of leadership gifts: the gifts of people who are in a position to make a greater financial committment. No fund raising effort, either in an annual or capital campaign, should proceed without knowing in advance both the number and size of leadership gifts needed and who will contribute them. Remember: some of these gifts should come from the board. If your board refuses to make them or cannot make them, your fund raising objective is probably too high.

XI. Lack Of A Coordinated Effort

Fund raising takes the time and commitment of many people. The efforts of these people should be superintended by a Coordinating Committee which is capable of providing the kind and depth of support which fund raising demands. One person alone cannot coordinate a successful fund raising effort, and no one should ask him to do so. Instead, assemble a committee of committed individuals who are willing to oversee your fund raising effort and to insure that the myriad tasks and questions involved are dealt with expeditiously.

XII. Not Saying "Thank You"

Once a gift has been received, all too many organizations simply lie back and (while grateful themselves) forget it. This is a fatal mistake. Gifts which are not handsomely acknowledged will be gifts that the donor will regret making; your organization will suffer accordingly. Thank every one: the more people who feel thay they have had any part in the gift, from suggesting the donor to actually making the donation, the better.

XIII. Failure to Seek Endowment Funds

The long-term solution to many of the financial problems non-profit organizations have today is the development of a "savings account", an endowment fund which can produce unrestricted operating income. No organization should set a fund raising objective without considering what percentage will be invested as part of its endowment. Few organizations will dispute the need for developing such funds; too many, however, procrastinate about beginning such an account.

Financial independence rests on the accumulation of capital. Without it, one is at the mercy of events; with it, substantial autonomy is possible. While gathering this capital may be difficult and may mean reducing programs and services in the short term, it is the only sensible course to adopt. A board which is unwilling to take steps to insure the development of an endowment is being negligent.

XIV. Waiting Too Long to Retain Technical Assistance Consultants

Far too often organizations will wait until their options are severely limited before they seek consulting assistance. This is suicidal. Either you are equipped to handle your own problems or you need outside assistance. Once you have made the determination that you need this assistance, go about acquiring it. The amount of lethargy in the nonprofit world is staggering. Don't be a party to it. Act today.

XV. Lack of Persistence

Fund raising is one of the slowest-moving games in the world. It takes time to cultivate people, time to develop links, time to do the necessary planning and prospect research. All of this is unavoidable. In the long run you will be successful to the extent that you are persistent. If you are willing to take "No!" for an answer, you should probably go into another line of work.

Equipped with what you know, however, you are ready to mount a successful fund raising effort.

Go to it!

There is still no feeling like having money in the bank.

APPENDIX I

TIME LINE FOR DEVELOPMENT PLANNING AND IMPLEMENTATION

Note: This Time Line is for raising unrestricted money for operating costs, endowment, &c.

November or early December: Needs Assessment and Development Planning Committee (NADPC) is formed and holds its first meeting.

January 1: Chairman of the Board outlines the planning process and presents his expectations of individual board members to serve on a fund raising committee and to donate money. NADPC may be formed at this meeting, but it is more efficient if it has already met by this time.

Chairman calls for a "sense of the board" that it supports the development planning process. A board resolution is passed indicating that the entire board is behind the plan. Absent members are canvassed by telephone.

January-May: Needs Assessment and Development Planning Committee meetings.

Mid-March: Preliminary report of NADPC to full board.

March 15: First Facilitating Session.

May 1-15: NADPC prepares its report of programmatic and fund raising recommendations and mails it to board members for future consideration.

Second Facilitating Session held, if necessary.

June 1: Chairman of the board calls for a motion of unanimous support from his members for the fund raising goals outlined in the NADPC report. Once this resolution is passed, the chairman calls for a second one. In this, the board must commit itself to raising the sum specified in the NADPC plan.

Note: if the board does not ratify this goal amount, a new fund raising objective must be set. The board's figure, multiplied by five, will be the grand total sought.

Once a goal has been set and unanimously ratified by the board:

- Fund raising committee are brought forward
- Individual committee goals are set
- Names of possible chairmen for these committee are suggested.

Note: It is perfectly acceptable to attend to the preliminary work on these matters beforehand.

Coordinating Committee appointed by board.

July 1: The board may use this meeting to ratify a revised plan or fund raising goal.

Chairman begins board solicitation.

Coordinating Committee meets.

Document development begins.

Initial approach to corporations and foundations following document development.

Individual fund raising committees finalized.

Special Events Committee begins planning October 1st kick-off.

August: Even if there is no board meeting, board chairman should solicit individual committee chairmen who are not board members. (**N.B.** He has already solicited board members).

Individual committees meet and staff themselves.

Committee chairmen solicit committee members.

Individual fund raising committees meet to: 1) define Universe of Prospects, 2) develop Top Prospect lists.

September 1: Individual fund raising committees submit Top Prospect lists to Coordinating Committee for approval.

Approaches to Top Donor Prospects.

First report from Coordinating Committee to board: board solicitation should be complete; also documents developed. Other matters proceeding on course. Coordinating Committee submits report on tasks completed, tasks pending.

September 15: All written materials should be developed, including: letter mail letters being sent to coincide with kick-off, public relations materials for kick-off, &c.

September 21-28: Volunteer Solicitor-Motivator Meeting. Copies of documents should be available for this meeting.

October 1: Fund Raising Kick-Off. Special event and media tie-ins.

October: Individual fund raising committees send letters, set up meetings, undertake solicitation visits with prospects.

Coordinating Committee continues to meet weekly.

Staff liaison reports on each committee's progress.

November 15: Second Volunteer Solicitor Motivator Meeting. Update on fund raising effort.

November 25: Direct mail letter to donors who have already given if campaign is 75-80% completed. This is the "We Are Nearly There, Put Us Over The Top" Letter. Should arrive first week of December.

December 1-10: Coordinating Committee presses hard for successful termination to fall fund raising effort.

December 15: Finale of fall fund raising effort. Thank-you party for volunteers. Possible second special event to raise additional unrestricted income and conclude fund raising.

If fund raising effort has not made its goal, first meeting of Coordinating Committee to discuss re-opening drive in March next year.

January 1: Board meeting. If necessary, Coordinating Committee presents plan for spring fund raising.

Chairman inaugurates planning process for fall fund raising drive.

March 15: If no fund raising is scheduled, organization sends letter to donors and other supporters with information on how money is being spent and the continuing good work of the organization.

SAMPLES CONTENTS

Essentials Of A Précis

• Print first page on your organization stationery. Other pages may go on plain white or colored paper.

• Include a list of your board of directors on the left hand side of page 1.

• If your fund raising project has a snappy or descriptive name, use it as a headline.

• Begin with a history of your organization: why was it created? 100-200 words.

• Detail your programmatic and organizational successes — in two separate sections. If you can, cite outside endorsements: newspaper stories, legislative testimony, evaluations, &c. Keep each success to about 25 words.

• List your institutional supporters for the last three years. Include government agencies, foundations, corporations, civic organizations, religious organizations, &c. Do not list the names of all contributing individuals but mention the range of their gifts and possibly the grand total of individual support. Show comparative progress if you can.

• Add 50 word biographies of the chairmen of the board and executive director. You may add 25 word biographies of other key individuals as needed.

• Speak to the critical role of your organization. You need between 100-200 words of persuasive rhetoric detailing the best reasons for supporting you.

• List your fund raising objectives, the amount sought per objective, and give reasons for your choices.

• Make sure you give your mailing address.

• You may also add a line suggesting that you are not spending vast sums on printing, &c so that contributions can go directly to the project in hand. (See Capital Campaign Précis on page 236).

SAMPLE PRÉCIS

THE CONTEMPORARY THEATRE

(list of Board)   The Contemporary Theatre Restoration Project

About The Contemporary Theatre, Inc.

The Contemporary Theatre, Inc. is a nonprofit community organization founded in 1977 to restore and preserve the historic Contemporary Theatre which first opened in 1914. More recently an abandoned porno movie house, The Contemporary Theatre was acquired by Richard Sims, a Boston producer and director, and converted into a performing and educational arts center.

The restoration of The Contemporary Theatre is part of the move to revitalize downtown Boston and preserve rare and historic buildings. Located on Washington Street in the Theatre District, The Contemporary Theatre is both of historic significance and essential to the whole revitalization campaign. The restoration of The Contemporary Theatre will have a significant impact on the rejuvenation of the rest of this previously-dilapidated urban area.

Offering a diversity of cultural events unparalleled by other Boston theatres, The Contemporary is unique in the City of Boston. Its programs include international, national and local theatre, jazz, contemporary music, mime, and dance.

The Contemporary Theatre Is A Success Story — Programmatically

- The Contemporary Theatre has presented over 200 theatrical events and educational workshops to ever-widening audiences. Last year alone, we presented 20 more programs than we had the year before. We anticipate continuing growth this year.

- The Contemporary Theatre actively participates in Arts/Boston, a citywide cultural service dedicated to audience development.

- The Contemporary Theatre is an ongoing worksite for such programs as Youth Enrichment Services (YES), Comprehensive Employment and Training Act (CETA), Action for Boston Community Development (ABCD), and the Massachusetts Internship Program. The *Boston Ledger* has written, "The Contemporary Theatre is one of the few places in the city where young people can find an introduction to the theater — on stage and backstage."

The Contemporary Theatre Is A Success Story — Organizationally

- When Richard Sims began The Contemporary Theatre it was an eyesore on abandoned property. It now has grown to include an all volunteer staff and Board of Directors. More than forty individuals serve The Contemporary in some capacity.

185

- The Director and Board of The Contemporary have taken a leadership role in the creation of the Washington and Tremont Street Neighborhood Association, formalizing the relationships between neighborhood merchants, city officials, local residents, and the District's theater owners. State Representative Vincent Carboza calls this Association "the key to the revitalization of the neighborhood" and has especially cited The Contemporary's role in fostering positive change.

- The Contemporary Theatre has balanced its books after only three years of existence. It is not only a viable organization but one which brings revenue to a depressed city neighborhood, creates jobs, and is helping to improve conditions in a difficult area of the city.

Ongoing Programs Of The Contemporary Theatre

- First Night, an annual New Year's Eve celebration. First instituted in 1978, this program drew more than 200 participants in its first year; last year there were more than 400.

- The Annual Boston Mime Festival. Conceived and organized by the staff of The Contemporary, this unique event first began in 1978 with three companies participating. Last year more than 150 performers took part. *Variety* calls it "An amazing, dazzling show."

- Matinees for children and senior citizens. Begun in 1979 The Contemporary now arranges programs for more than 500 children from the Boston City Schools and over 1000 senior citizens from neighborhood senior clubs and projects. The Boston City Counsil recognized the importance of this work by granting Lynn Centuri, Coordinator, an Official Citation in 1980.

- "Movies at the Modern," a repertory film series. With the assistance of a grant from the National Endowment for the Arts, this distinctive series of films by America's greatest filmmakers began in 1980. Films are accompanied by lectures by people who participated in their making. The *Boston Globe* wrote, "This isn't just another film series; it's American history being played out before us. My hat's off to The Contemporary for thinking up this wonderful idea."

- "The Jazz at The Contemporary" Series. This series, just begun this year, brought to The Contemporary thirteen well-known jazz ensembles for engagements of up to a week. Audiences were well above expectations and the press coverage was substantial. The Contemporary has made plans to expand this series next year.

Support For The Contemporary Theatre

The Contemporary Theatre has received government, foundation, corporate, and individual assistance.

Government Support

- Action For Boston Community Development (ABCD)
- Massachusetts Council on the Arts and Humanties
- Mayor's Office of Cultural Affairs

Foundation Support

- Eugene Fay Trust (1979, renewed 1980)
- Mabel Louise Riley Trust

Corporate Support

- Star Market
- Zayre Corporation

Individual Support

- In 1980, 520 individuals made contributions to The Contemporary of amounts between $2 and $1000. This was a 20% increase in contributors over the year before and a 40% increase in the amount contributed.

The Contemporary Theatre's Leadership

Mrs. Margaret Davis, Chairman of the Board. Mrs. Davis is well known to the Boston arts community. She served for seventeen years as manager of the Parkinson Theatre in Jamaica Plain; upon retirement she was elected one of its Trustees. She has been a Director of The Contemporary from its founding and has served as Chairman of its Nominating Committee and assisted with all previous fund raising efforts. She has been Chairman of the Board since 1979.

Richard Sims, Executive Director. Mr. Sims began his theatrical career as an actor with the Repertory Company of Wilmington, DE. He has a Master of Fine Arts Degree from Yale. He conceived the idea for The Contemporary in 1975 and worked for three years to gather the initial financing. He is active in all phases of The Contemporary's operation.

The Critical Role Of The Contemporary Theatre In The Boston Downtown Area

The restoration of The Contemporary Theatre is important to the successful renovation of the Washington-Tremont Street area. This area is desperately in need of extensive renovation. The Contemporary Theatre has a critical role to play in the revitalization of this area. It is located on a pivotal thoroughfare. It can help bring revenue to the district. It can preserve a significant cultural and historic monument, irreplaceable if lost. It can also, because of its unique nonprofit status, create a diverse series of programs, important in a city which values its artistic heritage.

What The Contemporary Theatre Needs To Succeed

In only a few short years, The Contemporary has found a niche in Boston's cultural world. The Board of Directors wishes this important work to continue and has, therefore, set an ambitious fund raising goal of $660,000 for the year. Each member of the Board has contributed financially to the realization of this goal and is energetically assisting the fund drive in other ways.

Here are the fund raising objectives for the next year:

- Building Acquisition

  In order fully to acquire The Contemporary Theatre, a sum of $300,000 must be raised over the next 28 months. Already over $250,000 in donated goods and services, volunteer labor, and actual capital funds have been invested to restore the building.

  Needed for building acquisition: $300,000

- Building Renovation

  The Contemporary Theatre, to realize its potential, must undertake certain renovations to its antiquated though structually sound edifice. The immediate renovation and equipment needs involve: complete architectural and engineering survey; rebuilding heating system; rebuilding the sprinkler system and addition of fire alarms; refurbishing seats, and restoring original ornamental detail of the stage, including the creation of a fly loft.

  Needed for building renovation: $155,000

- Equipment

  The Contemporary needs to install theatrical lighting, install a concert sound system with recording capability, and equip and refurbish the projection booth.

  Needed for equipment: $165,000

- Personnel

  At present The Contemporary has *no* paid staff. To facilitate its growth and stability, The Contemporary Board now wishes to raise moderate sums so as to be able at last to pay longtime, dedicated volunteers and to add a permanent fund raising assistant. Money will be devoted to the salaries of: the Executive Director, General Manager, and Director of Development.

  Needed for personnel: $40,000

Please note: All contributions to The Contemporary Theatre are fully tax deductible. Please mail your gift to:

THE CONTEMPORARY THEATRE
523 Washington Street
Boston, Massachusetts 02111

Essentials Of The Development Proposal

• Print the first page on your organization's stationery. All other pages may go on plain white paper. Colored papers should never be used.

• Problem Statement. Use your imagination in titling this section. I prefer something like "Why We Exist, What We Need." This section, of between 250-400 words, is intended to show the nonspecialist reader the serious nature of the problem you are in business to deal with. Give a sense of the dimensions of the problem and put it into perspective for the reader.

• History section. This section is optional. If your organization is well known in its marketing area, you may delete it. Otherwise give basic information about who started your organization and why in about 150 words.

• Cite your organization's successes programmatically. Three bullets of about 25 words each should suffice. If your program has several divisions (and they are pertinent to the fund raising objectives) give successes for each division.

• Cite your agency's organizational successes. Again, three bullets of about 25 words should suffice.

• Demonstrate your government, foundation, corporate, civic group, religious organization, &c support for the last three years.

• Discuss your organizational leadership. Fifty word biographies of the chairman of the board and executive director should be included and other key organizational personnel (in about 25 words) as needed.

• The Proposal Section should include the total amount of money sought.

• It should publicize the fact that each board member is supporting the fund raising effort financially.

• The introductory section of the Proposal Section should list the various fund raising objectives. Think up short, descriptive titles for each objective.

• The need for each fund raising objective should be clearly established in paragraphs of between 100-200 words. Use fewer words if you can.

• In the Critical Need Section, stress the best reasons for supporting your organization. This section should not be longer than 250 words.

• Line item budget. Provide a line item budget for each of your fund raising objectives.

• Indicate that certain supplementary materials are available upon request.

SAMPLE DEVELOPMENT PROPOSAL

A PROPOSAL ON BEHALF OF
LINCOLN HILL SUMMER PROGRAM

WHY WE EXIST AND WHAT WE DO

Under Public Law 94-142 (Equal Education for All Handicapped Children Act in 1975), and Chapter 766 of the Acts of 1972, special needs children in Massachusetts are guaranteed the right to a free, appropriate and adequate education. For many of these children, this education involves intense instruction year round.

According to a 1980 study by the Massachusetts Department of Education, 13.5% or approximately 135,739 out of 1,000,000 school-aged children in Massachusetts need special education services. It is also estimated that educational services for approximately 4.7% or 6351 out of 135,739 special needs students could not be provided in public school programs.

Since then, the public school systems have been challenged to continue providing these children with the intensity of services needed during the school year. This is especially true during the summer. For this reason, in July 1974 the Massachusetts Jaycees under the auspices of the Massachusetts Jaycee Charitable Trust established the Lincoln Hill Summer Program in Foxboro, Massachusetts on an existing 28 acre camp site with land and buildings rented from the Town of Foxboro.

The primary purpose of the Lincoln Hill Summer Program (LHSP) has always been and remains unique in its practice of providing quality intensive educational services during the summer to children ages 6-16 with the following kinds of problems:

> Severe deficiencies in a variety of skills areas including dressing, grooming, toileting, speech and language, play, motor coordination, peer interactions and social skills;

> Behavior problems which interfere with learning including aggressiveness (hitting, biting, pulling hair, kicking) towards others or oneself, or extreme refusal to participate in daily activities.

These problems interfering with their ability to participate in activities at home, at school, and in the community often exclude children from other summer programs. Those programs which do exist are generally not equipped to meet the needs of these children. Without an educationally-based summer program, these children may lose many of the skills gained during the year and are at higher risk of long-term placement in residential treatment centers/schools at the public's expense.

191

The LHSP is committed to working with the parents and siblings of these children providing them with the support and skills necessary to maintain the child's behaviors at home.

The LHSP also serves as a training ground for developing professionals by providing them with the tools and experience necessary to advance in their careers.

DIMENSIONS OF THE PROBLEM

Beginning in early February, the LHSP receives referrals from private sources: parents, local Associations for Retarded Citizens (ARCs), Federation for Children With Special Needs, National Society for Autistic Children, Children's Hospital Medical Center (Boston), New England Medical (Boston), Beth Israel Hospital (Brookline), Kennedy Centers (Brighton, Lakeville, New Bedford) as well as public sources: Department of Mental Health, Department of Social Services, Office for Children and local public school systems throughout the state.

LHSP's admission requirements are strict; nonetheless, 82% of each year's applicants are appropriate. If our physical site was larger, we could serve twice as many children each summer.

LINCOLN HILL SUMMER PROGRAM IS A SUCCESS STORY

LINCOLN HILL SUMMER PROGRAM IS A PROGRAMMATIC SUCCESS

Between 1974 and the present, the LHSP has successfully accomplished the following:

1) LHSP has provided quality educational services to children.

- Over 300 children have received intensive educational services during the summers.

- Approximately 15 children whose parents originally considered residential treatment centers/schools are still living at home with their families.

- 85% of all children who attended LHSP have learned new skills and decreased inappropriate behaviors.

2) LHSP has provided quality training and support to families.

- Over 300 families have received instruction in behavioral techniques for skill teaching and managing their children's behavior at home.

192

- Siblings of 8 children at camp attended our workshops to share feelings and learn useful techniques to work with their brothers and sisters.

- 28 families utilized LHSP staff as advocates to appeal inappropriate educational placements. In 1981-82, the LHSP helped 6 families win their cases before Chapter 766 hearing officers.

3) LHSP has provided quality training to new and existing professionals.

- Over 130 college students from various states participated in a multidisciplinary training experience to prepare them to work with special needs children.

- 68% of the staff trained at the LHSP continued to pursue careers or graduate study in special education, psychology, speech and language, social work and medicine.

- 3 community residences for retarded adults sent their new and existing staff members to the LHSP for training in educational and evaluative strategies since 1977.

LINCOLN HILL SUMMER PROGRAM IS AN ORGANIZATIONAL SUCCESS

In only eight years, the LHSP has successfully accomplished the following:

- The LHSP has been approved by the Massachusetts Department of Education as a private school under Chapter 766 since 1975. Only two other summer programs in the state have accomplished this, and each serves a uniquely different population.

- The LHSP received an award in 1979 from the *Exceptional Parent* magazine (published by the Council for Exceptional Children) as one of the nation's "Best Summer Programs of 1978 Involving Children with Disabilities".

- The LHSP staff established the Lincoln Hill Day School in 1979 to provide daily educational services to children ages 6-16 with severe learning and behavior problems. In 1980, the LHSP was approved by the Department of Education as a private school under Chapter 766.

- The LHSP has attracted professionals from Massachusetts, Wisconsin, California and Rhode Island to provide consultation and supervision to the teaching and administrative staff.

SUPPORT FOR LINCOLN HILL SUMMER PROGRAM

Since 1980, the LHSP has benefitted from the generosity of foundations, corporate foundations, corporations, community and public agencies.

GRANTS RECEIVED FROM FOUNDATIONS

Nathaniel Stevens Foundation
Elizabeth Stevens Foundation
Sherwood Forest Fund
Telephone Pioneers

GRANTS RECEIVED FROM CORPORATE FOUNDATIONS

Polaroid Foundation
Cowan Foundation Corporation
First National Bank Trust

GRANTS RECEIVED FROM CORPORATIONS

Bird and Company
IBM
The Foxboro Company
Cambridge Bank and Trust
Digital
American Chemical

Milton Bradley
Polaroid
Beatrice Foods (Dannon)
Mantusko Trucking
Rand and Company

GRANTS RECEIVED FROM CIVIC GROUPS AND COMMUNITY AGENCIES

Knights of Columbus (Webster and Holbrook)
Rotary Club of Wellesley
Lions Club of Beverly
Association of Retarded Citizens (North Shore)

CONTRIBUTIONS AND CONTRACTS
FROM THE COMMONWEALTH OF MASSACHUSETTS

Department of Public Health
Department of Mental Health
Department of Social Services
Office for Children

ON-GOING SUPPORT FROM THE MASSACHUSETTS JAYCEES

The Massachusetts Jaycees continue to make a yearly contribution to the program.
The following local chapters have made financial donations in the past:

Beverley	Winthrop	Somerville	Wellesley
Norwood	Sharon	Carver	Plainville
Lowell	Randolph	Greater Newburyport	Jaycee Women
Mansfield	Boston	Waltham	Jaycee Senate
East Longmeadow	Hudson	Springfield	Mass. Jaycee
Arlington	Reading	Pembroke	Executive
			Committee

The following local chapters have donated labor, equipment and supplies in the past:

Mansfield	Waltham	N. Attleboro	Rockland
Newton	Plainville	Riverside	Sharon
Boston	Stoughton	Randolph	Jaycee Women

ORGANIZATIONAL LEADERSHIP

John Lipa, Chairman, Massachusetts Jaycee Charitable Trust (Board of Directors). Mr. Lipa is employed by General Electric as the Labor Relations Negotiator. He has been a member of Massachusetts Jaycees for 8 years where he has served as a Chapter President, President of the Massachusetts Jaycee Credit Union and has been elected to the Jaycees' International Senate.

Ann R. Honigman, M.P.H., Executive Director. Ms. Honigman was associated with the LHSP as a direct service staff person in the program's first three years of operation. As head teacher of a special needs class, she gained experience in program evaluation, staff coordination and parent-training. She has also designed and participated in various research activities including staff-training in Michigan, deinstitutionalization in Massachusetts and evaluation of standards and regulations of board and care homes for special need populations throughout the U.S. Ms. Honigman, who is also the Executive Director of the Lincoln Hill Day School, has a Bachelor of Arts in Psychology from Brandeis University and a Masters of Public Health (Health Behavior and Administration) from the University of Michigan.

THE PROPOSAL

LHSP has a history of providing quality educational services to children with special needs and their families throughout Massachusetts.

To be able to carry out its demonstrated tradition of service, the LHSP now needs to raise $101,350. Each member of the Board of Directors has given financially to the realization of this goal.

The four current fundraising objectives are as follow:
1) Engineering Study To Determine Needed Sanitary Improvements
2) Sanitary Improvements Based on Engineering Study
3) Establishment of a Scholarship/Endowment Fund
4) Acquisition of 12-passenger van

AN ENGINEERING STUDY FOR SANITARY IMPROVEMENTS

The plumbing system at the LHSP dates back to the early 1900's and fell into disrepair during the years before 1974 when the site was not in use. Each summer, repairs and improvements must be made before the program can open. The recurring problems are as follow:

Cracked and/or broken pipes throughout the system must be located and patched before the water can be turned on.

Several pipes leak throughout the summer.

9 of the 18 (already too few) toilets throughout the site are inoperative during most of the summer.

2 of the 6 showers are inoperative during most of the summer.

There are no provisions for hot water in the bunkhouses (cabins) where children sleep.

There has never been in the history of the LHSP a major engineering study or renovation of the plumbing system. The Board of Directors has therefore determined that an engineering study of the existing sanitary facilities should be accomplished and that certain emergency repairs should be made for the summer program.

The purpose of the study is to determine the exact extent of the renovations and improvements and what needs to be done next.

Preliminary estimates provided to the Board for the proposed engineering project are as follows:

1) Engineering design	$6,000
2) Survey: 4 days @ $550/day	2,200
3) Construction plans with a cost estimate	5,800
SUBTOTAL:	$14,000

SANITARY IMPROVEMENTS BASED ON ENGINEERING STUDY

The Board of Directors has been given a preliminary estimate of the work which will need to be done. The exact extent is of course the objective of the engineering study. However, it is anticipated that the following tasks will need to be accomplished:

1) Installation of a water main with necessary connections	$20,000

2) Installation of 3 independent
   septic systems for:

   a) Dining Hall/Kitchen and
      Washroom/Showerhouse   17,000

   b) Infirmary, Director's
      Cabin, Small Washroom/
      Showerhouse and Cabins
      4, 5, and 6   12,000

   c) Cabins 1, 2, and 3   8,000

                        SUBTOTAL: $57,000

10% Contingencies as
Estimated by Engineer   5,700

                        SUBTOTAL: $62,700

SCHOLARSHIP/ENDOWMENT FUND

The LHSP has no scholarship funds itself, although the Associated Grantmakers of
Massachusetts gives approximately $4,000 in tuition assistance for children from the
Greater Boston area. The tuition charged ($1,862 for seven weeks) represents approx-
imately 50% of the actual cost per child to attend the program.

Using statistics from the Department of Labor, 73.8% of the children are from low-
income families and only 26% receive tuition assistance from their local public school
systems through the Department of Education. The differential must be raised from
private sources each year.

To deal with this problem, the LHSP wishes to establish a scholarship/endowment
fund. The Board of Directors determined for its first year objective for this fund the
sum of $10,000. It is anticipated that this fund will produce $900 a year in income.
This amount represents just one-half the tuition charged and one-quarter the actual
cost for one child to attend the LHSP.

                        SUBTOTAL: $10,000

ACQUISITION OF 12-PASSENGER VAN

The LHSP currently rents a 12-passenger van each summer at a cost of $4,200. This van is needed for general use around the physical plant transporting large materials/equipment and provides the opportunity for community skills (purchasing in stores, laundry, social skills, etc.) to be taught on-site.

The Board of Directors has determined that the long-term financial stability of the program can be better served by the purchase of a van.

1) Purchase of new van (12-passenger)	$12,000
2) Insurance for one year	650
3) Gasoline for one year	2,000
SUBTOTAL:	$14,650
GRAND TOTAL	$101,350

CONTINUED NEED FOR THE LINCOLN HILL SUMMER PROGRAM

Because of the LHSP, each year 42 children with special needs who would otherwise receive no services during the summer months learn new skills while interfering behavior problems are reduced and return to their families and schools with a decreased risk of long-term placement in residential treatment centers/schools.

Because of LHSP, each year 42 families know more about teaching fundamental skills to their children and managing their disruptive behaviors.

Because of LHSP, new and existing professionals are better trained in educational, behavioral and evaluative techniques to prepare them to work with individuals with special needs in other settings.

It is for these reasons, that we ask for your support of the Lincoln Hill Summer Program.

PROPOSED REQUESTED BUDGET

ENGINEERING STUDY FOR SANITARY IMPROVEMENTS

Engineering design		$6,000
Survey: 4 days @ $550/day		2,200
Construction plans with a cost estimate		5,800
	SUBTOTAL:	$14,000

SANITARY IMPROVEMENTS BASED ON ENGINEERING STUDY

Installation of a water main with necessary connections		$20,000
Installation of 3 independent septic systems for		
Dining Hall/Kitchen and Washroom/Showerhouse		17,000
Infirmary, Director's Cabin, Small Washroom/ Showerhouse and Cabins 4, 5, and 6		12,000
Cabins 1, 2, and 3		8,000
	SUBTOTAL:	$57,000
10% Contingencies as estimated by engineer		5,700
	SUBTOTAL:	$62,700

SCHOLARSHIP/ENDOWMENT FUND

	SUBTOTAL:	$10,000

ACQUISITION OF 12-PASSENGER VAN

Purchase of van (12-Passenger)		$12,000
Insurance for one year		650
Gasoline for one year		2,000
	SUBTOTAL:	$14,650
	TOTAL:	$101,350

The following items are available upon request:

1) IRS Tax Exempt Letter, 501 (c) (3)
2) List of board of directors
3) Audited financial reports, past three years
4) Current operating budget
5) Five Year Plan
6) Organizational brochure
7) Organization précis
8) Testimonials, letters of support

Essentials Of A Cover Letter To A Funding Source
Where You Have Had No Previous Dealings

• Letter should always be sent to a designated individual. Check with the funding source to be sure you are sending it to the correct person and that his name is spelled properly and his title is accurate.

• Letter may be sent either by the chairman of the board and/or executive director.

• Letter should be sent on organization's letterhead.

• State reasons in the opening paragraph why you feel the funding source is appropriate for you. Indicate, thereby, that you have done your homework.

• In second paragraph, describe in concise detail the project for which you are approaching the funding source. Do not leave the selection of what might be funded to the funding source. This is your responsibility. 200 words should be sufficient for this synopsis.

• In third paragraph indicate how the project was developed. Show that you have given it your thoughtful consideration.

• In the fourth paragraph suggest the level of support you are seeking.

• Conclude by indicating how you will follow up this letter: with a telephone call, visit &c. and when this will occur.

SAMPLE COVER LETTER

Mr. Jeffery Giroux
Director of Employee Relations
National General Corporation Foundation
365 Wisconsin Avenue
Burlington, VT 08867

Dear Mr. Giroux:

We are aware of the long-time interest of the National General Corporation Foundation in juvenile welfare projects in the Burlington community. Recent grants made by your Foundation and publicized in both the *Foundation News* and your Annual Report confirm this interest.

Given this fact, it is my hope and that of my fellow directors of the Inner-City Juvenile Project that you would be willing to consider a proposal on our behalf. Specifically, we would like to approach you for our new School Reading Program. As you know, the reading scores of our high school students aged 14-18 are well below the national average. I enclose an article on the subject from the *Burlington Times* which outlines in detail the dimensions of the problem. This is, however, an area in which our organization has been working for some time; again, I refer you to the enclosed article which gives you some idea of our work.

For the last year our Needs Assessment Committee has been working directly with members of the Burlington School Committee, high school administrators, teachers and students in an attempt to formulate a new, innovative program to deal with this severe problem. The enclosed proposal represents the fruit of this work. Given the fact that this project will not only aid the youth of Burlington but also provide a model for the nation, I hope we may count on your interest and support.

It is our hope that you will be willing to consider a contribution of $3000 to this project, 25% of what we are seeking. To begin discussions on your possible support, I would like to call on you with our executive director, Mary Cahill, and a member of our Needs Assessment Committee, Michael Carruthers. A member of the staff of the Inner-City Juvenile Project will call you shortly to arrange this meeting.

I look forward to meeting you and to discussing this important project for our city's young people.

Sincerely,

Chairman of the Board

FACILITATING SESSION CONTACTS QUESTIONNAIRE

1. Name: _____

2. Home Address: _____

   _____

3. Home Telephone: _____

4. Business Address: _____

   _____

5. Business Telephone: _____

6. Business Position and Title: _____

   _____

7. Spouse's Business Affiliation and Position: _____

   _____

8. Spouse's Business Address: _____

   _____

9. Spouse's Business Telephone: _____

10. Business Affiliations of Adult Children or Other Close Family Members:

   _____

   _____

   _____

   _____

   _____

11. High or Prep School Attended: _____

12. Graduation Date: _____

13. College(s) Attended: _____

   _____

14. Graduation Date(s): _____

15. Your Insurance Company: _____

   Name of your local agent: _____

   Name and location of agent if not local: _____

   _____

Do you have any friends who work for insurance companies? _____

Do any of them live in our area? _____

_____

16. Your bank(s): _____

Name of your local bank(s): _____

Do you know anyone at the bank(s): - officer _____

                                    - home mortgage rep. _____

                                    - director _____

Do you have friends who work at banks: _____

_____

17. Do you have a local lawyer? _____

What is his name? _____

If not local, where is your lawyer located? _____

Do you have any friends who are lawyers? _____

What are their names and addresses: _____

_____

18. Membership in local organizations: _____

_____

Do you belong to any civic or fraternal organizations? _____

_____

If so, what are their names and addresses: _____

_____

19. Do you belong to a church? _____

If so, who is the pastor? _____

What is the address of the church? _____

_____

20. Do you belong to any national organization(s)? _____

If so, what is its address: _____

Do you know any members of this organization? _____

If so, give their names and addresses: _____

_____

205

21. Do you know anyone who works in any position for a local corporation? Please give the names of the friends, their corporations and their positions, if known.

_____

_____

_____

_____

22. Do you know anyone who works for a corporation outside our area? Please give the same information:

_____

_____

_____

23. Which local businesses do you frequent and who do you know at them?

- food _____

- pharmacy _____

- household goods _____

- auto _____

- hardware _____

- appliances _____

- restaurants _____

- other _____

24. Who is your doctor? _____

25. Who is your dentist? _____

26. Do you have any trade union connections? _____

27. Please list the names and address and zip codes of 10 friends you would ask to give contributions of under $100 to our organization.

    1. _____

    2. _____

    3. _____

    4. _____

    5. _____

    6. _____

    7. _____

8. _____

9. _____

10. _____

28. Is there any other information you think would be helpful to us or lead us to potential fund raising sources you would care to give?

_____

_____

_____

_____

_____

_____

_____

_____

_____

_____

_____

Essentials Of The Letter From Individual Committees To Their Prospects

Note: This letter is one used by the Civic Organizations Committee. It can be readily adapted to suit all other committees. **N.B.** Top Donor Prospects are usually contacted by telephone or by a brief personal note asking for a meeting. This letter is usually reserved for individuals below the rank of Top Donor Prospect.

• Letter goes on agency letterhead to a specific individual. The spelling of this individual's name, his or her title, and the correct name of the organization should be verified.

• Opening paragraph should talk about successes already logged in fund raising effort. You want the potential donor to become a member of a team already in place.

• Second paragraph discusses the benefits provided by the organization within its marketing area. You want the prospective donor to think after reading this section, "Of course, this kind of organization deserves my support!"

• Third paragraph discusses the specific fund raising items of this effort. It suggests the need for them.

• Fourth paragraph suggests both the size of the overall goal and this committee's specific objective.

• Letter concludes by suggesting what follow-up will take place and when.

Note: This letter should be as personal as possible. Make a special effort to make it informal, upbeat, and persuasive.

SAMPLE SOLICITATION LETTER FROM INDIVIDUAL COMMITTEES TO THEIR PROSPECTS

Mrs. Janet Wethersfield, President
Catholic Women's Club
6 South Cedar Street
Wakefield, MA 01648

Dear Janet:

Last summer we began approaching the many civic groups of Wakefield to gain their support for the fund raising effort of the Wakefield Girls' Club. My committee members and I have been very gratified by their enthusiastic response. Already we have been joined by seven organizations, including (list). We hope that you, too, will join us.

As you know the Wakefield Girls' Club is a significant community organization. Virtually everyone in Wakefield benefits in some way from its activities. We have a variety of family programs, including recreational and counseling services. We provide young girls with leadership, athletic and recreational programs. We offer fitness and conditioning programs for both adult men and women. And I'm sure you know about our fine aquatic program. This year the High School Diving Team won the Massachusetts State Finals!

Now we find ourselves in yet another fund raising drive brought about by the community's continuing need for improved athletic programs for both children and adults. Specifically, we are both renovating and building new construction which will leave the Wakefield Girls' Club superbly equipped for the next century.

This year we are trying to raise $130,000 in Wakefield towards this end. We have set as our fund raising objective for Wakefield civic organizations the sum of $10,000. Already we have $5,000 of this in hand.

The success of our fund raising effort is important not just for the Girls' Club but for the revitalization of our entire community. Therefore, we look to your committee for support. Next week I shall call to arrange an appointment at which we can discuss it.

With all good wishes and thanks,

Sincerely,

Chairman of Civic Organizations Committee

Essentials Of A Letter From A Direct Link To A Foundation Trustee

• Letter should be sent on individual's personal stationery.

• Writer should mention his connection to the organization.

• The letter may be sent either to the trustee's home or business address.

• It should be informal in tone and personal.

• The letter need not dwell on the project. It should, however, indicate that the writer understands that the source is an appropriate one. The purpose of this letter is to get a meeting and create a direct link between the grantseeking organization and the foundation trustee.

• Writer should ask whether the trustee would rather deal with the matter directly or refer it to the foundation staff. (Writer should know before sending this letter whether such staff exists.)

• Writer should indicate how follow-up is to be handled.

• Appropriate materials (including précis and development proposal) may be sent to familiarize trustee with organization.

• A copy of this letter should be sent to the executive director for filing.

Note: The same points apply to the following letters:

   • Direct Link to Corporate President

   • Direct Link to Corporate Professional Staff

SAMPLE LETTER FROM A DIRECT LINK TO A FOUNDATION TRUSTEE

Mr. Peter Grimes, Trustee
The Andover Foundation
435 Smythe Street
Hatfield, MA 01564

Dear Peter,

As I'm sure you've heard me talk about, I am a great fan of the Greater Pittsfield Youth Symphony. In fact, I've been a trustee for years. As you'll not be surprised to learn, this worthy organization, like most arts groups, is in need of funds.

Now I believe that The Andover Foundation has, from time to time, supported arts organizations. I hope to be able to persuade you to support ours, too.

I should very much like to bring the executive director, Marion Davies, by and introduce her to you. She makes a very persuasive case on behalf of the good work the organization is doing, and I'm sure you'd enjoy meeting her. I don't, however, wish to overturn any apple carts; it may be that you'd like to refer us, first, to the professional staff of the Foundation. I could then let you know what happens.

To get your opinion, I'd very much like to call next week. In the meantime, I'm sending materials which I trust will be of interest to you about the fine work of the Greater Pittsfield Youth Symphony.

Give my best to Mollie and the girls; Helen joins me in wishing you the best, as ever.

Sincerely,

Friend of the Foundation Trustee

Essentials Of A Letter To An Indirect Link Connected To A Foundation Trustee

• Letter should be sent on writer's personal or business stationery, not on agency letterhead.

• Writer should mention his connection to organization.

• Letter may be sent to the Indirect Link's home or business address.

• The Letter should be informal in tone and personal.

• The letter need not dwell on the project. It should, however, indicate that the writer understands that the source is an appropriate one. The purpose of this letter is to transform the Indirect Link into the agent and friend of the organization so that he will help make the direct connection with the foundation.

• The writer should never be coy about his purpose. He should say what he hopes will transpire.

• Writer should request a meeting with Indirect Link and organization representatives. A meeting with an Indirect Link to familiarize him with the organization is virtually always necessary.

• Writer should suggest how follow-up to this letter will be accomplished.

• Appropriate materials should be enclosed.

• A copy of this letter should be sent to the executive director.

Note: The same points apply to the following letters:

  • Indirect Link to Professional Staff of a Foundation

  • Indirect Link to Corporate President

  • Indirect Link to Corporate Professional Staff

SAMPLE LETTER TO AN INDIRECT LINK
CONNECTED TO A FOUNDATION TRUSTEE

Mrs. Melanie Gross
135 Church Hill Lane
Hatfield, MA 01564

Dear Melanie,

As I'm sure you know (from hearing me speak about it so often and at great length!), I am a great fan of the Greater Pittsfield Youth Symphony. In fact, I've been a trustee of the organization for years. As you'll not be surprised to learn, this worthy organization, like most arts groups, is in need of funds.

Before you run for cover, let me say that this letter is not a solicitation of you (although it would be very nice if you'd consider a donation). Rather, it's my attempt to begin persuading you to become our advocate with Peter Grimes, your cousin. Peter, as you well know, is a Trustee of The Andover Foundation, and, after research, the executive director of the Youth Symphony, Marion Davies, tells me that they have supported many, many arts organizations over the years. I'm hoping you can help us persuade Mr. Grimes to support us, too.

I should very much like to bring Marion by and introduce her to you. She makes a very persuasive case on behalf of the good work of the organization, and I'm sure you'd enjoy meeting her. Perhaps at that time you can advise us on the best means to make this approach; I'm hoping you might even come with us.

To get your opinion, I'll call next week. In the meantime, I'm sending materials which I trust will be of interest to you about the fine work of the Greater Pittsfield Youth Symphony.

When last we spoke you were feeling a bit under the weather. I trust you are much better now. No doubt your trip to Bermuda helped!

Talk to you next week,

Sincerely,

Friend of Indirect Link To Foundation Trustee

Essentials Of A Letter From This Indirect Link To The Foundation Trustee

• Letter should be on Indirect Link's stationery.

• It may be sent either to the trustee's home or business address.

• The letter should stress the interest of the Indirect Link in the organization and his connection to the original writer.

• The letter should ask for a meeting with the trustee. Given the kinds of connections which are involved, this meeting is important whether or not there may be professional staff. If such staff exist, the foundation trustee can refer the executive director to the appropriate person later. Further links at this point, however, might confuse matters.

• Ideally, the Indirect Link indicates his willingness to schedule the meeting and attend. If not, work your way down the Pyramid of Contacts.

• Follow-up should be handled by the Indirect Link whenever possible.

• Indirect Link should enclose appropriate materials or indicate they are coming from the organization.

• A copy of this letter should be filed with the executive director, although it may be difficult to obtain.

Note: The same points apply to the following letters:

• Converted Indirect Link to Foundation Professional Staff

• Converted Indirect Link to Corporate President

• Converted Indirect Link to Corporation Professional Staff

SAMPLE LETTER FROM THIS INDIRECT LINK
TO THE FOUNDATION TRUSTEE

Mr. Peter Grimes, Trustee
The Andover Foundation
435 Smythe Street
Hatfield, MA 01564

Dear Peter,

I've become involved with a wonderful organization I'd like to tell you about: the Greater Pittsfield Youth Symphony. I believe you know about it and you've probably heard of Erich Rich, one of its trustees, and Marion Davies, the executive director. I myself have known Erich for years and have often heard him rhapsodize about the Youth Symphony. Now I know why.

You've probably guessed the purpose of this letter: like all other arts groups, the Youth Symphony is looking for additional funds. They tell me The Andover Foundation supports many arts organizations and given your own interest in the arts, Peter, I'm not at all surprised.

My question: Would you be willing to meet with Erich, Marion Davies and me and discuss the possibilities for Foundation support? I'd like to call you next week and schedule a meeting; you can tell me then whether I'm on the right track.

Marion Davies will be sending you some material about the Youth Symphony in advance of the meeting. You should get it in a day or two.

Needless to say, I'm looking forward to seeing you and hope you will feel as I do about the Greater Pittsfield Youth Symphony.

As ever,

Melanie Gross

Essentials Of A Letter From A Direct Link To Foundation Professional Staff

• Letter should be sent on writer's personal or business stationery, not agency letterhead

• Writer should mention his connection to the organization.

• Letter should be sent to professional staff's business address, although the home address may also be used.

• The letter should be informal in tone and personal.

• This letter need not dwell on the project. The purpose of the letter is to arrange a meeting at which the executive director of the organization or another organizational representative may be introduced. The writer needs to signal the foundation staff, however, that this foundation has not been chosen idly. If there is a reason you feel any support might be forthcoming, say so.

• Writer should indicate how follow-up will be handled. It is better if the writer arranges any subsequent meeting.

• Appropriate materials about the organization should be included. These may come either from the writer or the executive director.

• A copy should be filed with the executive director.

Remember: Be creative in establishing links to people who can help your organization. Consider the following:

    • An alumnus of a college may write to another prominently-placed alumnus whether known to him or not. The chances of a reply are very good.

    • An employee may send an interoffice memorandum to either the president of his company (where there is no corporate contributions program) and/or the corporate contributions officer, if there is.

    • A depositor of a bank may send a letter to the bank president.

    • A policyholder may send a letter to the president of an insurance company.

    • A stockholder may send a letter to the president of a company in which he holds stock.

Use your imagination!

SAMPLE LETTER FROM A DIRECT LINK
TO A FOUNDATION PROFESSIONAL STAFF

Marcia Taggert, Administrator
Lucia Mott Hamilton Foundation
6790 Woodward Avenue
Des Plaines, IL 60504

Dear Marcia,

As you know my brother is the Coordinator of the Senior Housing Division of the Des Plaines Neighborhood Improvement Association. He's been there now for seven years and has always kept me abreast of their ambitious plans. I believe you are already familiar with their new nonprofit housing development on Oak Bluff.

As you may imagine this organization is always looking for new sources of revenue, but particularly just now. They have recently been putting together a unique Senior Crime Patrol working with students at the local college and the Des Plaines Police Department. Like most new projects, this one could benefit by having some "venture capital." Specifically there is some anti-crime equipment they would like to purchase, and they are seeking funds to do so.

After looking into the matter, John Haggerty, the executive director, informed me that he thought the Hamilton Foundation might be a place to look for support. When I said I knew you I was quickly "volunteered" into writing. I don't mind, since the program seems an excellent one and is, I know, very much needed.

What I'd like to do is to bring both my brother and John Haggerty to see you and let them explain just what they've got in mind. I'm enclosing their introductory proposal which I think covers the ground very well, but I know they will want to expand upon this necessarily brief description.

I'll call next week, since I'd like to come along, too, and see you in action. Perhaps we can all have lunch together.

With thanks and good wishes,

Sincerely,

Friend of Foundation Professional Staff

Essentials Of The Offset Letter

Note: This letter may also be produced by word processor. Ordinary xerox techniques are not recommended.

• Letter goes on agency letterhead, although individual directors may wish to produce their letter on their personal letterhead. This is acceptable.

• **All** directors of the organization should send **at least** ten of these letters. All names must be approved by the Coordinating Committee so that there are no duplications and so that individuals are not approached for a moderate donation who are known to be capable of something more substantial. This letter goes specifically to people who will give $100 or less.

• First paragraph mentions that writer is a director of the organization. Employees, of course, and others may also send a letter tailored for them.

• Second paragraph discusses the good work of the organization. It is important to bring home to the reader that the organization has a substantial community impact, and, if possible, betters the reader's life directly.

• Third paragraph presents the current fund raising objectives and cites the goal to be raised. This paragraph may mention how much has already been raised. It must also say that **all** directors have given themselves.

• Fourth paragraph mentions the need for the reader's contribution. You may cite an amount you would like him to give (the usual amount is $25). If you can produce this letter with differing amounts, $25, $50 or $100, to be sent to differentiated donor prospects, do so.

• The writer should include with the letter a stamped self-addressed envelope. He wants the donor to send **him** his contribution rather than forward it to the agency directly. Those who have given want the writer to know they have done so.

• Writer should personalize the letter by adding a post script in his own hand directed to the donor prospects.

• Enclose a précis with this letter or other appropriate materials; do not send the development proposal.

Note: For best results, those who have not yet given should be called in two weeks after the letter is sent. Letters should be sent at the beginning of a month; at the next full board meeting each director should be asked for a progress report.

SAMPLE OFFSET LETTER

Note: Do not write a "Dear Friend" salutation. Either hand write in the name or use a word processor to type it. Your letter should be as personal as possible.

Dear Mary,

I am writing to you on behalf of the Boston Special Needs Adoption Agency, Inc. I am myself a director of this organization and am, as such, most enthusiastic about its important work. It is my hope to be able to get you to share my enthusiasm and become a supporter, too.

The Boston Special Needs Adoption Agency works exclusively with hard-to-place children. Its clients are the mentally retarded, physically disabled, adolescents and minorities — all once thought to be "unadoptable." The work of the Boston Special Needs Adoption Agency has conclusively refuted this belief.

In the last two years alone it has helped place nearly 100 special needs children in loving families. Think of it! These are children who would otherwise have been institutionalized — at great cost to themselves psychologically and to the taxpayers financially. No wonder I'm so high on this organization: it's humane and it's also good business.

We are trying this year to raise funds for our Post Placement Services Project. Under this project the adoptive parents of these often-difficult children will be given special services and sustained attention by social work professionals beyond the initial transition period. These services are not available through either the state or federal governments and, as such, we must raise $50,000 this year to provide them.

Each member of the board — including me — has already given a gift towards this effort. Now I am asking you to join us.

It is my hope that you will consider sending us a check for $25 in the enclosed envelope. Please make it payable to the Boston Special Needs Adoption Agency. It is, of course, fully tax deductible.

I look forward to having you as a supporter of the profoundly important work of this agency.

With thanks,

Sincerely,

Friend/Director of Agency

Foundation, Corporation and Top Prospect Log Sheet

Name of Prospect: _____

Address: _____

Telephone Number: _____

Foundation or Corporation Decision Maker: _____

Our Contact Is: _____

His Title Is: _____

His Address: _____

His Telephone: _____

Other Pertinent Contact Information _____

_____

Complete Record Of Contacts

Date	Person Dealt With	Synopsis of Meeting	Suggested Follow-Up

SAMPLE PLEDGE CARD (Obverse)

Note: Consider printing a perforated card which fits into a regular sized business envelope.

First Section

• This portion is about 1½″ long.

• It is confidential and should be marked as such. It includes the following language: "Detach this stub before presenting card to prospect. It is hoped that this donor prospect might consider a gift (or investment) in the range of $_____."

• Allow space for notes in this section.

Second Section

• This portion is about 5-7″ in length.

• For ease of filing, allow space for the donor's name at the top of the card, surname first.

• Allow several lines for the donor's name, address and telephone. Allow space for his business address and telephone, too. Don't forget space for the name of a business!

• Always include the name of your organization, its address and telephone number on this portion of your pledge card.

• This section should include the following language: "To provide (purpose of fund raising), I subscribe the sum of (written amount), (amount in figures).

Or give the following securities or other property: (List)"

Payments will begin (Date) _____ and will be paid

Annually ☐   Semi-Annually ☐   Quarterly ☐   Monthly ☐

Allow space for the donor's signature and the date.

You may wish to add a line at the foot of this section of the card for the solicitor's name.

Third Section

This is the Temporary Receipt.

Include:

- Contributor Name
- Total Pledge Amount
- Amount Paid
- Balance Outstanding
- Solicitor Name

Make a notation that all contributions are tax deductible.

Sample Pledge Card (Reverse)

The second side of the pledge card functions as a payment record. The following information needs to be logged:

- Amount pledged
- Date Pledged
- Amount sent
- Balance remaining

You may also like to leave a space for the initials of the individual recording the payments.

It is also helpful to have a section on the pledge card indicating the dates letters were sent reminding people that a payment was due on their pledge. This section may be titled "Billed."

Remember: You may also wish to consider having your pledge card printed on your return envelope. This is perfectly acceptable and cuts down the size of your pledge card. If you adopt this course, however, you'll have to adopt another method of handling billing information

**Essentials Of The Letter Sent To Proven Givers When Fund
Raising Effort Nears A Successful Conclusion**

• Letter is sent by chairman of the board on agency letterhead.

• It should be sent to **all** those who have pledged or donated to current funding drive including the organization's board members.

• This letter must have a confident, upbeat tone.

• First paragraph thanks donors for their support.

• Second paragraph reports progress both in the raising of funds and gives a preliminary indication of how money already raised is being spent on fund raising objectives(s).

• Third paragraph asks proven giver to dig deeper and pledge more. This paragraph suggests that chairman of the board has himself given again. A suggested amount of contribution should be made.

• A stamped addressed envelope is included. Remember: these are your proven givers.

• Consider asking these people to the party that concludes your fund raising effort. It's a graceful gesture.

SAMPLE END OF FUND RAISING DRIVE LETTER

Note: Always send this letter to a specific individual. A word processor can be most valuable.

Dear Dr. Johnson:

A few weeks ago the Milwaukee Girls Club contacted you concerning our annual fund raising drive. You responded promptly with a generous donation. I thought you'd like to know where this drive now stands.

We had, as you'll remember, a goal of $100,000 to be used for renovating our girls athletic facilities, which are quite run down. I am delighted to tell you that we have now raised approximately $80,000 of this amount and are within sight of a successful conclusion. Anticipating this result we have already begun to take the first steps towards the long-overdue renovations, and we feel that the facilities will be entirely operational within six months.

As someone who so evidently believes in our work, Dr. Johnson, it is my hope that you would be willing to go just a little farther for the Milwaukee Girls Club. I have myself. I have made an additional pledge of 20% on what I previously gave, and I hope you will consider doing the same.

For your convenience, I enclose a stamped addressed envelope, which I hope you will use.

We shall be concluding our fund raising drive with a party in honor of our volunteers and donors at our headquarters three weeks hence. I enclose information about it for you, and trust I shall have the pleasure of greeting you there and thanking you personally for your continuing, generous support.

With good wishes and thanks,

Sincerely,

Chairman of the Board

Essentials Of A 'Cold' Letter To Individuals Not Known To Organization

Note: This letter is usually sent by the chairmen of individual fund raising committees. It should only be **considered** after the chairman himself has given, has solicited his committee members, the Top Donor Prospects for the committee have been sought out, **and** more moderate donors have been solicited. In other words, this is the last thing for a committee to consider doing.

• Letter should be sent by an individual chairman on agency letterhead.

• It should always be sent to a specific individual.

• First paragraph should indicate writer's connection to soliciting organization.

• Second paragraph should detail benefits organization provides within marketing area.

• Third paragraph should indicate amount of fund raising goal, what percentage has already been raised.

• Fourth paragraph should request donor prospect's help and indicate what specific follow-up there will be to this letter: either that a member of the committee will visit or that a telephone call will be made, &c.

• Précis and pledge card should be enclosed with the letter.

SAMPLE 'COLD' LETTER TO INDIVIDUALS
NOT KNOWN TO ORGANIZATION

Sally Hawkins, Esq.
Hawkins & Smythe Attorneys
345 Grove Street
Parksville, PA 18906

Dear Ms. Hawkins:

As you may know, I am a fellow attorney practicing in Parksville and am also serving as a volunteer fund raising solicitor for the Parksville Summer Camp Program.

As you probably know, the Parksville Summer Camp Program has existed for over 12 years. It provides nearly 250 children with the opportunity to have at least two weeks of supervised camp experience in the nearby Gray Mountains. These are children who often come from broken homes, very often from institutional settings and who have never had the opportunity so many of us have had of enjoying good healthy recreational — and educational — opportunities in such a setting. There is no other program like this in our community, and that's why I'm so enthusiastic about what it does.

Programs like this cost money, of course. Further, the Parksville Summer Camp Program is entirely supported through the voluntary donations of individuals. This year we are raising $85,000. Some of this sum is going for needed repairs to the camp facility, but most ($60,000) will provide whole or partial tuition assistance for the children, aged 6 to 15, who need it. So far, I'm glad to tell you that $65,000 of this sum has already been raised from a wide variety of sources, including many local professionals like you and me, (for I am an enthusiastic contributor).

I am writing to you today to see whether you would join with us on the last lap towards raising the money we need for this summer's program? Further information is enclosed, including a pledge card. Since I would welcome the chance to discuss this fine program with you and your involvement in it, I'll call your office in the next few days.

I look forward to having you join the team of enthusiastic boosters of the Parksville Summer Camp Program.

Sincerely,

Member Area Professionals Fund Raising Committee

Essentials Of Progress Report Letter

• This letter should be sent on agency letterhead by the chairman of the board.

• This letter should be sent about 4-5 months after the conclusion of your fund raising effort to those who have given to support it. Consideration should be given to contacting media sources concurrently with the progress report so that other people can be made aware of what has happened. Consideration should also be given to sending your entire mailing list an update in the form of a newsletter or letter from the chairman of the board. The important thing is to keep your constituency (particularly proven givers) abreast of what you are doing.

• The salutation to this letter may be "Dear Friend" or something comparable.

• First paragraph should again recognize individual as a donor and thank him for helping make the fund raising effort a success.

• Second paragraph should discuss what is being done to realize fund raising objectives. Substantial progress should be reported.

• Third paragraph should hope for donor's continuing interest and support. No explicit request for money should be made, however.

• Include pledge card and return envelope.

SAMPLE PROGRESS REPORT LETTER

Dear Friend:

Nine months ago or so we contacted you regarding the Greenville Community Hospital drive for a new Cancer Research Laboratory. You responded promptly with a handsome donation to the cause. Although we have thanked you before, let me take this opportunity to thank you both personally and in my capacity as chairman of the board. Thanks to the generosity of people like you this drive has proved to be a resounding success. We exceeded our goal of $250,000 by $15,000. Again my thanks.

Since you made a generous gift, I felt it incumbent upon me by virtue of my position in the hospital to report to you on what we have been doing with your money. I hope you will agree with me that substantial progress has already been made in realising our announced goal of constructing within the Hospital the county's first Cancer Research Laboratory.

Just before the successful completion of the fund raising drive, the Hospital contracted with the architectural firm of Sperry & Rees from Columbia. Working with our facilities advisory committee made up both of doctors from the Hospital and members of the board, they have produced an admirable, cost effective set of plans for the laboratory. The board recently gave these plans their unanimous approval.

Construction of the laboratory has now just begun. It will take about a year before this facility is fully operational. In the meantime, however, some preliminary cancer work is being undertaken through Dr. Laurence Star of the Hospital staff. Dr. Star will be the Laboratory's Director once it is completed.

The citizens of this county have, I think, long felt the need for this Cancer Research Laboratory. The resounding success of the fund raising drive proved that this was a felt need with broad based support. Soon our dream will be a reality — and we can continue the fight against a dread disease.

Again, let me thank you. We are privileged to live in a country where community-minded citizens can themselves band together to accomplish this kind of significant goal. I pledge that we shall continue to use your money wisely as we move forward with our plans.

Sincerely,

Chairman of the Board

Essentials of Donor Meeting Synopsis

• Give name of Donor Prospect (individual or institutional)

• Mention who represented your organization at meeting.

• List all items needing follow-up, including:

      i)   points to be dealt with in cover letter
      ii) objective for which you are requesting funds
      iii) amount being requested
      iv) further documents or materials needed by funding source
      v) anticipated date of decision
      vi) individuals who need to have these facts communicated to them

SAMPLE MEETING SYNOPSIS

Mary Danvers, executive director, met with Win Schiff, corporate contributions officer, Maltravers Company Foundation on October 15, 1989. It was agreed that our organization should request $5000 for our ambulance acquisition campaign. WS suggested we stress benefits to company marketing area in our cover letter. Letter of request will come from MD and will include a copy of our development proposal, our 501 (c)(3) letter and list of the board of directors. Decision will be reached by the end of February. MD needs to tell Joe Brown, our contact within the company.

Essentials Of The Capital Campaign Précis

Note: The précis for a capital campaign is similar to that used in an organization's annual fund raising effort. Here are the major differences:

• The campaign chairman or co-chairmen should be listed along with Board members. Add the names of others who are prominent in the campaign as necessary.

• The document may be twice as long as a regular précis; the two (back-to-back) pages will be attached so that you have a pamphlet.

• The document should be written so that the objectives of the full multi-year campaign are outlined. Each separate annual objective should be detailed.

• Individual fund raising committees can be listed along with their chairmen and their fund raising objectives for the year.

Western Bible College
DENVER, COLORADO

PARTNERS IN PROGRESS

A Campaign on Behalf of Western Bible College, 1982-85

Thirty-five years ago in Denver a partnership of concerned Christians with a dream made a God-directed decision. Their dream was a college in the Rocky Mountain region, solidly grounded in the Word of God to train committed men and women for ministry in service for Jesus Christ. Western Bible College is the realization of that dream and is today the *only* fully-accredited, four-year, evangelical and interdenominational Bible college in the entire Southern Rocky Mountain region.

OUR PURPOSE

Western Bible College is an undergraduate institution specializing in Biblical studies and dedicated to the preparation of purposeful believers in career and lay ministries for fruitful Christian service in the modern world.

WESTERN BIBLE COLLEGE IS A SUCCESS STORY

With limited material resources—but with the unlimited resources of God—Western Bible College has achieved a series of notable successes. The number of graduates has grown from only four in the class of 1951 to the Western Bible College alumni family which now numbers over 1,300:

- Forty-one Western Bible College alumni are serving as foreign missionaries in Kenya, Japan, Okinawa, Venezuela, Bolivia, Guatemala, Brazil, Philippines, Argentina, Germany, Canada, Italy, Bermuda, France, Spain, Liberia, New Guinea, Austria, England and Uruguay. Joseph Lulich ('59) is one of them. He heads a radio and evangelism ministry in his native Italy.

- Seventy-four Western Bible College alumni are in full-time career ministry across the United States as pastors and home missionaries. Tom Rempel ('76) is one of them. His ministry as pastor of First Baptist Church in Gothenburg, Nebraska has been marked by significant growth in church membership.

- Western Bible College alumni are well-recognized for their work in music and academic education in private and public institutions across the country. Robert Vogel ('71), who is Professor of Homiletics at Western Conservative Baptist Theological Seminary in Portland, Oregon is one of many such distinguished graduates.

16075 West Belleview Avenue, Morrison, Colorado 80465 • Telephone (303) 697-8135

- Not all Western Bible College alumni are in career ministries. But all spiritually influence their homes, churches and communities as lay and professional Christians. Arleigh Bee ('65), owner of the largest bookstore in the Cheyenne, Wyoming region, and Duncan Wilkie ('69), Assistant Chief of the Denver Fire Department, are only two who have benefited from their Christian education at Western Bible College.

● ● ●

Western Bible College is also involved in vigorous institutional outreach through its radio station KWBI and its External Video Studies program:

- **Radio Station KWBI:** Western Bible College operates a 24-hours-a-day, seven-days-a-week, FM-stereo radio station, KWBI, which meets the spiritual needs of the Denver community. It has quality Christian music, counseling and Bible teaching. Typical of listener response was a letter recently received at KWBI which stated, "KWBI has been company to the lonely, encouragement to the troubled and help to those who need it." Dr. James Dobson, nationally-known child psychologist-counselor-teacher whose program is aired daily on the station, recently wrote KWBI, "Thanks for letting me be part of a radio station which is having such a ministry in the Denver area."

- **External Video Studies:** Through its External Video Studies program Western Bible College provides an important service to the Christian community worldwide. Using state-of-the-art video equipment and its well-equipped campus communications studio, College personnel videotape actual Biblical and Theological courses. These are made available for college credit to people in such areas as Overseas Christian Servicemen's Centers, mission stations, and churches and Christian schools where teachers and administrators need further education but cannot attend classes on campus.

OUR ACADEMIC PROGRAMS

Western Bible College is small in size but clear about its purpose—the training and preparation of believers for career and lay ministries through Biblical studies. We have made the decision to be selective and deliberate about our academic programs, offering only those which help achieve our purpose:

DEGREE PROGRAMS	MAJORS
● Bachelor of Biblical Science	● Pastoral Studies
● Bachelor of Sacred Music	● Missions
● Bachelor of Biblical Education	● Youth Ministries
● Associate Degree of Biblical Education	● Sacred Music
● Biblical Certificate (1-Year)	● Christian Teacher Education

COLLEGE AND CAMPAIGN LEADERSHIP

WILLIAM D. BOYD – PRESIDENT, WESTERN BIBLE COLLEGE
President, Western Bible College, 1978-present; previously Academic Dean and Chairman of the Christian Education Department

J. RAYMOND CHEYNEY – CHAIRMAN OF THE BOARD, WESTERN BIBLE COLLEGE
District Representative, Village Missions, since 1971; Board Member, Western Bible College, for 14 years and Chairman since 1978

GUY E. BOYER – CAMPAIGN CO-CHAIRMAN
Executive Vice-President, Chief Operating Officer and Director, Western Federal Savings & Loan Association, Denver, since 1970; Member of the Board, Western Bible College, since 1966

STANLEY A. HARWOOD – CAMPAIGN CO-CHAIRMAN
President, Willow Springs Enterprises, Incorporated, since 1972; Board Member, Western Bible College, 21 years (Chairman from 1961-71)

CAMPAIGN OBJECTIVES

In order to sustain the successful ministry of the College the Board of Trustees has set the following fund-raising objectives for 1982-85:

- CONSTRUCTION OF 12-APARTMENT STUDENT DORMITORY
- WATER SYSTEM
- RENOVATION OF OLDER CAMPUS BUILDINGS
- MAINTENANCE AND HEATING
- SALARY INCREASES/NEW PERSONNEL
- LANDSCAPING AND PAVING
- CURRENT OPERATING EXPENSES

**TOTAL COST:
$2,210,000**

The Board has determined that in the first year the goal is $900,000. To help realize this goal *each* Board member has contributed financially and is working diligently in the fund-raising effort.

CAMPAIGN OBJECTIVES FOR YEAR I (1982-83) — $900,000

1. CONSTRUCTION OF A 12-APARTMENT STUDENT DORMITORY
A new dormitory is needed because enrollment is projected to increase from the present 190 students to approximately 250 over the next three years. Realization of this objective will enable Western Bible College to build a three-story building containing 12 two-bedroom apartments and a central laundry facility. It can house 60 single students or can be easily converted for married students. The design chosen is similar to an existing dormitory and will be in harmony with the rest of the campus and inexpensive to design and build. To meet the requirements of the local fire department improvement of the water system is included in this project.
COST: $450,000

2. RENOVATION OF SELECTED OLDER BUILDINGS
In 1960 surplus housing units from Lowry Air Force Base were purchased and moved to the new foothills campus of Western Bible College. With improvements and modifications these 30 buildings have served as dormitories, classrooms, offices, dining hall, chapel and library for over 20 years. Major renovation is now necessary to make them serviceable for continued use. This renovation includes painting inside and out, new drapes and carpet, new bathrooms, new furniture throughout, roof repair and heating and plumbing system repair and improvements.
COST: $75,000

3. HIRING OF ADDITIONAL PERSONNEL/IMPROVEMENT OF FACULTY AND STAFF SALARIES
In order to meet the demands of expanding programs and increasing enrollment a number of additional personnel will be hired over the next year. In order to attract gifted and capable personnel, as well as keep the competent and dedicated employees now at Western Bible College, salaries must be raised to an adequate level of compensation.
COST: $71,000

4. CURRENT OPERATING EXPENSES
As at other independent colleges tuition revenue alone cannot cover the cost of an education at Western Bible College. In order to keep the cost affordable to the student gifts required to meet current operating expenses are included in this campaign.
COST: $304,000

CAMPAIGN FUND-RAISING COMMITTEES AND OBJECTIVES

The following committees have been established and fund-raising objectives set for 1982-83:

COMMITTEE	OBJECTIVE (YEAR I)	CHAIRMAN
Board of Trustees	$133,000	Raymond Cheyney
President's Council	36,000	William Boyd
Western Witness (Quarterly College Newspaper)	15,000	Cecil Cole
Founders Banquet (October 1, 1982)	25,000	Guy Boyer/Stanley Harwood
Faculty/Staff	15,000	Rick Pinkham
Student Body	10,000	Colin Green
Alumni	50,000	Elsie Fick
Women's Auxiliary	8,000	Elaine Boyd
Parents	15,000	Edward German
Churches	85,000	Raymond Cheyney/Ken Kilinski
Independent Businesses	35,000	David Blakemore
Radio Station KWBI	35,000	Claud Pettit

WE NEED YOU

We firmly believe that God in His perfect timing is leading Western Bible College into a new and exciting period of growth and that He would have us move forward *now* to make an impact for the Kingdom of God.

The same kind of partnership which caused a dream to become the reality of Western Bible College is needed *now* as God leads the College forward.

Please consider your active involvement as a Partner in Progress.

NAMING OPPORTUNITIES: There are numerous options available for those Partners who are interested in having the new dormitory, individual rooms or a renovated building named after an individual of their choice. For a list of naming opportunities to be mailed to you, write: **Partners in Progress Naming Opportunities,** Western Bible College, 16075 West Belleview Avenue, Morrison, Colorado 80465.

NOTE: This document and all campaign materials have been prepared as inexpensively as possible so that your contribution will go to realize the objectives of the campaign.

Western Bible College is a member in good standing with ECFA, the Evangelical Council for Financial Accountability.

Essentials Of Top Donor Solicitation Report

Note: It is the responsibility of the solicitor to prepare a brief report on each Top Donor Prospect he visits for submission to the Coordinating Committee. The solicitation process is not concluded until this report has been prepared. This report should contain as much information about the visit and Top Donor Prospect as possible including:

- Name of Top Donor Prospect

- Home address

- Home telephone

- Business position and address

- Business telephone

- Solicitor name

- Suggested level of contribution

- Previous donation information (last three years)

- Indications of donor interest (if any)

- Did solicitor communicate a specific figure to Top Donor Prospect

- How did Prospect respond (be specific)?

- If a pledge is possible, when will it be forthcoming? Did Prospect give any indication of how pledge would be paid?

- If Prospect declined interest, what was the stated reason?

- Is there anything else about this meeting that should be noted?

- In solicitor's estimation, was the level of this gift set properly?

SAMPLE TOP DONOR SOLICITATION REPORT

Name of Top Donor Prospect: Dr. Phillip Edgerly

Home Address: 435 Edgehill Road, Weston, MA 02193

Business Address: Dr. Edgerly is president of Consolidated Electronics, Inc., 10908 Waverly Circle, Watertown, MA 02135

Business telephone: (617) 457-0690

Solicitor name: John James, Director

Suggested level of contribution: $5000 per year for three years

Previous donation information: 1981-82 (latest) - $1,500
                                      1980-81 - $500
                                      1979-80 no contribution

Indication of donor interest: Dr. and Mrs. Edgerly consistently attend organization functions. Dr. Edgerly was once approached to be on the board but declined citing other responsibilities. He said we could ask again later, however.

Did solicitor communicate a specific figure to Top Donor Prospect? Yes

How did Prospect respond? Dr. Edgerly said that he would have to think about this level of support. Would I call him again? I said I would call in another week and we arranged a time. When I called back he was unavailable, so I called again the next evening. At that time I made a second appointment. At this appointment, Dr. Edgerly said he would make a gift to the capital campaign but could not be certain of the amount. I said it was important to know for planning purposes and could he give me some indication. He then said it would probably be between $2000-$4000 for the first year.

When will pledge be forthcoming: Probably not until the end of the first year of the campaign.

Anything else that should be noted: Dr. Edgerly mentioned that his brother, a physician in New York, is quite friendly with one of the senior directors of Coca Cola. I got the impression that Dr. Edgerly would pursue this matter if asked in the right way by the chairman of our board.

Was gift level set properly: Possibly a little high.

Essentials Of Direct Mail Letters To Individuals Familiar With Your Organization Or Your Cause Who Have Not Yet Given

Note: The following letters are examples of the kind of direct mail you should send to individuals who may already have heard of you or who are familiar with your cause, but who have not yet given to it. You will need to make modifications in this letter to send it to current and/or lapsed donors.

First Letter

• The first letter should be sent so as to arrive in early October.

• It may come either from the chairman of the board or executive director.

• It must stress the organization's history of good work and its important place within its marketing area.

• It should set forth the fund raising goals for the year and prove the need for the objectives selected.

• It should ask for the reader's support but should not name a suggested figure.

• This letter should be accompanied by a précis, pledge card and unstamped return envelope.

Second Letters

There must be at least two kinds of follow-up pieces prepared, three if you use a newsletter.

i) To Proven Givers. This letter follows the elements outlined in the Letter Sent To Proven Givers (See Samples, page 224). It is an extended thank-you letter indicating what progress is occuring both with the fund raising effort and the program objectives. A pledge card and return envelope are included in the package but are not referred to.

ii) To Donor Prospects. This letter begins pressing home the point that contributions are needed — now. This letter communicates the importance of both cause and donor but without any hint of anxiety. "We're surprised we haven't heard from you yet," this letter says in effect, "After all, we know you believe in our work."

• These letters should be sent to arrive the first week of December.

Note: An organization may choose to update its entire mailing list with a newsletter. (See Samples, page 247). This is entirely acceptable. Different cover letters from your organization can accompany the newsletter depending on whether the individual has contributed or not.

Third Letters

• The final letter for the year should arrive in March or April.

• This letter may take one of two tacts:

> With Donors: A continuing update on the progress of both the fund raising drive and project realization.

> With Donor Prospects: "We're baffled. We know you like our work, so we're confused about why we haven't heard from you yet. Let's tell you why it's important we do — now."

Remember: If you are using a newsletter you can simply mail out differing cover letters to those who have donated and those who have not yet done so.

SAMPLE DIRECT MAIL LETTER TO INDIVIDUALS FAMILIAR WITH YOUR ORGANIZATION OR YOUR CAUSE WHO HAVE NOT YET GIVEN

Letter I

Note: Use a general salutation for your letter.

Dear Fellow Resident:

You probably already know about the Swansea Visiting Nurse Association. I certainly hope so.

For seventy-five years the Visiting Nurses have been providing a wide variety of necessary health care services to the greater Swansea area. I'm sure you've seen our nurses in their distinctive grey uniforms with the red berets riding their bicycles through town. Perhaps you already have benefitted from their many services:

- They help the sick in their own homes by providing check-ups and post-operative care.

- They call on soon-to-be mothers and recently-delivered mothers with good baby advice.

- They provide health care to the elderly in Swansea's senior centers.

- They teach the essentials of good nutrition in the city's public schools.

Our home health care aides, too, are very active around town. They bathe the elderly, clean house, do the shopping, and even manage the day-to-day bills and finances of many sick and older people.

In fact, it's hard to think of Swansea without our nurses or our home health care aides, don't you agree?

This year we've launched a vital new program which I'd like to bring to your attention — the Swansea Hospice.

Perhaps you know about the hospice concept. It's quite simple really. Many people nowadays want to end their days not in a hospital or nursing home, but where they've spent their happiest moments — right at home. The hospice program allows them to do so.

Under our new hospice program, we shall provide up to twenty-four hour care to the gravely ill and disabled in their own homes. We shall also provide bereavement counseling and social services to the survivors of those who die.

We hope you'll agree with this humane alternative. We aren't, of course, criticizing hospitals or nursing homes — many people benefit from them after all — but we do want to provide a comfortable alternative.

To do so, we need to raise about $75,000 this year. This money will enable us to hire a full time Director and an around-the-clock team of medical and social service workers.

Won't you please help us implement this good idea — and give us the ability to provide another needed community service?

I enclose for your consideration a pledge card and some additional information about the Swansea Visiting Nurses Association. Don't think of this as just another solicitation letter. Remember, we provide services. Perhaps you know someone who needs us. If you do, will you kindly let us know so that we can do what we do best — help.

Sincerely,

Executive Director

SAMPLE DIRECT MAIL LETTER TO INDIVIDUALS FAMILIAR WITH YOUR ORGANIZATION OR YOUR CAUSE WHO HAVE NOT YET GIVEN

Letter II

Dear Fellow Resident:

Several weeks ago I had the pleasure of writing you about the Swansea Visiting Nurses Association and our new Hospice Program. I regret that we haven't heard from you yet. Modern life, I know, has a way of distracting us even from the most important concerns — like good health. Still, I'm sure you'll want to know how both our Hospice Program is proceeding and our effort to raise the funds we need to sustain it.

Of the $75,000 we need we have now raised $40,000. This sum has come from over 250 people including each member of our board of directors. This is a very gratifying beginning.

With these funds we have been able to take the first steps toward starting the Swansea Hospice. Let me tell you about them.

Two months ago we were very fortunate to find Dr. Herbert Kahn. We have now hired him to be the first Director of our Hospice. Dr. Kahn comes to us from Angle Memorial Hospital where, among many other things, he created the hospital's first hospice program. I enclose an interview with Dr. Kahn from the local newspaper so that you'll get a good idea of how he will approach his important, sensitive task.

Dr. Kahn has already made contact with all the local hospitals, nursing homes, and senior clubs and facilities in town to acquaint them with our services. We have already had our first referrals and work is already beginning on the chief task of the Hospice: to assist the dying and to make their final days as comfortable as possible in circumstances they know well—their own homes.

I hope you will join with us in creating the Hospice. Your gift is important and necessary in enabling us to bring Swansea this very important new service. May we count on you?

I enclose for your convenience a pledge card. I look forward to hearing that you are among the supporters of this significant new community project.

Sincerely,

Executive Director

SAMPLE DIRECT MAIL LETTER TO INDIVIDUALS FAMILIAR WITH YOUR ORGANIZATION OR YOUR CAUSE WHO HAVE NOT YET GIVEN

Letter III

Dear Fellow Resident:

I have already written twice to you about our significant new Hospice Program. Although I have not yet heard from you, I wanted to bring you up-to-date on developments.

As you may remember, our original goal was to raise $75,000. This sum would enable us to appoint a full-time Director and an around-the-clock medical-social service team to help the dying and disabled in their homes. Some of these funds, too, would go to providing bereavement counseling.

I am glad to tell you that we have now raised $68,000 towards our goal: the end is indeed in sight!

Our Director and team are now entirely in place. We already have 20 clients. To give you some idea of why we feel so enthusiastically about the work they are already doing and the importance of the program, let me share with you just one letter from the adult daughter of an 80-year old cancer victim who was served by the Hospice. She recently wrote me, "Mother didn't want to die in a hospital. I didn't want her to, either. But with a full-time job, I couldn't provide her with the home care she needed. The Hospice did. You made my mother's last weeks comfortable and even cheerful despite her pain. Thank you. I've enclosed a donation for your program. It's not substantial, but it is heartfelt."

Put yourself in the same place. Do you have elderly parents who may need help? Are you elderly yourself? What will you do when the time comes?

God willing, the Hospice will be there to serve you and yours as it did the woman who wrote to me about her aged mother.

God willing, that is — and with your help.

Please make your donation today.

And, please remember, if you know of individuals who need the assistance of the Visiting Nurses be it for nursing, home care or hospice care, let us know. That's why we're here.

Sincerely,

Executive Director

Essentials Of A Newsletter

• The newsletter can be written and produced by the executive director.

• It should deal with four main subjects:

      i)   Programmatic successes of the organization

      ii) Agency's organizational successes

      iii) What organization needs to continue its fine work

      iv) Actual fund raising drive — its inauguration, progress and successful conclusion.

• Newsletter should focus on:

      i)   People who have helped fund drive

      ii) Major gifts made

      iii) Purposes to which money is being put

• Newsletter should answer any leading questions about fund drive which may emerge.

• A newsletter can be published in early October, early December and in March or April. Three issues a year are usually sufficient.

Partners In Progress Update

Vol. 1, MELROSE YMCA

By JUDITH W. HARRINGTON
and RICHARD A. WHITWORTH

Capital Fund Reaches $490,000

As of May 1, the YMCA's Capital Campaign had reached $490,000 in pledges. This places the "Y" at one-third of its total goal of $1.5 million for the entire project. This is, of course, a pleasant milestone and will give further impetus to completing the campaign.

In term of specific goals for 1982, the "Y" is trying to raise an additional $300,000 in contributions. With this sum, construction on Phase II will begin. Toward this end, the YMCA has raised $33,413 in new funds this year.

The fund-raising committees are hard at work trying to meet their individual goals and put the campaign over the top for the current year. The "Y" can always use more help in its pursuit of a new building. If you are interested in helping, please contact Richard Whitworth or Jean Gorman at the YMCA.

New Building Has Several Naming Opportunities

The new YMCA will have several possibilities for permanent recognition of individuals who have contributed to its construction. These naming possibilities provide an excellent opportunity for the recognition of support to the YMCA in particular and the community in general. This will be permanent recognition that will be viewed by hundreds of thousands of community residents in the years to come.

The following is a list of the naming possibilities within the new "Y":

> Gymnasium
> Health Club (2)
> Weight Training Center
> Youth Lockerrooms (2)
> Adult Lockerrooms (2)
> Track
> Youth Lobby
> Racquetball and Squash Courts (3)
> Lobby Area
> Fitness Room
> Multipurpose Meeting Rooms (3)
> Staff Offices
> Sauna and Steam Rooms (4)

If you or anyone you know may be interested in such a possibility, please contact Richard Whitworth at the YMCA.

Special Events

A new committee called "Special Events" has been added to our list of fund-raising committees, and Board Member Paulette McCabe has been named Chairperson. Paulette has chaired many very successful charitable fund raisers for other organizations, and she and her committee are busy making exciting plans for the near future.

One of these events will be the second annual "Day at the Races," which is scheduled for Sunday, October 3, with Paulette and her committee at the helm.

Paulette's husband, Ed, an attorney and well-known Melrose resident, is busy with his own subcommittee. His group is specializing on an emphasis on public relations and visibility for our campaign. He has a great group with lots of ideas and plans! Keep an eye out and an ear open — you'll soon be seeing and hearing the results of their efforts.

Special Events Committee members include:

> Steve and Debbie Anderson
> Paul and Shelly Draper
> Marcy Holbrook
> Tony and Margie Koles
> Sally Lerman
> George "Red" and Sue Lynde
> Dick and Barbara Shea

"Y" Receives Two $10,000 Foundation Grants

The Melrose YMCA has recently secured two major foundation grants toward the Capital Campaign. One is in the form of an outright grant, while the other is a challenge grant.

The first grant of $10,000 came from the Adelaide Breed Bayrd Foundation. The money is to be applied to the Phase II portion of the campaign and marks the third grant which the Bayrd Foundation has made to the local YMCA in the past several years.

The second grant is a $10,000 challenge grant from the Agnes M. Lindsay Trust of Boston. The Trust has challenged the "Y" to raise an additional $150,000 by October 31 of this year to receive the funds. Presently, the "Y" is seeking the funds to meet this challenge.

These two grants act as a further indication of the faith which the foundation community has in the overall plan of the Melrose YMCA. The demands on foundation funds are heavier now than at any previous time and the securing of these grants is a major accomplishment.

New Faces at the Melrose YMCA

The "Y" Board's Annual Meeting was held March 8 at Bellevue Country Club. At this meeting, Judith Harrington succeeded Col. Thomas Wright as President of the Board. "Tom" has spent three very busy, very challenging and very successful years as President. Judy becomes the first woman to serve in this office. She is married to Roland Harrington, who grew up in Melrose. They have three children, Pamela, who is married to Albert Cairns, Scott, and Paula. Judy graduated from Lynn schools and attended the University of New Hampshire. She was graduated from the Katharine Gibbs School, Boston, and from Northeastern University. She is a Real Estate Broker associated with Bjorkman & Lann of Melrose. Previously, Judy has served as President of the Melrose Circle of the Florence Crittenton League and the YMCA's Auxiliary. She is a member of Phi Theta Xi, the League of Women Voters, and Sharing & Caring. She has also been a member of the Community Council, North Shore Benefit League, Melrose High School Scholarship Committee and the Bicentennial Committee. She has been a member of the YMCA Board since 1974.

At this Annual Meeting, five new Board Members were also welcomed aboard. They are Thayer Fremont-Smith, J. Michael Hughes, Mary Kiddie, Anthony Koles, and Sally Lerman.

Thayer Fremont-Smith is a well-known trial lawyer associated with Choate, Hall & Stewart in Boston. He is a member of the Melrose Planning Board, as well as a member of several bar associations. He has been admitted to practice in the U. S. Supreme Court as well as Massachusetts and New Hampshire Federal Courts. He is married to the former Anne Jeffery, a lifelong Melrose resident, and they and their four sons reside on Bellevue Avenue.

Mike Hughes is a C.P.A. with offices in Melrose and Boston. Mike graduated from Northeastern University in 1964 and did post graduate work at Bentley College. He has been involved with the Mount Hood Park Association for the past five years, serving alternately as President, Vice President and Treasurer. He is presently Co-Treasurer of the Horace Mann P.T.O. He and his wife, Mary, have lived in Melrose for 12 years and are the parents of three children, Maureen, Michele, and J. Michael, Jr., all students at the Horace Mann School.

Mary Kiddie and husband, Alex, live on Sunset Road and have two daughters, Mrs. Diane Duratti of Wakefield, and Mrs. Linda Archer of Pembroke. Mary has been active in Melrose since she and her family arrived in 1956. She was with the Melrose Girl Scouts for nine years acting as a leader, organizer, consultant, city-wide activities chairman, and orientation instructor. In the past, she

has served as President of the Melrose Mother's Club and of Phi Theta Xi. She has recently stepped down after three years as Chairman of the Melrose High School Permanent Scholarship Fund. She has been a member and officer in the Horace Mann P.T.O., Melrose YMCA Auxiliary, the Melrose Circle of the Florence Crittenton League. She is presently a Trustee of the Melrose-Wakefield Hospital Association and a Corporator of the Melrose Savings Bank. Recently Mary was honored by the Melrose Chamber of Commerce for her outstanding contribution to the Melrose Scholarship Fund. She is employed as a secretary at the Horace Mann School.

Tony Koles has lived in Melrose all his life. He attended Melrose schools and graduated from Wentworth Institute in 1963. He is President of Montvale Tire Company of Melrose and Stoneham. Tony is Past-President of Kiwanis and has served on the Board of Directors of the Melrose Chamber of Commerce. He is still active in both organizations. He and his wife, Majorie, and two children, Scott and Susie, live on Windsor Road in Melrose.

Sally Lerman is an attorney, and she and her partner, Daniel McCarthy, have their office at 50 Tremont Street, Melrose. Sally graduated from Brandeis University, did graduate work at Brown University, and received her law degree from the New England School of Law. A relatively new Melrose resident, Sally grew up in South Bend, Indiana, where she and her nine (!) brothers were active "Y" members. Her family, including her mother, are still active in the South Bend "Y". Sally said, upon being asked to join the YMCA Board, "As the Melrose YMCA moves ahead with its building plans, I hope that I can contribute to the success of this endeavor and, in some way, reflect the positive experience which my family and I have had with the 'Y'."

These new, talented and enthusiastic members of the Board are sure to be assets in our continuing "Partners In Progress" capital campaign.

Other Board Members include: Jeanne A. Borenstein, Vice President, Peter E. Garipay, Vice President, Richard S. Barton, Treasurer, Judith A. Tierno, Secretary, Rufus L. Briggs, Isabelle K. Brown, Lester H.N. Burnam, Edward F. Cassidy, Jr., Thomas F. Deehan, Ralph C. Delorie, James F. Driscoll, Jr., Charles E. Gill, George A. Glines, M.D., Henry D. Haynes, M.D., John J. Hickey, Jr., Robert B. Holden, M.D., L. Bradley Hutchinson, John J. Kelliher, D.M.D., Carol A. Landry, James A. McAvoy, Jr. Paulette G. McCable, Christopher J. McCarthy, Donald R. Putney, Richard Quinlan, Harland W. Robinson, III, O.D., Reverend John R. Schroeder, Richard Shea, Robert J.W. Stone and Thomas H. Wright, LTC (Ret).

APPENDIX II

HOW COMPUTER-ASSISTED MARKETING CAN HELP IMPROVE THE EFFICIENCY OF YOUR NONPROFIT ORGANIZATION

People involved in nonprofit marketing, public relations and fund raising (all marketing activities, by the way) are constantly complaining to me about how much they have to do and how little time they have to do it.

Before I can decide whether to be sympathetic. . . or angry. . . with their situation, I need more data:

"Are you computerized?", I ask the wailing one.

If he's not, my anger is immediate. An organization that doesn't possess a computer and word processor is engaging in the same kind of worker abuse that in earlier times resulted in sending children into coal mines.

These days with computer prices at an all time low, there is no reason for an organization not to be computerized and to let the machine do what it does best: both store and sort data and carry out routine tasks involving the dissemination of identical information.

People who have not yet understood what the computer can do for their organization constitute, by definition, a sort of managerial underclass, permanently doomed to do and redo and do yet again the most mundane tasks. Every day they do these tasks themselves, instead of enlisting the assistance of available machinery, they fall farther and farther behind in the struggle for increasingly scarce resources. In scarcely takes a world-class doomsayer like Cassandra to predict that the influence of such ill-prepared organizations will always be limited. . . and their futures uncertain.

For these people I have just one piece of advice: beg, borrow or fund raise for a computer and word processor — at once. As this section ought to convince you, any other course makes no sense whatsoever.

When The Person Says His Organization Is Computerized

But what about when the person says, "Oh, yes, we've been computerized for years"?

Are they, I wonder? Questions like these enable me to find out in a jiffy:

- "When a foundation or corporation rejects your proposal, do you have to compose an individual response, or do you have a template letter already available?"

- "When a donor gives you money, does it take you weeks to get a thank-you out? Or do you use an impersonal card or letter? Or do you have a template letter already available for personalization and personal executive signature?"
- "When a media source calls and asks your executive director for an interview, do you have to scramble to create a press kit . . . or simply let the opportunity go by because you can't respond fast enough?"

If the answer to any one of these questions — or dozens like them — indicates that this person is engaged in creating individual responses to regularly recurring situations, then this person isn't computerized. He merely has the equipment. He neither understands what it is to be used for, how to create the various document files he needs, and how and when to use them. In short, he's part of the problem, not part of the solution.

Some Necessary Background About Marketing

Marketing is a persuasion business. It has as its sole task identifying someone who has something you want . . . and motivating that person to give it to you as soon as possible. Markets can be as small as a single individual and as large as tens of millions of people.

By its very nature, marketing is a repetitive process. That is, there are tasks which must be done again and again and again. The people you seek to motivate will have many reasons why they can't do what you ask of them now. You must therefore keep approaching them in the expectation of motivating them later . . . while at the same time identifying others whom you also wish to motivate.

What's crucial to the marketing process, whether you're involved in getting clients for your organization, selling its products, getting free media attention or raising money from individuals is this. You must:

- identify a coherent group of people who could do what you want them to do;
- find out what they get from doing what you want them to do;
- create a plan that persuades them they can get what they want by doing what you want;
- work the plan until either they do what you want . . . or until it is abundantly clear they will never do what you want.

Marketing, in short, is a focused and relentless art.

Thinking Before Acting

Right now, my guess is that you spend a good deal of your day doing the same kinds of things you do most days . . . and yet you approach these things as if you have never done them before . . . and will never do them again. This, of course, is nonsense.

The seasoned marketer (be she a fund raising or public relations specialist) understands that she must spend her professional life doing just two things: creating a marketing plan and implementing that plan. Both are equally important, but clearly creation comes first.

I'd lay odds that not even 1% of nonprofit organizations have such a written marketing plan, however. This is where their problems begin. A plan indicates:

- what marketing objective you are trying to reach;
- what people you will be going to to achieve this objective;
- what reasons they have for doing what you want them to do;
- what precise methods you'll be using to approach them;
- what you intend to do when they say no;
- what you intend to do when they say maybe;
- what you intend to do when they say yes;
- what you intend to do to follow up at regular intervals, *etc*

In short, a plan gives you both a precise objective and the exact means you need to reach it and under what circumstances you'll use them. It thereby suggests what marketing documents you need. . . so you can create them before you need them. REREAD THIS LAST SENTENCE!

Most nonprofit personnel create marketing documents in response to situations. Marketers consider what situations are virtually certain to emerge in the process of their work. . . and create the necessary documents *in advance* so that they can move quickly whatever their prospect says.

Let's look at an illustration. Say that you're trying to raise $10,000 to purchase a computer and word processor and necessary software. This is the marketing objective you are trying to reach.

The people you're going to approach constitute the data base for this project. That is, they are people known to you through your research to be interested in providing either funds or actual computer equipment.

In approaching these people, you can logically deduce just what is likely to happen:

- some people will never respond at all;
- some will say no;
- some will say not now;
- some will agree to a meeting;
- some will want to visit your office;
- some will say yes if you can find others to get involved;
- some will say yes.

Now, you have two options. Most nonprofit people wait to think through what they will do until their prospect has actually said or done one of these things. They are therefore constantly placed in a defensive position, reacting to events.

The marketing specialist is different. He knows that achieving his objective is likely to take longer than most people anticipate... and that there will be lots of contacts with his prospects. He knows that the success of his business is not just identifying people who will say yes right away... but persuading people who either say no or do nothing to say yes in due course.

In other words, the marketer prepares for the long haul... and gets everything he needs accordingly.

Which is where the computer comes in.

Marketing And Your Computer System

Knowing what is likely to happen, the marketing specialist now uses his computer to prepare for it. This specialist knows he is playing a game, a very real game to be sure with very real prizes, but a game nonetheless. His objective is to win, and he knows there are always many fewer winners than losers. His goal is therefore to maximize his chances of winning by maximizing the resources he has... including his computer.

Thus, since more people are likely to turn down his request for a new computer than give it to him, he needs to develop a template (that is, form) letter that responds to their negative... and yet moves them closer either to supporting this project at a later phase... or another project of the organization. The marketer knows, you see, that the game doesn't end with this negative... unless there are solid reasons why this prospect should never have been considered a prospect at all; (in this case, because this source never funds computer equipment.)

The marketer's job is therefore to:

- understand what the prospect may do;
- know that the process of developing a link with this prospect doesn't end merely because the prospect has declined this request, (unless the prospect is not a real prospect);
- decide what an appropriate next approach is to the prospect;
- create the right response letter that moves the organization closer to this next approach... and to the ultimate objective of getting support.

It's important to remember that all this can be done ONCE THE PROSPECT IS KNOWN BUT BEFORE THE PROSPECT IS EVEN APPROACHED AND SAYS ANYTHING AT ALL!!!

252

The marketer's job is also to identify all the other responses the prospect can give and to prepare suitable documents for all the other situations in which he's likely to find himself, ranging from the first approach to a prospect . . . to a prospect's continuing failure to respond to any of the previous approaches.

What is crucial in the marketing sequence is that there be no surprises. The seasoned marketer is never taken off guard. Why should he be? He has identified his prospects in advance and considered every conceivable move they can make. His planning — including the creation of every necessary document — has followed as a matter of course. He is therefore ready whatever happens.

Being so prepared has several advantages:

- In virtually all cases, you know precisely what to do. You don't have to ponder your move. You simply make it.
- Because you don't have to spend a lot of time thinking what you'll do and creating documents accordingly, you'll move a lot faster. When your responses are swift and sure, you look like a much better candidate for whatever you're asking for than the lackluster organizations that operate in the traditional "muddle through", "do it whenever" fashion.
- You work with confidence and assurity. People like to deal with people who show they know what they're doing.
- You get more work done. People who anticipate what their prospects are likely to do and prepare accordingly are people who can get much more work done than the kind of nonprofit bumblers we are all familiar with.

Implementing Your Plan

Now that you've got your plan and have created all the necessary response documents, it's time to start marketing.

For tested marketers, the implementation stage of marketing means that to a considerable extent they are on "automatic pilot." What they are aiming for is this:

- they always remember what they are trying to get the prospect to do;
- they know that they may not get what they want immediately;
- they know, however, that their job is to move, cajole, push and wheedle their prospect closer, closer, ever closer to what they want with every contact;
- they are prepared to assist this movement whatever the prospect says, so long as they still regard this individual as a prospect.
- they are prepared so that this movement takes place as soon as it can after the prospect's own action.

Thus:

- You are trying to raise money for a computer: your submission letter and proposal should be available on computer.
- You call your prospect time and again to find out if he needs any further information: after the second and certainly after the third call, you send your already composed follow-up note indicating your attempt to call, the reasons why this prospect should support you, your hope he'll call you... and an indication of what you intend to do if he doesn't.
- Your prospect says he's not interested in supporting you now: your template letter lets him know how important your computer will be... not to the organization, mind... but to the people you serve. It also announces you'll be back in touch as developments warrant.
- Your prospect says he's coming for a site visit: your template letter tells him how glad you'll be to receive him. It provides certain crucial information about your organization... and how the computer you want will serve the people the funding source is interested in helping.

Get the idea?

It is not, you see, that nonprofit marketing personnel are so severely overworked. After over a decade in the business, I just don't buy that. Instead they:

- don't understand marketing;
- don't understand computers;
- don't have a plan;
- don't create the necessary documents to achieve the plan's objectives, and
- don't use their marketing savvy, their computers, their plan and template documents to get prospects to do what they want.

I cannot be any plainer than this. Don't say this isn't you, because my experience says it is.

Now it's up to you. Will you tomorrow do again and from scratch all the tasks you did today without attempting to do what's necessary to routinize them and so increase your efficiency and control? If so, you are a lost soul, indeed. Even so, I don't feel sorry for you for a minute. I'm reserving my pity for the poor people your organization is in business to serve... but who have to rely on this kind of breathtaking managerial myopia to get the help they need.

YOUR WORST FEARS REALIZED, OR WHAT TO DO WHEN THE CORPORATION OR FOUNDATION DECLINES YOUR PROPOSAL

Author's Note: Because so many people have asked me what I do (and what I advise my clients to do) when (as inevitably happens) one or more of their well-considered proposals is turned down by a corporation or foundation, I wrote the following article which first appeared in **Nonprofit World**, a publication of The Society of Nonprofit Organizations. If you follow its suggestions closely, you will noticeably improve the success-rate for all your proposal submissions. Remember: persistence is a necessary prerequisite of successful fund raising.

Anyone who has ever tried to raise funds from corporations and foundations knows the following scenario only too well. You've been expecting a letter from the donor prospect and at last it's come. You are a little nervous as you open the envelope. In an instant you know your worst fears are being realized.

Your fine proposal, you are told, has been declined. The letter is short and offers no help, no hope, no possibilities for the future. It's as close to a perfect vacuum as you'll find outside a scientific laboratory.

Such letters are sent out by the thousands these days. The essence of successful fund raising from corporations and foundations lies in taking such an unpromising response and turning it into a fruitful relationship with the donor prospect.

The First Necessity: Dealing With Your Anger

The tendency in reading such a letter is to be angry — angry about all the unrecompensed work, about the effort which has now so evidently failed, about the fact that the project for which the money was requested cannot now be accomplished, no matter how urgently it needs doing. Despite the fact that the fund raising literature is almost universally silent on this issue, anger, irritation, and, yes, humiliation are parts of fund raising. No one likes to be turned down; in this business, everyone is. The difference between those who succeed and those who fail is directly related to how they cope with the rejection.

Those who are going to receive funding have a way of disposing of their anger which does not jeopardize the possibility of a future productive relationship with the donor prospect. One helpful way of dealing with your anger is to develop a relationship with someone else who's doing the same sorts of things you are, who understands your problems, and with whom you can discuss your feelings. To succeed in fund raising, you must recognize that there will be angry moments, and you must learn to deal with them constructively.

After You've Calmed Down: Reviewing Your Situation

After you've dealt with the anger, it's time to review your situation and figure out how to salvage it. First, you need to find out whether your rejection could have been predicted. If so, your homework was faulty. Ask yourself these questions:

- Did you ask the prospect for the right thing? Fund raising requests fall generally into three categories: capital requests, project or program requests, and operating requests. If you have asked a source for a type of funding they usually don't give, they'll be perfectly justified in rejecting you.
- Did you ask for the right amount? If you did your homework, you should have known how much to ask for. If not, the source can comfortably reject you.
- Did you provide the attachments requested, and did you follow up close to the source's meeting time to ascertain whether your file was complete? The prospect may not have had all the information about your organization that he or she needed (and may not have told you so).
- Did you look like a good "investment" to the source? Did you make a case as to why the funds you were requesting would either be a "final" grant, one which would not need to be requested annually, or a "multiplier" grant, one which would produce a disproportionate benefit?
- Are you in the geographical area served by the prospect?

If the answers to these questions are positive — that is, if they conclusively demonstrate that you were applying to the right place for support — then it is your obligation to take the necessary steps to develop a relationship.

The Principle of Assertive Courtesy

Successful fund raisers presume upon a funding source; they presume, before there is any hard evidence to sustain this point of view, that if they do their work properly they will, in due course, build a constructive relationship with the donor prospect. The principle under which this work takes place is the "principle of assertive courtesy." With this principle, you assume that the prospect really wants to help you, really wants to learn how to work with you to solve the problem your organization is working to solve. You begin operating under the principle of assertive courtesy the minute you know that the prospect can in fact give you a grant, for it's pointless to keep asking people to support you when they have made it very clear they cannot.

Calling the Prospect

Within 48 hours after your application has been declined, and as soon as you have reaffirmed that this source can help you, place a call to the person who signed the rejection letter. This call is difficult to make, but it is absolutely essential. You need to know why you've been turned down, and you need to start building a relationship with the prospect.

Before you make the call, prepare yourself. Sit at a clean desk with your initial proposal, the rejection letter, your calendar, and a log form so you can enter what you are told. Now call. If you don't get the source on the telephone right away, leave a detailed message about who you are. If your call isn't returned in 48 hours, call again.

At last you will succeed in getting the prospect on the telephone. Begin the conversation thus: "Ms. Donor Prospect? This is Mr. Fund Seeker. I'm calling to follow up on your recent correspondence. I see that you are unable to fund us just now, and I'm calling to find out how we can work together in the very near future."

Starting the conversation this way minimizes the tension you feel and the defensiveness it is easy to create in the prospect. The prospect must not feel criticized. The prospect needs to understand that you are serious about gaining future support. That your organization still needs help. That there are people to serve. And the prospect must feel that you are behaving in a difficult situation in a supremely professional way.

Ask the prospect to help you determine:

- what would have made the proposal stronger
- what comments her board members had about your organization and/or proposal, or what concerns they are feeling
- when it will be possible to return to them and what other materials it would be helpful for the board to see
- whether a site visit might help change their minds
- what other sources of funding the prospect might suggest.

Since this situation is one fraught with risk and one which most people shy away from, keep this book in front of you as you talk, and work your way through the above points. You are looking for (1) answers that will help in your next approach, and (2) an opening which you can effectively use in your follow-up.

Before you end the conversation, suggest keeping in touch about your organization's work. Say something like this: "Ms. Prospect, since I know you are interested in the problem of long-term care for the elderly of our county, I'd welcome the possibility of keeping you informed about our work." There's scarcely a prospect in the world who won't say, "Fine!". Remember: this conversation is stressful for the prospect, too. How often do people who reject you want to be called upon to explain their actions?

Your Move Again

The minute you are off the telephone, pat yourself on the back. Such a call is hard to make, and you deserve to be congratulated. But there's more work to do.

The next step in developing your nascent relationship with the prospect is to send a letter confirming your understanding of what you've just been told. Begin this letter by, first, thanking the prospect for the time she or he has given you. No matter how uncooperative the prospect has been, she has nonetheless given you something which is irreplaceable: her time. Express your gratitude.

Having begun with a thank you, proceed by confirming your understanding of what the prospect has told you and what you intend to do as a result. If the prospect has said that your proposal is weak in a certain section, indicate that you're going to strengthen it and that you'll be sending the prospect a copy of the new document when it's ready. You want the prospect to know that you have heeded her advise.
Also, put the prospect on your mailing list. Send her your newsletter as it appears, your annual report, and information about your organization. Don't forget invitations to the fun things: your annual meeting, the Christmas party.

Moreover, as your fund raising efforts proceed, send the prospect periodic updates (every six months will probably do). The prospect needs to be assured that you are a get-ahead organization. Your successes in other quarters will provide this necessary impression.

Note that it is perfectly acceptable to return to the prospect for support when you are about 75 percent of the way to your goal on the project for which you originally requested money, even if it has not been a year since you last asked for help. Success always changes the configuration of events.

Your Next Formal Submission

Eventually, it will be time to submit another formal proposal. The cover letter accompanying the submission needs to indicate that you have a relationship with the prospect. "When we last talked/corresponded, you indicated that we should be submitting about this time, for this project, for this amount." Make this letter as specific as you can, and indicate very, very clearly that you are following directions. Remember: the prospect wants to know that you are a good investment, and the likelihood of persuading her of this necessary fact is substantially increased if she knows you have listened to her.

Your Chances of Success

By following these suggestions, the likelihood of your winning the grant is substantially increased. And if you have any doubts, just think about it. A large number of submissions reviewed by the prospect are coming from organizations she knows nothing about. But she does know about you, quite a lot. A large proportion of the organizations you were competing against last time are not now your competitors. Having been rejected, they have simply dropped out.

You didn't. You handled rejection with professionalism and aplomb. You have requested the assistance of the prospect, and you have followed at least some of her suggestions — and you've let her know you've been attentive.

In short, you are now admirably positioned to obtain the fund support you want and need.

You lucky dog.

SELECT BIBLIOGRAPHY

A note on how to use this bibliography. The literature of nonprofit organizational development does not fit neatly into sharply-defined sections. Therefore this bibliography doesn't either. Thus, in reading this bibliography be aware (as noted) that most of the companies listed also produce other materials which will be of interest to you. Most of them are also major mailers who will keep you abreast of their new products and update services without charge. Addresses are given with the producer's first entry.

FUND RAISING AND GENERAL NONPROFIT DEVELOPMENT INFORMATION

Annual Register Of Grant Support: Directory Of Funding Sources, 1993 Edition. Covers all types of funding sources (non-traditional, corporate, foundation and public). Arranged by organization and program, by geographic location, by personnel, and by subject. Also includes a 7-step proposal-writing guide on how to write a winning proposal. Reed Reference Publishing, P.O. Box 31, New Providence, NJ 07974. 800-521-8110. $165.

Bergan, Helen. **Where The Money Is, 2nd Edition.** Equips development officers, prospect researchers, and executive directors with concrete methods of uncovering information they need to identify, cultivate, and successfully solicit major prospects. BioGuide Press, P.O. Box 16072, Alexandria, VA 22302. $29.95.

Blimes, Michael and Sprat, Ron. **More Dialing , More Dollars: 12 Steps To Successful Telemarketing.** Shows you just what you need to know to raise money on the phone. Learn how to target your audience, set dollar objectives, develop scripts that get people to give, and more. American Council For The Arts, 1 East 53rd Street, New York, NY 10022. 212-223-2787. $8.95.

Brentlinger, Marilyn E. and Weiss, Judy. **The Ultimate Benefit Book: How To Raise $50,000-plus For Your Organization.** Here's the book you need to plan to use volunteers to create a profitable special event. Get the low-down on selecting the right chairperson, ticket pricing strategies, recruiting and motivating committee members, working effectively with paid staff, and handling the inevitable crises. Available from Octavia Press, 3546 Edison Road, Cleveland, OH 44121. 216-729-3252. $22.95.

The Compleate Professional's Library. To find out what's new and helpful in fund raising management and marketing for your nonprofit organization, here's your prime source. Ask for a free copy of their catalog. It includes many of the books mentioned in this bibliography as well as a whole lot more. The Compleate Professional's Library, 634 Commonwealth Ave., Suite 201, Newton, MA 02159. 617-964-2688.

Computer Resource Guide For Nonprofits. Over 700 pages of the most accessible, up-to-date and comprehensive data available on computers and the nonprofit world. Vol. 1 deals with available software. Vol. 2 deals with funding sources for computers and software. Available from the Public Management Institute, 358 Brannan Street, San Francisco, CA 94107. 415-896-1900. Public Management Institute has many items of interest to nonprofit organizations. Write for their current catalog.

Faust, Paul, Editor. **An Introduction To Fund Raising: The Newcomers' Guide To Development.** In 92 pages, 14 fund raising experts take the novice through the basics of theory and practice, organization and technique. Council for Advancement and Support of Education (CASE), P.O. Box 90386, Washington, DC 20090. 800-554-8536. $20.00/members and $24.00/non members.

CASE, a well-known name in fund raising, publishes many other helpful materials. Write for their catalog.

Flanagan, Joan. **The Successful Volunteer Organization.** How-to manual for any type of nonprofit organization. Explains everything from tax exempt status to five-year plans for both leaders and staff. Contemporary Books, Inc., 180 N. Michigan Ave., Chicago, IL 60601. 312-782-9181. $14.95.

Giving U.S.A. Provides estimates of the extent of charitable giving in any year. Very much a standard source. American Association of Fund-Raising Counsel, 25 West 43rd Street, Suite 1519, New York, NY 10036. 212-354-5799. $45. Also publishes Giving U.S.A. Update. $35.

Hopkins, Bruce R. **The Law Of Tax-Exempt Organizations, 4th edition.** A comprehensive working guide for the tax lawyer or accountant who needs specific information on the Federal tax law and its impact on tax-exempt organizations. John Wiley & Sons, 1 Wiley Drive, Somerset, NJ 08875. 800-225-5945. $115.

How To Conduct Successful Capital Campaigns. Over 1,200 pages on what you need to know to make your next capital campaign a success. Public Management Institute.

How To Establish & Fund An Association Foundation. Developed by the ASAE Foundation, this book provides development strategies, tax/legal considerations and operational guidelines for setting up a foundation. ASAE Publications, 1575 Eye Street NW, Washington, DC 20005. 202-626-2748. $45.25

Huntsinger, Jerry. **Fund Raising Letters, 3rd Edition.** Jerry Huntsinger has spent over 30 years writing personal, readable and effective fund raising letters. This book demonstrates that he is a master of the art. Emerson Press, P.O. Box 15274, Richmond, VA 23227. $110 plus postage and handling.

King, George V. **Deferred Gifts: How To Get Them.** A nuts and bolts approach for starting and maintaining a deferred gifts program. A non-technical book emphasizing the practical promotional and managerial aspects of deferred giving. Contains a directory of major firms supplying deferred giving services. The Taft Group, 5031 MacArthur Blvd., NW, Washington, DC 20016. 800-877-8238. $44.95.

Kiritz, Norton J. **Program Planning And Proposal Writing.** Gives detailed descriptions of each component of the grant proposal: summary, introduction, problem statement, objectives, methods, evaluation, future funding sources and budget. Available from The Grantsmanship Center, P.O. Box 17220, Los Angeles, CA 90017. 213-482-9860. $4 per copy plus $2 shipping and handling. Also write for your free copy of "The Whole Nonprofit Catalog," a major compendium of nonprofit wit, wisdom, insight and materials you'll want to have in your library.

Margolin, Judith B. **The Individual's Guide To Grants.** Step-by-step methods for getting funds for your project. Plenum Press, 233 Spring Street, New York, NY 10013. 212-620-8000. $19.95. Plenum Press publishes many resources of interest to nonprofit organizations. Write and request a complete list.

The Nonprofit Board Book. You need an active Board, committed to the agency, involved in its work. Here's how you get it. This resource addresses such key topics as Board recruitment, orientation, and training; board and staff relations, holding productive board and committee meetings, and, of course, the best way to use the board for fund raising and public relations. Independent Community Consultants, P.O. Box 141, Hampton, AR 71744. 501-798-4691. $24.95 plus postage and handling.

O'Rourke, Helen. **Standards for Charitable Solicitations.** Simplified guide to nonprofit fund raising and public disclosure requirements. Recommended for fund raising staff and volunteers. Philanthropic Advisory Service, Council of Better Business Bureaus, Inc., 4200 Wilson Blvd., Suite 800, Arlington, VA 22203. Free.

Plessner, Gerald. **Charity Auction Management Manual.** Charity auctions can make you big bucks... and/or give you big headaches. Get more bucks and fewer headaches when you use this manual. You get information about timetables, budgets, worker's job descriptions, sample letters, checklists and flow charts. Fund Raisers Inc. 59 W. La Sierra Dr., Arcadia, CA 91006. $39.

Plessner, Gerald. **Golf Tournament Manual.** Here's what you need to know about how to create and run a lucrative golf tournament. Fund Raisers Inc. $39.

Plessner, Gerald. **Testimonial Dinner And Industry Luncheon Management Manual.** Running testimonial events is a good way to make people happy, get good PR and raise money, too. Here you find out how to select the right honoree, work within a budget, create a professional script and presentation, and handle the guests efficiently and courteously. Fund Raisers Inc. $39.

(NOTE: The above three books by Gerald Plessner are available for $100 for the combined set.)

Plinio, Alex J. **Resource Raising: The Role Of Non-Cash Assistance In Corporate Philanthropy.** Of course you want money. But there are lots of other things for you to get, too, including products, services, and personnel. This is a new trend in resource development. Make sure you know how to take advantage of it. Independent Sector. P.O. Box 451, Annapolis, MD 20701. $10 plus postage and handling.

Pray, Francis, C., Editor. **Handbook For Educational Fund Raising. Principles and practices of successful fund raising for colleges, universities and schools.** Jossey-Bass, 433 California Street, San Francisco, CA 94104. 415-433-1767. $42.95.

Schlachter, Gail Ann. **Directory of Financial Aids for Women 1991-92.** Identifies millions of dollars set aside as financial aid for women and women's organizations. TGC/ Reference Service Press, 1100 Industrial Road, Suite #9, San Carlos, CA 94070. $49. Also publishes Schlachter's Directory of Financial Aid for Minorities 1991-92. $51.50.

Scribner, Susan and Green, Florence. **Asking For Money.** Basic techniques to use when making face-to-face requests for donations. The Grantsmanship Center. $5.

Seymour, Harold. **Designs for Fund-Raising, 2nd Edition.** Widely regarded as one of fund raising's classics, this book, first published in 1966, is packed with information that will help you raise money. Includes critical details on proper and sustained prospect cultivation, writing case statements, strategies for recruiting campaign workers, donor motivation, staff and volunteer relations and much more. The Taft Group. $34.95.

Skloot, Edward. **The Nonprofit Entrepreneur.** Shows how to set up earned income enterprises that are consistent with the goals and purpose of your nonprofit organization. The Foundation Center, 79 Fifth Ave., New York, NY 10003. $19.95.

Sladek, Frea E. and Stein, Eugene L. **Grant Budgeting And Finance: Getting The Most Out of Your Grant Dollar.** Advice on how to spend grant and contact money most efficiently. Plenum Press. $39.50.

White, Virginia P. **Grants For The Arts.** Handbook for finding appropriate funding and budget planning. Plenum Press. $32.50.

White, Virginia P. **Grants: How To Find Out About Them And What To Do Next.** Overview of potential funding sources. Plenum Press. $32.50.

Williams, M. Jane. **Big Gifts: How to Maximize Gifts from Individuals, With or Without a Capital Campaign.** Clearly shows you how to identify, cultivate, and solit major donors. Provides convincing evidence that every nonprofit, regardless of size, can attract major gifts. The Taft Group. $79.

Williams, M. Jane. **The Annual Giving Book.** Since raising money annually is going to be a part of your life, here's a book that can help you do it right! Williams provides details on identifying prospects, staffing and budgeting, volunteers, gift clubs, challenge programs, special events, and more. The Taft Group. $39.95.

NEWSLETTERS AND UPDATE SERVICES

"ARIS Funding Reports." Provides information about grant opportunities, fellowships, awards, and contracts from federal and private sources in three areas: biomedical sciences, social and natural sciences, and creative arts and humanities. Academic Research Information System, Inc., 2940 16th Street, Suite 314, San Francisco, CA 94103. 415-558-8133. $125 to $210 (8 issues plus supplements).

"Campaign Letter." Monthly information update on managing a successful campaign. 4516 Emery Industrial Parkway, P.O. Box 18044, Cleveland, OH 44128. $180.

"The Chronicle of Philanthropy." Covers all aspects of nonprofit and philanthropic activity, including books, coming events, foundation reports, grants, model programs, management, and professional opportunities. The Chronicle of Philanthropy, P.O. Box 1989, Marion, OH 43306. $60/year.

"Contributions." Published bimonthly, this is now America's leading "how-to" publication on fund raising, management, and nonprofit marketing. Contributions, 634 Commonwealth Ave., Suite 201, Newton Centre, MA 02159. 617-964-2688. $18/year.

"Ford Foundation Letter." Describes new project announcements and recent grants. Ford Foundation, Office of Reports, 320 East 43rd Street, New York, NY 10017. 212-573-5000. Free (six times a year).

"FRI Monthly Portfolio." Reviews the fund raising activities of more than 2,000 nonprofit organizations. Searches out and evaluates new fund raising techniques and ideas. The Taft Group. $65/year.

"Fund Raising Management." Covers general fund raising issues. Hoke Communications, 224 Seventh Street, Garden City, Long Island, NY 10530. 516-746-6700. $54/year (12 issues). Also publishes "FRM Weekly Newsletter." Reports on current events, issues, lists meetings. $115.

"Government Relations Info and Action." Regularly publishes information on what is happening at the federal level of interest to nonprofit organizations. Independent Sector. Free to association members. A good source of information on topics of concern to all nonprofits.

"Grants Magazine." Contains articles on government, foundation, and corporate grants and discusses current trends and issues affecting public and private philanthropy. Plenum Publishing Co. $32.50/year (institutions). $130/year (individuals).

"LRC-W Newsbriefs." Covers events, resources, private sector and federal grants. Lutheran Resources Commission-Washington, 5 Thomas Circle N.W., Washington, D.C. 20005.

"The Nonprofit Counsel." Monthly newsletter edited by well-known authority Bruce R. Hopkins. Provides analysis of current developments in tax, fund raising, and related law for nonprofit organizations and their professional counselors, in easily understandable language. Published by John Wiley & Sons, Inc., 605 Third Ave., New York, NY 10158. $96/year.

"Nonprofit Management Strategies."
Provides needed information for nonprofit
executives. The Taft Group. $150/year. Taft
is one of the largest producers of information
for nonprofit organizations. They publish a
very extensive catalog of what they produce.
Make sure you're on their mailing list.

"The Nonprofit Times." Timely information
on boards, development, foundations,
management, books, employment market-
place, and more. The Nonprofit Times, 190
Tamarack Circle, Skillman, NJ 08558. You
may qualify for a free subscription; otherwise
$39/year.

"Nonprofit World." Focuses on leadership
and management issues, including fund
raising, income generation, current legisla-
tion, and book review. Published by The
Society for Nonprofit Organizations, 6314
Odana Road, Suite 1, Madison, WI 53719.
608-274-9777. $69/year (bi-monthly).
Free to Society members. The Society also
publishes an extensive book list of the best
current resources for nonprofit organizations,
all available at a discount to Society members.

"The Philanthropic Trends Digest."
Provides information on charitable trends and
techniques. Douglas Lawson Associates,
Inc., 545 Madison Avenue, New York, NY
10022. 212-759-5660. $36/year.

FOUNDATION GRANT AND RESOURCE INFORMATION

Comsearch Printouts. Contains grants of
$5,000 or more awarded in the preceding year
by 500 foundations within 62 subject categories, including communications, education,
health, humanities, population groups,
physical and life sciences, social sciences,
welfare, *etc*. The Foundation Center, 79
5th Avenue, New York, NY 10003. 212-620-
4230. Published annually in the spring. $60 a
category on microfiche. The Foundation
Center is a key resource if you expect to raise
money from foundations. Make sure you are
on their mailing list.

**Corporate Foundation Profiles, 7th Edi-
tion.** Over 500 corporate foundations included with profiles and program and financial analysis of the 200 largest givers. The
Foundation Center. $135.

**Directory of Building and Equipment
Grants.** Money sources for building, equipment, and renovation. Research Grant Guides,
P.O. Box 1214, Loxahatchee, FL 33470. Also
publishes the Handicapped Funding Directory
and Directory of Computer and High Tech-
nology Grants.

**The Foundation Center National Data
Book, 16th Edition.** Gives fiscal profiles,
addresses and chief officers of all 24,000 U.S.
foundations. Vol. 1. is an alphabetical list by
name. Vol. 2 lists foundations within each
state in descending order of grants made. The
Foundation Center. $135.

**The Foundation Center Source Book
Profiles.** Provides grant analysis and policies
of the 1,000 largest foundations in loose-leaf
form. The Foundation Center. $195.

The Foundation Directory. Provides
information on over 4,000 of the largest
foundations. Entries include financial data,
directors, officers and trustees, areas of
interest, addresses, and application information. The Foundation Center. $175.

Foundation 500. An index to the 500 largest
foundations in the United States with their
giving patterns broken down into 66 different
categories and a listing of how many grants
were made in each state by each foundation.
Douglas M. Lawson Associates, Inc. $39
plus $3 shipping and handling.

**Foundation Fundamentals: A Resource
Guide For Grantseekers.** Guide to success-
ful grant seeking in workbook format. The
Foundation Center. $19.95.

Foundation Grants Index Annual. Lists grants of $5,000 or more awarded in the preceding year by 500 foundations, alphabetically by state, and includes amount, date of grant, location of recipient, and description of grant. The Foundation Center. $125.

Foundation Grants To Individuals, 7th Edition. Give information on approximately 950 foundations making awards directly to individuals. The Foundation Center. $40.

Foundation News. Published 6 times yearly, this is the official publication of The Council on Foundations, the body to which many foundations belong. Here's where you get insight into the grantmaker's mind. Council on Foundations, 1828 L Street N.W., Suite 1200, Washington D.C. 20036. 202-466-6512. $29.50.

CORPORATE GRANT AND RESOURCES INFORMATION

Corporate Giving Watch. Provides detailed information on where corporations are giving their money and how much they are giving. Published by the Taft Group, which has long specialized in providing information on corporate giving. $139/year.

Poor's Register Of Corporations, Directors And Executives. Provides information on 45,000 U.S. companies, their corporate family interconnections, products and services, locations, and key executive personnel. Available from Sales Support Department, Standard & Poor's Corporation, 25 Broadway, New York, NY 10004. 800-221-5277; in New York call collect 212-208-8812). $475/year.

Who's Who In America. More than 75,000 of America's most influential people. Reed Reference Publishing. 2 volumes. $335 plus $10 shipping and handling.

FEDERAL FUNDING INFORMATION

Catalog Of Federal Domestic Assistance. Annual publication of federal grant programs. Office of Management and Budget, Government Printing Office, Washington, D.C. 20402. Stock #941-001-00000-9.

The Commerce Business Daily. Lists contract and research opportunities from many federal agencies. U.S. Department of Commerce, Government Printing Office, Washington, D.C. 20402. Stock #703S013-00000-7.

Federal Assistance Monitor. Twice-monthly newsletter of federal funding announcements, private grants, rule changes and legislative actions affecting all community programs, including social services, arts, education, and health. CD Publications, 8204 Fenton St., Silver Spring, MD 20910. $239/year.

Federal Funding Guide. 700+ page guide answers questions about federal funding programs for governments and community organizations. Government Information Service, 1611 N. Kent Street, Suite 508, Arlington, VA 22209 703-528-1082. $176.95.

Federal Register. Provides daily accounts of federal grant awards. Office of Management and Budget, Government Printing Office, Washington, D.C. 20402. Stock #722-004-00000-1.

Krauth, Diana, **How To Use The Revised Catalog Of Federal Domestic Assistance.** The Grantsmanship Center. $3.

ABOUT THE AUTHOR

Surrounded by a mountain of paper, an underused exercise machine and the incessant hum of his computer, Dr. Jeffrey Lant confronts each day with one insistent question: "How can I help even more people develop their businesss by helping them raise the money they need, by helping them sell more of their products and services?"

He's answered — and continues to answer — this question in a variety of ways. Over the last 13 years, he's created the 8 volume "Get Ahead" Series that presents the exact steps people need to sell any product or service. In addition, he's written the standard book on how nonprofit organizations can raise the money they need from corporations, foundations, and individuals. His other books include a volume he edited on Harvard College and a rollicking history of Queen Victoria's Court that was presented to Queen Elizabeth II on a blue silk pillow.

Jeffrey also created and regularly writes the Sure-Fire Business Success Column now reaching over 1.5 million people monthly in about 200 print and electronic information sources in many countries… puts out the quarterly Sure-Fire Business Success Catalog… his quarterly Sales & Marketing Success card-deck… and is president of JLA Ventures, which develops and markets many different products and services. Further, he is a well-known speaker on many business development and fund raising topics, offering programs around America and in other countries.

Holder of four earned university degrees, including a Ph.D. from Harvard, Jeffrey and his work have been honored by many institutions, both public and private. In 1991, he was raised to the dignity of The Rt. Hon. The Count of Raban by His Beatitude Alexander II, Patriarch of Antioch, Syria. This title was originally held by one of Jeffrey's ancestors who traveled with King Richard I of England to the Third Crusade, 800 years ago. Through his mother, a peeress in her own right, he is also heir to both the Barony of Barlais and the Barony of Kezoun, Crusader titles 8 centuries old.

At some point, like millions of people around the world who first connected with Jeffrey through a workshop, media program, audio or video cassette, article or book, you'll want to be in closer touch with this man to see how he can help you better. No problem! Whenever you're ready, simply call (617) 547-6372 or write 50 Follen St., Suite 507, Cambridge, MA 02138 to request your free year's subscription to his quarterly catalog (a copy of which concludes this book). He's ready for you *now*!

267

Jeffrey's new book — his 11th — tells you how to cash in selling your service...

> # NO MORE COLD CALLS!
> ## THE COMPLETE GUIDE TO GENERATING — AND CLOSING — ALL THE PROSPECTS YOU NEED TO BECOME A MULTI-MILLIONAIRE BY SELLING YOUR SERVICE

If you're running a service business — any kind of service business — and are not yet a millionaire, listen up. This book was written explicitly for you.

Jeffrey's books are famous for their unrelenting detail... precise guidelines and step-by-step techniques for doing what he says they do. This one is no exception.

Are you a doctor, lawyer, dietitian, consultant, engineer, tinker, tailor, private investigator, dog walker, house sitter, landscape architect... or any one of millions of service providers in this country who hasn't yet turned your service business into the certain means of making yourself a millionaire? Then this giant resource has just what you need...

In 16 information-dense chapters you discover how to:

- avoid the thirty major mistakes service providers who aren't yet millionaires are making... and how to solve them and start making more money immediately;
- create the multi-million dollar plan that'll turn your service business from work... into a process that produces the money you need to achieve millionaire status faster;
- identify the right prospects for your business and find out what they want (so you can give it to them);
- create motivating cash copy... yes, you'll learn how to turn every word you write into a hook that gets your prospects to respond faster... and your customers to buy again sooner;
- create fast, effective, economical marketing communications that make your prospects and buyers move. We're talking about ads, flyers, cover letters, brochures, media kits... all the things you may be wasting your money on now;
- turn your computer into a client-centered marketing department of awesome power and speed;
- generate *all* the low-cost leads you need through free media, talk programs, direct response marketing, classified and small space ads, and through such specialized marketing programs as card decks, electronic moving message display signs, and package stuffer programs;
- create an aggressive, focused leads-closing system so you can get more business from all the leads you've generated;
- work with clients so you can upgrade the value of their business and get more business faster;

- keep more customers and benefit from them longer;
- develop your organization when you're generating more leads than you can possibly handle;
- turn your service expertise into information products like Special Reports, audio & video cassettes, booklets, books... and more... so you make money every single day.

And you'll find out what you have to do to turn the ever increasing profit from your business into capital and investment income, the basis for both financial independence and the lifestyle you want for yourself and your family.

> Caution: this book is only for those service sellers who seriously want to become millionaires. It lays out the exact guidelines you need to do this. If achieving millionaire rank as a service seller is what you want, you cannot afford to be without this new book... the most detailed ever written on what it takes to turn your service business into a wealth-producing machine.

Item #B9

675+ pages.
$44.95 postpaid.

> *"Your card deck is by far the best deck I've received!"*
> Abigail Houtchens, Pismo Beach,

CASH COPY: HOW TO OFFER YOUR PRODUCTS AND SERVICES SO YOUR PROSPECTS BUY THEM... NOW!

#B6 Cash Copy
NEW REVISED EDITION!!!
JUST UPDATED!!!

Look at the marketing "communications" you're putting out... ads, flyers, post cards, cover letters, proposals... and all the rest.

Is the first thing you see... your name? Your company name? Your photograph? Your address? Your logo? THEN YOU'RE PRODUCING SELFISH, "ME-CENTERED" MARKETING DOCUMENTS... INSTEAD OF CASH COPY... and your sales are suffering!!!

> *"CASH COPY and MONEY MAKING MARKETING have taught me more than I learned in the classes at college on marketing and business."*
> Richard Irby, Warrenton, VA

Over 98% of the marketing communications you're producing right this minute are ending up in the trash. They don't get anyone to act. They don't get anyone to buy. Yet because you're spending a pile on producing this junk you think you're "marketing". GET OVER IT!

The marketing communications you're using are failures unless they get people to ACT... unless they get people to BUY. There is never another reason for producing any kind of marketing communication — certainly massaging your ego isn't one!

That's why you need CASH COPY in your office... now! Learn:
- the 21 biggest copywriting mistakes you're making — and how to avoid them;
- directions for turning your copy around so it's about your prospects... and not about you;
- how to turn product/service features into the benefits that really get people to buy.

You'll learn how to:
- turn every word, every line, each paragraph and page into hooks that motivate your prospects to buy NOW;
- get and use client-centered testimonials;
- create offers that motivate buyers...

And much, much more.

> *"I am currently reading your book CASH COPY. Rarely have I benefited so greatly in so little time from any book that I have purchased. Thank you for writing such a helpful book for business owners."*
> James Telford, Fruitland, NM

Thousands of business of every kind all around the world are profiting from this book. It's time you did, too.

Over 15,000 in print!
480 pages. $38.50

> *"Jeffrey, it's embarrassing but true that reading CASH COPY has been an enlightening, near-religious experience for me, so much so that I've become keenly evangelical about prospect-centered results-oriented marketing for my small-business clients... Jeffrey, CASH COPY is so good that I'll continue to reread it until your marketing philosophy and fundamental principles are indelibly etched on my brain."*
> J. Frederick Blais, Jr., Richmond, VA

#T1
CASH COPY AUDIO CASSETTE PROGRAM

Do you learn better by hearing? Then get the cash copy message in 12 hard-hitting audio cassettes based on the book. You get 18 hours of focused, profit-making advice, exactly what you need so you stop wasting your marketing dollars producing selfish, me-centered marketing.

These tapes are for people who are truly committed to getting more prospects to respond to their marketing communications faster... doing everything that's necessary to reduce the waste in their marketing budgets and substantially increase the return.

If that's you, here is it. $125

> *"Thank you for your book CASH COPY — it should be made mandatory reading for all corporate communications people."*
> Gregg Siegel, Wilmington, DE

#C1
CASH COPY AUDIO CASSETTE AND BOOK PACKAGE

Get the complete CASH COPY package, including 480 page book and 18 hours of audio tape. Just $140. Save $23.50. This is the most comprehensive package ever assembled for creating marketing communications that get people to respond fast. You know this is what you want. This is, therefore, what you need.

269

THE UNABASHED SELF-PROMOTER'S GUIDE

What Every Man, Woman, Child And Organization In America Needs To Know About Getting Ahead by Exploiting The Media

Thousands and thousands of people around the world are already profiting from this book. They range from people running small businesses to two sitting members of the United States Senate, from people with the most idealistic motives to those who have no other motive than simply wanting to get filthy rich. Members of state legislatures and celebrities with well-known names are using this book to build their stature and promote their interests... entrepreneurs swear by it because it promotes their products and services to targeted markets.

> **"Your knowledge of the subject of marketing is mind-boggling!"**
>
> *Richard Lawrence, Lowell, MA*

You need this book if you're:

- running *any* kind of business entity;
- selling *any* product or service;
- running *any* charitable or nonprofit organization;
- a professional who's tired of laboring in obscurity!

> **"THE UNABASHED SELF-PROMOTER'S GUIDE is for everybody. I don't care what you're doing!"**
>
> *KIEV Radio, Los Angeles*

You get 364 of Jeffrey's characteristically information-dense pages. Learn how to:

- create Quintessential American Success Images... and avoid Failure Images;
- produce the documents you need to deal with the media. It's all here from media advisory, standard media release, biographical documents, fact sheets, chronology, position papers, prepared statements, media schedule, clip sheet, announcements, etc. *Every* form you'll ever use when dealing with the media is already done... and immediately available for you;
- create and maintain a media Self-Promotion Network;
- produce all the print articles you'll ever need... you get exact formats the print media use every day and how and when to use them;
- handle every kind of media interview... including hostile ones;
- get just the right photographs... and how to use them;
- constantly appear on radio and television programs... and know what to do to promote your products/ services when you get there;
- get "waves" of media... not just isolated, single-shot appearances;
- create and promote books through free media... yes, there isn't an author or publisher in the world who should be without this book!
- use negative media... to enhance your image.

And much, much more.

Over 20,000 copies in print!

Item #B2
365 pages. $39.50 postpaid!

271

IF YOU'RE NOT MAKING AT LEAST $100,000 EVERY YEAR AS A SUCCESSFUL CONSULTANT, CALL JEFFREY IMMEDIATELY TO ACQUIRE THESE TWO ESSENTIAL RESOURCES:

#B1
THE CONSULTANT'S KIT: ESTABLISHING AND OPERATING YOUR SUCCESSFUL CONSULTING BUSINESS

This is the *only* book on consulting recommended by the U.S. Small Business Admin. to people who want to get off to a fast start in consulting... and there's a real good reason why. Jeffrey doesn't fool around. If you have specialized or technical skills and want to build a profitable consulting career fast, start here. This is his essential book for beginners... people who have been in business under a year... or are having trouble getting their act together.

Here's the help you need to:
- define your speciality to make the most money
- develop a contact network and get business fast
- market and promote your expertise
- upgrade a lead into a contract
- write contracts that protect your interests (yes, you get the *exact* language you need for letters of intent, commission engagements and full contracts)
- set up shop
- incorporate
- handle bookkeeping, accounting and tax matters

and much, much more.

Over 26,000 people worldwide have used this crucial resource to launch their consulting businesses in every imaginable field. How good is it? IBM just bought a bunch of them to give to top execs taking early retirement. If it's good enough for Big Blue... it's precisely what you need, too!

208 pages. $38.50

> *"Three distinguishing characteristics of all books in the Lant series are long titles, fat books, and meaty contents. HOW TO MAKE AT LEAST $100,000 EVERY YEAR AS A SUCCESSFUL CONSULTANT IN YOUR OWN FIELD ranks among the longest, fattest, and meatiest... A great piece of work from start to finish."*
> Nationally syndicated columnist
> Stew Caverly

#B4
HOW TO MAKE AT LEAST $100,000 EVERY YEAR AS A SUCCESSFUL CONSULTANT IN YOUR OWN FIELD: THE COMPLETE GUIDE TO SUCCEEDING IN THE ADVICE BUSINESS

Once you've mastered the consulting basics, here's where you go. This is the book that'll give you exactly what you need to make at least $100,000 every year as a consultant.

> *"Jeffrey Lant is one of America's top consultants!"*
> The Associated Press

There has never been a resource this detailed about what it really takes to make a six-figure consulting income. You find out how to:
- raise your fees higher than your competitors — and still seem like a bargain;
- get the big retainer contracts that get you income every month, whether you're working for the client or not;
- develop a national — or even international — consulting business — in person and by phone;
- get the best results for the client — so you can leverage these results to get more clients in the same field... fast;
- develop the "passive income" sources that enable you to make money every day whether you're otherwise working or not... we're talking about books, booklets, audio cassettes, special reports, and more.

You'll get the low-down on how to use your computer for maximum efficiency (and where to get state-of-the-art hardware and software for rock-bottom prices); how to get detailed problem-solving information fast. There's even ready-to-use information on time management, stress reduction, and traveling smart.

This book — like everything Jeffrey produces — is packed with detailed money-making follow-up information. You get the names, addresses and phone numbers of the experts who can help you make the big money now. And complete details on dozens of other resources you'll want to know about and use to your advantage.

315 pages. $39.50

#C8

Get a deal on a combined package including THE CONSULTANT'S KIT and HOW TO MAKE AT LEAST $100,000 EVERY YEAR AS A SUCCESSFUL CONSULTANT IN YOUR OWN FIELD.

Stop wondering how to launch your consulting practice and squeeze it for all the profit possible. The information you need is right here, right now.

Just $68. Save $10.

#B3
MONEY TALKS: THE COMPLETE GUIDE TO CREATING A PROFITABLE WORKSHOP OR SEMINAR IN ANY FIELD

> *"I have in hand a copy of MONEY TALKS: THE COMPLETE GUIDE TO CREATING A PROFITABLE WORKSHOP OR SEMINAR IN ANY FIELD which I obtained at the local library. I had heard of your publications through a seminar some time ago, and I find your material refreshing and enthusiastic."*
>
> Rick Hogan, Tacoma, WA

These are the only reasons for giving talk programs:
- you make money from them directly;
- you can use them to sell your products and services to people who attend;
- you can generate heaps of favorable publicity from them and build your reputation and perceived value.

Is this happening to you every time you give a talk program? If not, you need The Rev. Second Edition of **MONEY TALKS.**

For years now, this has been widely recognized as the most complete resource ever written on what it really takes to make money from talk. And with this revision, everything in it is up to date!

You'll find out how to:
- get sponsors for your programs;
- make the best deals with people who hire you;
- write descriptions of your programs that make people want to attend;
- make big money from back-of-the-room sales... even when you don't have products of your own;
- develop the audio & video cassettes, booklets, special reports and books you need to make really big money. I'm talking about over $10,000 a day... and, if you assiduously follow the directions, a whole lot more;
- squeeze the most publicity from every engagement;
- develop a networking system that generates a steady stream of speaking leads.

And a whole lot more.
308 pages. $35.

> *"Your MONEY TALKS was just the publication I was looking for to help me get my new venture off the ground."*
>
> L.W. Peterson, Paso Robles, CA

Now you can earn up to $3,000 easy dollars for just a few minutes work... and you can earn this much over and over again.

Who isn't looking for some easy money these days? I'm sure YOU are. Now you can get it... all by recommending Dr. Jeffrey Lant as a speaker to:
- business and professional groups
- colleges and universities
- trade shows and conferences... and any one else who needs a profit-making speaker.

When your recommendation results in an assignment, you get 10% of Jeffrey's honorarium... and product sales the day of the program. This can add up fast — up to $3,000 for you!

Here are just some of Jeffrey's popular topics:
- How to sell another million dollars of your product or service... now;
- Ten marketing mistakes you'll never make again;
- How to create marketing communicationns that get people to respond fast... and what to do when they do;
- How to make big money from your home-based business;
- How to make at least $100,000 every year as a successful consultant in your field;
- How to raise money for your nonprofit organization from corporations, foundations and individuals...

and many more!

> *"Until now, COSMEP has never invited a speaker to give a presentation two years in a row. This year is an exception. In 1991, at our 24th conference, in Cambridge, Massachusetts, Jeffrey Lant gave a half-day seminar that was so intense, fast-moving, humorous and useful that we knew that we had to have him back in 1992. Not only did our members describe Jeffrey as 'outrageous and stimulating,' or 'electric, up-beat,' they told us that his talk had been the highlight of the conference...."*
>
> COSMEP, The International Association of Independent Publishers

How do you get on this gravy train? Contact the groups you're a member of... the businesses and professional associations you belong to... and recommend Jeffrey to them. Make sure they can either pay his minimum daily fee ($5000) or are willing to work with him to create a deal that generates this much money from a combination of fee and product sales. Then call Jeffrey at (617) 547-6372, and he'll take it from there. He has the necessary audio & video cassettes, books, articles, testimonials and recommendations to close the deal! As soon as he gets paid... you get paid. And remember, you can do this over and over again... and keep getting paid!

Meeting planners: Call now for complete details about how you can book Dr. Jeffrey Lant for *your* programs. Jeffrey is a knowledgeable, enthusiastic and often electrifying platform speaker with a client-centered marketing message that will not merely inform and entertain your audiences but transform their business and personal lives.

273

#B7
HOW TO MAKE A WHOLE LOT MORE THAN $1,000,000 WRITING, COMMISSIONING, PUBLISHING AND SELLING "HOW-TO" INFORMATION

> *"I love HOW TO MAKE A WHOLE LOT MORE THAN $1,000,000... TREMENDOUSLY! Thanks for writing it."*
> Don Floyd, Gainesville, FL

Stop trying to make your million dollars selling yourself by the hour. That's stupid. Learn what it takes to find problem-solving information and turn it into a multi-million dollar information empire.

This is the most detailed resource ever created — all 552 pages of it — providing you with *precisely* what you need to make real money from how-to information.

You get exactly what you need to:

- create the information products people want to buy;
- produce products you can profit from for a lifetime... not just a season;
- produce your products fast, accurately and for the least money;
- make tens of thousands of extra dollars from end-of-product catalogs;
- save money — and avoid problems — by following Jeffrey's product production guidelines. You also get the names, addresses and phone numbers of reputable production people who won't rip you off;
- turn your personal computer into the most effective customer service center imaginable;
- get other people to produce money-making products for you so you can

make your million-dollar fortune faster;
- get all the free publicity you can handle for your products from radio, television, newspapers, magazines... in this country and abroad;
- master the essentials of direct response marketing so you bring your message to just the right people — and get them to buy your products fast;
- make big money through talk programs, bookstores, libraries, overseas rights, exhibits... and more.

This book is packed with the names, addresses and phone numbers of dozens of people who can help you sell more products fast. As with all Jeffrey's books, he doesn't just provide the step-by-step details you need... he directs you to the specific people you need to make money fast.
552 pages. $39.50

HEY, BARGAIN HUNTERS... HERE ARE FOUR PACKAGES THAT'LL SAVE YOU MONEY AND GIVE YOU MORE DETAILED, PROFIT-MAKING INFORMATION THAN YOU'VE PROBABLY EVER SEEN IN ONE PLACE IN YOUR LIFE.

#C4

Combined offer for the future information millionaire...

Four fast-paced, densely detailed books by Jeffrey give you a fast start towards becoming a million dollar+ producer & seller of books, booklets, audio cassettes and Special Reports. Whatever your field! Get **HOW TO MAKE A WHOLE LOT MORE THAN $1,000,000 WRITING, COMMISSIONING, PUBLISHING AND SELLING "HOW-TO" INFORMATION; CASH COPY; THE UNABASHED SELF-PROMOTER'S GUIDE** and **MONEY TALKS.** Just $115. You save over $35!

#C6

Combined offer for the people who want to sell more of their products and services faster...

Now benefit from Jeffrey's step-by-step marketing advice and learn how to sell more of your products and services for the least possible cost. Get a deal on **THE UNABASHED SELF-PROMOTER'S GUIDE, MONEY MAKING MARKETING** and **CASH COPY.** $80 for all three. You save $23.45.

#C7

... when you want to master all the master's profit-making techniques.

Get all eight books in Jeffrey's "Get Ahead" Series, including **CASH COPY, THE CONSULTANT'S KIT, THE UNABASHED SELF-PROMOTER'S GUIDE, MONEY TALKS, HOW TO MAKE AT LEAST $100,000 EVERY YEAR AS A SUCCESSFUL CONSULTANT IN YOUR OWN FIELD, MONEY MAKING MARKETING, HOW TO MAKE A WHOLE LOT MORE THAN $1,000,000 WRITING, COMMISSIONING, PUBLISHING AND SELLING "HOW-TO" INFORMATION and NO MORE COLD CALLS!** Well over 3,000 pages of detailed step-by-step guidelines on achieving success by creating and selling products and services. No other specialist — anywhere — has ever written such complete instructions on what it takes to make money — lots of money. We'll be flabbergasted if you don't make back the cost of this package many hundreds of time. Get all eight for just $240. Save nearly $60! You automatically qualify for a free 60-minute cassette with this order!!!

#C9

Combined offer for service sellers who won't rest content until they're millionaires...

Now get a deal on the four essential resources that'll turn your service business into a cash-generating process that'll make you a millionaire. Package includes **NO MORE COLD CALLS!; CASH COPY; MONEY MAKING MARKETING,** and **THE UNABASHED SELF-PROMOTER'S GUIDE.** Just $110. You save $47!

YOUR NONPROFIT OR CHARITABLE ORGANIZATION IS LOOKING FOR MONEY. HERE'S WHAT YOU NEED TO GET IT...

#B8 New Edition! Just Published!

DEVELOPMENT TODAY: A FUND RAISING GUIDE FOR NONPROFIT ORGANIZATIONS

> *"DEVELOPMENT TODAY isn't for the faint of heart or those with a penchant for pondering. Lant orders you into the heat of the battle and barks "Fight!" His is a refreshing approach, one especially suited for those unafraid of braving the fund raising trenches. We recommend it!"*
>
> *Contributions*

Tens of thousands of nonprofit organizations around America have made this book by Jeffrey the premier fundraising resource of its kind. Why? Because by following its detailed step-by-step guidelines, you raise the money you need for your capital, program and operating needs... even when money is tight.

You'll learn how to:
- determine how much money you can realistically raise;
- create the plan that'll get it for you;
- get even recalcitrant Board members to assist;
- pick just the right corporations and foundations to solicit;
- write fund raising proposals that get results and...
- ... follow up proposals that get rejected... so you can turn a no into a yes;
- raise money from community residents and businesses;
- use direct mail effectively and raise more money faster;

- mount profit-making special events... year after year;
- do your own capital campaign needs assessment and save tens of thousands of dollars;
- find volunteers... and get them to do what needs to be done...

and much, much more — including one of Jeffrey's characteristically packed Samples Sections containing ready-to-use documents, letters, log forms, etc. 282 pages. $29.95

PG#2

THE COMPLETE GUIDE TO PLANNED GIVING: EVERYTHING YOU NEED TO KNOW TO COMPETE SUCCESSFULLY FOR MAJOR GIFTS.

Look who's recommending Debra Ashton's definitive planned giving book these days:

American Association of Museums
American Lung Association
CASE
Christian Management Association
National Catholic Stewardship Council
National Hospice Organization
National Easter Seals
National Society of Fund Raising Executives
Planned Parenthood
Public Broadcasting System
Society for Nonprofit Organizations
and many, many more.

Why? Because if you expect to raise money from major gifts, the experts agree you must have this book.

> *"This is the most complete, practical guide ever written on planned giving!"*
>
> *Frank Minton, President, National Committee on Planned Giving*

Awesomely detailed information on how to:
- start a pooled income fund and gift annuity program
- use life insurance to facilitate major gifts
- conduct screening sessions to identify prospects capable of making major gifts
- find & use planned giving software & consultants;
- build board support for planned giving;
- use planned gifts to solve major donor problems
- develop a 12-month plan ensuring success for your program!

Based on current tax laws, this is a book you cannot afford to be without. 400 pages. $54.

BOTH THESE BOOKS ARE RECOMMENDED BY THE AMERICAN LIBRARY ASSOCIATION. IF YOUR CASH IS TIGHT, YOUR LOCAL LIBRARY WILL EITHER HAVE THEM... OR GET THEM FOR YOU! ASK!!!

> *"I'm midway through HOW TO MAKE A WHOLE LOT MORE THAN $1,000,000... and had to stop to order additional books from you. I've read such junk published by hucksters, I wanted to let you know how grateful I am for your book. Besides being incredibly informative, it's downright funny! Thanks."*
>
> *Frances O'Brien, Westport, CT*

Special Reports

We've already sold tens of thousands of these quick and dirty profit-making reports (#R1 – #R88). They're densely written five-page, single-spaced computer print-outs personalized with your name so you know you're supposed to follow the good-for-you directions. Don't expect fancy packaging. Just solid, up-to-date information you can use right now. Each report is packed with use-it-now details so you can achieve what the title promises. No one else in the country offers this kind of instantly available, eminently practical information in this form or gets them to you this fast. Stock up on 'em. **Just 6 bucks each, 3 for $14.**

#R1

THE SECRET TO BECOMING A MILLIONAIRE SELLING "HOW-TO" INFORMATION: 10 STEPS FOR CREATING, COMMISSIONING, PUBLISHING AND SELLING PROBLEM-SOLVING BOOKS, BOOKLETS, SPECIAL REPORTS AND AUDIO CASSETTES. In honor of his new book **HOW TO MAKE A WHOLE LOT MORE THAN $1,000,000 WRITING, COMMISSIONING, PUBLISHING AND SELLING "HOW-TO" INFORMATION,** Jeffrey lays down the rules for profitably selling problem-solving information. $6

#R2

SIX STEPS TO MORE SUCCESSFUL NEWSLETTERS. If you're putting any money into producing either a free or subscription newsletter... or even thinking about it... don't do anything until you get Roger Parker's steps for designing the product so it accomplishes your objectives. Roger's one smart cookie, and he knows what it takes to get people to pay attention to your newsletter. Here he shares this vital information with you. $6

#R3

WHICH 2% WILL YOUR AUDIENCE SIT STILL FOR? In honor of the publication of her new book, Jeffrey interviews author Marian Woodall on how to find the focus that is appropriate for each audience. Too many speakers try to cram everything they know into their talk... and end up alienating their audience. Not you. Here you learn exactly what you've got to do to give the right talk to the people you're speaking to. $6

#R4

HOW TO ELIMINATE JOB STRESS AND INCREASE PROFITS AND PRODUCTIVITY THROUGH STRESS MANAGEMENT. Jeffrey interviews author Dr. Andrew Goliszek about what you can do to cut stress in the office. Stress doesn't just debilitate and even kill you... it cuts your profits! Here's what you can do to help yourself and break your stress habit. $6

#R5

MEGATRAITS: 12 TRAITS OF SUCCESSFUL PEOPLE. Jeffrey interviews Doris Lee McCoy, author of a new book based on interviews with several hundred successful people, and identifies the crucial traits, the "megatraits", they possess in common that helped get them where they are. $6

#R6

HOW TO MAKE YOUR PR MAKE MONEY. For most businesses, public relations is a useless activity that is not tied to the profit picture. Now Jeffrey tells you how to turn your expensive public relations into a money-making activity that will sell your products and services faster. $6

#R8

OVERWORKED ENTREPRENEURS' GUIDE TO LUXURIOUS CRUISE DISCOUNTS. Jeffrey interviews Captain Bill Miller, author of the superb new book Insider's Guide To Cruise Discounts, and provides you with specific information on how you can take some of the world's best and most luxurious cruises for ridiculously low rates. $6

#R9

WHAT EVERY INVENTOR ABSOLUTELY MUST DO BEFORE CONTACTING ANY MANUFACTURER. Jeffrey interviews consultant Arnold Winkelman, author of the new book The Inventor's Guide To Marketing, about precisely what you've got to do before you show any manufacturer your creation so that your rights are fully protected. Must reading if you're an inventor! $6

#R10

EIGHT SELF-DEFEATING BEHAVIORS PREVENTING YOU FROM BECOMING THE MILLIONAIRE YOU *SAY* YOU WANT TO BE... AND WHAT TO DO ABOUT THEM! Here Jeffrey lays out eight significant behaviors making it difficult, if not impossible, for people to become millionaires and tells them just what to do to overcome them. If you keep talking about wanting to be a millionaire but just can't seem to get started... or keep failing along the way... these behaviors are probably bedevilling you. Learn what they are... and how to get rid of them. $6

#R11

EVERYTHING YOU NEED TO KNOW TO PREPARE YOUR OWN WILL — WITHOUT THE EXPENSE OF A LAWYER! Eight out of ten people in America die without a will, throwing their accumulated possessions and savings into the hands of the court system which then allocates what's available. To stop this idiocy, Jeffrey interviews Attorney Daniel Sitarz, author of the new book Prepare Your Own Will And Testament — Without A Lawyer. Here's exactly what you need to do to prepare your own legal will without a lawyer, securing your estate and saving the lawyer's fees. $6

#R12

WHY MOST CONSULTANTS CAN NEVER MAKE AT LEAST $100,000 A YEAR... AND WHAT TO DO SO YOU WILL. Jeffrey shows you why most consultants fail to make at least $100,000 a year... and provides specific steps to follow so you will. $6

#R13

HOW TO GET FREE AND LOW-COST SOFTWARE FOR YOUR IBM AND IBM-COMPATIBLE COMPUTER. Jeffrey interviews John Gliedman, author of the new book Tips And Techniques for Using Low-Cost And Public Domain Software, on how to get your hands on some of the stupendous amount of free and low-cost software currently available for IBM and IBM-compatible personal computers. Gliedman provides the names, addresses and phone numbers of just where to go to save big money on your software and techniques on how to use it effectively. $6

#R14

HOW TO CREATE CLASSIFIED AND SMALL SPACE ADS THAT GET YOUR PROSPECTS TO RESPOND... AND WHAT TO DO WHEN THEY DO! Jeffrey gives you the low-down on how to create classified and small space ads that get people to respond... and how to create an effective, profit-making program so you can turn your new prospects into buyers... fast! $6

#R15

SETTING AND GETTING YOUR FEE. Jeffrey interviews author Kate Kelly upon the occasion of a new edition being published of her well-known book How To Set Your Fees And Get Them. People selling a service either run the risk of pricing themselves too low (and working for too little) or too high... and losing the business. Kate tells you just what you need to do so you price your services just right... for fast sale and maximum return. $6

#R16

HOW TO MAKE MONEY BUYING PRE-FORECLOSURE PROPER-TIES BEFORE THEY HIT THE COURTHOUSE STEPS. Jeffrey interviews property investment advisor Tom Lucier, author of the new book How To Make Money Buying Pre-Foreclosure Properties Before They Hit The Courthouse Steps, on just what it takes to make big money in pre-foreclosure properties. New workshops have sprung up recently charging as much as $6000 for a weekend providing this kind of advice. Why pay 6G's when specialist Tom Lucier provides the detailed steps right here? $6

#R17

HOW TO DEVELOP AND USE A CLIENT-CENTERED QUESTION-NAIRE THAT GETS YOUR PROS-PECTS TO TELL YOU WHAT THEY WANT... SO YOU CAN SELL IT TO THEM. In this report, Jeffrey helps people who hate making cold calls... and can't figure out how to get their prospects to tell them what they want. If you can solve this problem, you can sell any product or service. Here are the guidelines you need to create this unique client-centered prospecting questionnaire... and how to use it. When you do, your prospects start telling you precisely what they want... all you have to do is give it to them. $6

#R18

HOW TO DO "HOW-TO" (BOOK-LETS AND BOOKS, THAT IS). Here Jeffrey tells you exactly how to produce a how-to booklet or book that really tells your readers how to do what your title promises. Most how-to products are dismal failures, because they don't provide the details your readers need to achieve what they want. Don't let this happen to you. Learn how to create a truly useful how-to. $6

#R19

HOW TO MAKE OVER $100,000 *EVERY* YEAR WITH YOUR OWN CATALOG SELLING PROBLEM-SOLVING INFORMATION PROD-UCTS. Most people in mail order try to make a big kill from a single problem-solving information product... or just a few. Here Jeffrey shows you why that's futile... and how to go about establishing a client-centered catalog selling how-to information products that will make you at least $100,000 every year... and maybe a whole lot more. $6

#R20

HOW TO USE JOB ADS TO LAND THE JOB YOU *REALLY* WANT. If you've ever tried to get a job using classified job ads you know how time consuming and frustrating it is. Here Jeffrey interviews jobs-finding special-ist Kenton Elderkin, author of the new book How To Get Interviews From Job Ads: Where To Look, What To Select, Who To Write, What To Say, When To Follow-Up, How To Save Time. With these techniques answering job ads can lead to the interviews you need... and the good job you want. $6

#R21

YOUR WORST FEARS REALIZED, OR WHAT TO DO WHEN THE CORPORATION OR FOUNDA-TION DECLINES YOUR PRO-POSAL. The competition for corporate and foundation dollars for non-profit organizations has never been greater... and will get worse. You can count on getting turned down, often. What you do next determines whether your organization will ever get the money it needs from these sources. Here are Jeffrey's guidelines for turning a no into a yes, for doing what it takes to build a lucrative relationship with a funding source that has just turned you down. Since this will happen to you (if it isn't happening already), prepare for it now. $6

#R22

IT ISN'T JUST SAYING THE RIGHT THING THAT MAKES A SUCCESSFUL PRESENTATION... OR WHAT YOU'VE REALLY GOT TO DO TO CONNECT WITH YOUR AUDIENCE AND PERSUADE THEM TO LISTEN TO YOU. This isn't a report about speech content... it's a report about how to deal with your audience so they like you and want to listen to what you have to say. Verbal presentations aren't just about imparting information; they're about persuading people to do things. Here's what you've got to do to achieve this crucial objective. $6

#R23

HOW TO CREATE A BROCHURE AND COVER LETTER YOUR PROSPECTS WILL RESPOND TO... NOW! In honor of the new second printing of his book CASH COPY: HOW TO OFFER YOUR PRODUCTS AND SERVICES SO YOUR PROSPECTS BUY THEM... NOW!, Jeffrey tells you how to solve one of the most basic marketing problems of any business: what it takes to create a brochure and cover letter that gets people to respond, instead of being tossed. $6

#R24

HOW TO RAISE MONEY FOR YOUR NON-PROFIT ORGANIZATION WITH AN ANNUAL PHON-A-THON. Jeffrey tells you what you've got to do to use telemarketing to raise money for your non-profit organization... when you've got to work with community volunteers and can't afford professional help. $6

#R25

HOW TO BRING ORDER TO DESK CHAOS, OR ESSENTIALS OF ORGANIZING YOURSELF. Jeffrey talks to organizational specialist Kate Kelly, author (along with Ronni Eisenberg) of the best-selling book ORGANIZE YOURSELF!, about what you've got to do to control clutter and get all those papers in your business life under control. $6

#R26

HOW TO AVOID DESKTOP DIS-APPOINTMENT, OR WHAT YOU'VE *REALLY* GOT TO KNOW TO MAKE DESKTOP PUBLISH-ING WORK FOR YOU. Jeffrey interviews desktop design specialist Roger Parker, author of Looking Good In Print, on what to do to avoid the pitfalls of desktop publishing and use design to create compelling marketing communications. $6

#R28

HOW TO CREATE A MARKETING PLAN THAT SELLS YOUR SER-VICE... WITHOUT COSTING YOU ALL YOUR MONEY. Most people selling a service are "winging it" with predictable results: their marketing is episodic, spasmodic... unproductive. Jeffrey tells you how to create a market-ing plan that will sell a service for the least possible cost and greatest results. $6

#R29

TELESELLING: HOW TO GET THROUGH THE SCREEN THAT'S KEEPING YOU FROM YOUR PROSPECT. Jeffrey talks to Art Sobczak, editor of Telephone Selling Report, on what you've got to do to get through your prospect's screens... switchboard operators, secretaries... anybody who stands between you and your next sale. $6

#R30

HOW TO OPEN A TELEPHONE SALES CALL WITH EITHER A PROSPECT OR A CUSTOMER... SO YOU GET THE BUSINESS. Jeffrey again talks to Art Sobczak, editor of Telephone Selling Report, on what to say during those crucial opening moments with a telephone prospect... and how to build profitable relationships by phone with existing customers. $6

#R31

HOW TO CREATE A PROPOSAL THAT A CORPORATION OR FOUNDATION WILL FUND. Jeffrey tells you and your non-profit organiza-tion what it takes to create a proposal that a corporate or foundation funding source will give money to support. $6

#R32

WHAT YOU HAVE TO DO TO SELL YOUR PRODUCTS AND SERVICES THROUGH A FREE CLIENT NEWSLETTER. Jeffrey tells you how to produce free client newsletters that get your prospects to buy your products and services. $6

#R33

HOW TO CREATE INEXPENSIVE, EFFECTIVE AUDIO CASSETTES TO GET MORE OF YOUR PROS-PECTS TO RESPOND FASTER... AND MAKE EXTRA MONEY, TOO. Jeffrey tells you how to create inexpen-sive 60-minute audio cassettes in your home or office that you can use to induce more and faster sales... and sell profitably, too. $6

#R34

HOW TO PROFIT BY INVESTING IN USED AND BRUISED HOUSES. Jeffrey gets step-by-step advice from Florida author and investor Thomas Lucier on how to make money in real estate through affordable used and bruised houses, one of today's smart investments for people with a moder-ate amount to spend. $6

Jeffrey's Summer Vacation

People are always telling me I work too hard... and it's true you'll usually find me at the phone talking to customers. But this summer I allowed myself to be persuaded to go to London... and spend some of the ample amounts of money my good customers send my way. I'm happy to report I acquired an excellent 18th century English portrait of the Rev. John Upton by the eminent portrait painter George Knapton, Keeper of the King's Pictures. Painted and signed in 1740, it's a superb edition to my burgeoning collection of fine, fine art. If you visit me (like so many people do nowadays), I'll happily show it to you... And remember, when you buy something, the money goes into my next acquisition fund!

#R35

HOW TO USE WORKSHOPS AND OTHER TALK PROGRAMS TO GET CLIENTS. In honor of the publication of the new Second Edition of his well-known book MONEY TALKS: HOW TO CREATE A PROFITABLE WORKSHOP OR SEMINAR IN ANY FIELD, Jeffrey tells you how to use lectures and talk programs to get clients. $6

#R36

THINKING ON YOUR FEET, ANSWERING QUESTIONS WELL WHETHER YOU KNOW THE ANSWER — OR NOT. People who can't deal effectively with questions present a poor self-image and can harm a company. Here Jeffrey interviews Marian Woodall, author of a popular book on the subject, about how people can master the crucial "thinking on your feet" strategies. $6

#R38

WHY YOU NEED SPECIAL REPORTS: HOW TO WRITE THEM, USE THEM TO GET PEOPLE TO BUY WHAT YOU'RE SELLING NOW, TO PUBLICIZE YOUR BUSINESS, AND MAKE MONEY! The secret to successful marketing is making people take action NOW to get what you're selling. Jeffrey shows you how to create inexpensive but powerful Special Reports and how to turn them into compelling marketing tools that get your prospects to respond NOW, and that you can also sell profitably. $6

#R39

COPY FLAWS THAT DOOM YOUR EXPENSIVE MARKETING DOCUMENTS TO LINE BIRDCAGES IN SAINT LOUIS. Jeffrey tells you just what you need to know to write marketing copy that gets people to buy. Key rules of profit-making copy. $6

#R40

YOUR GRAND OPENING: HOW TO START YOUR MARKETING DOCUMENTS SO PEOPLE *BUY* WHAT YOU'RE SELLING. If your marketing documents don't draw people in immediately, you — and your next sale — are lost. Jeffrey tells you precisely what to do to begin documents so your prospects read what you have to say — and buy what you have to sell. $6

#R41

COMPUTER-ASSISTED MARKETING: HOW TO INCREASE YOUR PRODUCTIVITY AND MAKE EVERY PROSPECT AND CUSTOMER FEEL YOU'RE DELIVERING *EXACTLY* WHAT HE WANTS. People have computers but aren't using them effectively. Now learn to turn the computer into your best marketing tool. You'll read things here you've never seen before and increase your marketing productivity astonishingly. $6

#R42

MONEY MAKING MAIL, OR HOW TO AVOID THE TEN BIGGEST MAIL ORDER MISTAKES. Every day I get deluged with mail order offers that make me weep for the trees that have died. What rubbish! There are rules to succeed in mail order. Here's what you should avoid — and what you should do. $6

#R43

HOW TO CREATE AND USE OFFERS YOUR PROSPECTS FIND IRRESISTIBLE. The trick to marketing is to create and sell offers — not products and services. Here's what you need to know about offers, how to create them and use them so that your prospects will buy. $6

#R44

KNOWING WHAT TO DO WHEN PEOPLE OWE YOU MONEY, OR HOW TO GET PAYMENT IN FULL. Don't give way to the rage and frustration of being owed money by deadbeats. Get what you're owed. Here's what you need to do in practical detail. $6

#R45

HOW AUTHORS AND THEIR PUBLISHERS MUST WORK TOGETHER TO SELL MORE BOOKS. Follow these precise steps to construct a profitable author-publisher partnership, so each of you makes money from the book. $6

#R46

YOUR IRA: WHY YOU *STILL* NEED IT, WHAT YOU NEED TO KNOW ABOUT INVESTING IT. If you've lost interest in the IRA, think again. Tax-free compounding of earning's no joke, and millions can still take their contribution off their taxes. Here's the low-down. (By the way, last year IRA contributions were substantially up. This report no doubt helped!) $6

#R47

TELESMARTS: EFFECTIVELY USING TELEMARKETING TO SELL YOUR PRODUCTS AND SERVICES. Most people are hideously ill-equipped to use the phone to sell anything. Here are the basics (and some advanced tips, too) on how you can turn the phone into a profitable business tool. Have I reached out and touched you? $6

#R48

HOW TO OVERCOME SALES OBJECTIONS, INCLUDING THE BIGGEST ONE OF ALL: "YOUR PRICE IS TOO HIGH!" If you're in sales (and if you're reading this, you are), you've got to learn how to deal with objections. Here's what you need to know so that you can. $6

#R49

HOW TO STOP BEING THE LOWLY ORDER-TAKER, BECOME THE CONSUMMATE MARKETER, AND GET MORE SALES FROM NEW BUYERS. The dumb marketer simply sells a prospect what that prospect wants to buy. The expert marketer learns the prospect's problem and persuades him to take an upgraded solution. Here's how to do that. $6

#R50

TESTIMONIALS FOR YOUR PRODUCT OR SERVICE: WHY YOU NEED THEM, HOW TO GET THEM, HOW TO USE THEM. If you aren't using testimonials now, you are missing a prime marketing device. If you are, make sure you're doing it right! $6

#R51

UNDERSTANDING AND PROFITING FROM THE RULE OF SEVEN: CONNECTING WITH YOUR BUYERS AND CONNECTING WITH THEM AGAIN UNTIL THEY BUY WHAT YOU'RE SELLING. Most marketing gambits don't work. In part this is because you don't hit your prospects sufficiently often to interest them in what you're selling. Now learn how you can. The Rule of Seven is the prime rule of marketing. $6

#R52

MARKETING YOUR BOOK BEFORE IT'S PUBLISHED. Stupid authors and publishers wait to begin marketing and making money from their books until they are physically available. Don't you be one of them. Follow the detailed guidelines in this report and make money long before your book is even printed. $6

#R53

WHAT TO DO WHEN YOUR PROSPECT SAYS NO. We all get turned down. Now what? Tears? Rage? No! Use Jeffrey's step-by-step guidelines to get the sale after all — or do what it takes to get the next one! $6

#R54

ESSENTIALS OF MONEY MAKING MARKETING. Successful marketing is the key to business success. Now learn precisely what you have to do to improve your marketing. Follow these steps; sell more. $6

#R55

WHY YOU NEED A BUSINESS PLAN, WHY YOU RESIST CREATING ONE. Makes a clear case for why you must have a business plan to succeed, how to overcome your resistance to creating one, and what should go in it. A must, particularly for new and struggling entrepreneurs. $6

#R56

HOW TO GET THE LOWEST CARD-DECK ADVERTISING PRICES AND MAKE THE MOST MONEY FROM CARD-DECK ADVERTISING. Card-decks can get you maximum response for the least price. Now in honor of Jeffrey's Sales & Marketing SuccessDek, you can learn the secrets of how to get the lowest prices and biggest response. $6

#R57

TEN THINGS YOU CAN DO RIGHT NOW TO GET MORE MONEY FROM YOUR NEXT FUND RAISING LETTER. If you're running a non-profit organization and expect to raise money using fund-raising letters, read this report first. Jeffrey's been writing profit-making fund-raising letters for non-profits for over a decade. Here's what he's learned to make you more money. $6

#R58

HOW TO GET THE MOST BENEFIT WHEN WORKING WITH CONSULTANTS: THE 10 BIGGEST MISTAKES YOU'RE NOT GOING TO MAKE. All too often organizations hiring consultants don't get their money's worth. This won't happen to you if you follow the guidelines in this sensible report. $6

#R59

WHAT YOU THINK MAY BE A COPY PROBLEM MAY REALLY BE A STRATEGIC MARKETING PROBLEM ... HERE'S WHAT YOU CAN DO TO SOLVE IT. All too often what people think is a copy problem is actually a strategic marketing problem. Your marketing strategy has got to be right before you can create the most effective copy. For just $6 you learn how to create the strategy that gets people to buy what you're selling. (Then you can use CASH COPY to create the copy itself!)

#R60

HOW TO HAVE AN EFFECTIVE MEETING, OR WHAT YOU'VE REALLY GOT TO DO TO STOP WASTING YOUR TIME AT NON-PRODUCTIVE BUSINESS GET-TOGETHERS. Before you waste another senseless minute in a pointless meeting (or, God forbid, chair such a meeting) get this report and learn how to structure meetings so you get what you want — the only reason for having a meeting in the first place. $6

#R61

HOW TO TURN YOUR (PREVIOUSLY UNREAD) ANNUAL REPORT INTO AN ACTION ORIENTED MARKETING DOCUMENT THAT GETS PEOPLE TO DO WHAT YOU WANT THEM TO DO! For most organizations — profit and not-for-profit — annual reports are a complete waste of time and money. Who reads them? But properly created annual reports can become powerful marketing documents that get you new business. Here's what you need to know about creating them. $6

#R62

HOW TO GET YOUR CLIENTS TO GET BUSINESS FOR YOU. There are tricks for getting your existing (and past) customers to get new business for you. Here they are. When you have a customer you get not only current income but future business ... if you use these techniques. $6

#R63

HOW TO SET UP AN INDEPENDENT AGENT REFERRAL SYSTEM AND GET HUNDREDS OF PEOPLE TO REFER YOU TO ORGANIZATIONS NEEDING PAID SPEAKERS. Talk programs remain a superb way to make money — often astonishingly large amounts of money. Problem is: booking agents don't want you until you're a celebrity and cold calling is an agony. The solution? Set up your own Independent Agent Referral System to generate a constant stream of program leads. Here Jeffrey — one of America's best-known speakers — explains just how to do it! $6

#R64

HOW YOU CAN MANAGE YOUR BUSINESS' CASH FLOW EFFECTIVELY. Prosperity in the 'nineties means getting your hands on money earlier and managing that money more effectively. Here Jeffrey gets tips from Les Masonson, author of a new book intriguingly titled *Cash, Cash, Cash*, about the secrets of better cash management. Details about how to work with your bank you've never seen before. $6

#R66

HOW TO WRITE A BUSINESS PROPOSAL THAT GETS YOU THE BUSINESS. If you have to write proposals to get contracts, learn Jeffrey's secrets for creating proposals that get you the business — instead of wasting your time and money. $6

#R68

MARKETING IN THE BAD TIMES: HOW TO SELL MORE OF YOUR PRODUCTS AND SERVICES EVEN IN A RECESSION! If you didn't read this in my syndicated column and are still in a part of the country (as I am) where the recession isn't over, here are detailed suggestions to keep selling your product/service — yes *more* of your product/service! — even when times are bad. $6

#R69

WHAT YOU'VE GOT TO DO BEFORE YOU WRITE ANY MARKETING COMMUNICATION — FLYER, PROPOSAL, AD, COVER LETTER, ETC., OR DOING THE HOMEWORK THAT PRODUCES THE MARKETING COMMUNICATION THAT GETS YOUR PROSPECT TO BUY WHAT YOU'RE SELLING In honor of the publication of the new Revised Second Edition of his well-known book MONEY MAKING MARKETING: FINDING THE PEOPLE WHO NEED WHAT YOU'RE SELLING AND MAKING SURE THEY BUY IT, Jeffrey tackles one of the most important marketing problems: showing how lack of client-centered preparation makes it impossible to produce marketing communications that get people to respond. Here are the steps you need to take so you'll regularly produce profit-making marketing documents. $6

#R70

FIVE CRUCIAL THINGS YOU NEED TO KNOW TO MAKE REAL MONEY IN YOUR HOME-BASED BUSINESS. Up to 22,000,000 Americans derive some or all of their income working from home. Yet the vast majority gross only about $15,000 yearly — peanuts! Here Jeffrey, who's run a home-based business for over 12 years and became a millionaire in the process, provides crucial information on how to create a business at home that will produce $100,000 a year — or more. $6

The list of Special Reports continues on page 284. First look at the Special Offers on pages 282 & 283!

Jeffrey Lant's Sales & Marketing Successdek

Are you selling nationwide? Are you offering a product/ service that will increase another business' profitability? How about a health, travel or investment service? Or a business opportunity? Do you offer business equipment or products? Or have you got a way of making a business more efficient? Are you interested in getting thousands of qualified leads for the least possible cost and so making money faster? If you've answered yes to any of these questions, and you're not already in my card deck, ARE YOU CRAZY?

"We received over 2,100 leads on our first insertion alone," says multi-time card-deck advertiser Robert Blackman of Diversified Enterprises. "We'll be advertising with you every time! Thanks for all your advice, too. You've been a big help in showing us how to make more money!!!"

Every 90 days I send out 100,000 of these decks for advertisers who want more high quality leads fast. These advertisers have made mine one of America's two largest card decks... for very good reasons:

- **price** — my prices are by far the lowest in the industry. I charge just $1199 for 100,000 two-color cards; just $650 for 50,000 two-color cards and $1350 for 100,000 four-color cards. Other decks charge up to $3000 more for the same thing. If you get a discount from them, you have to negotiate for it. With me, you get the rock-bottom lowest cost offered by any deck in America — and you get it immediately.
- **free color**. Other decks charge you for a second color. You get it free from me.
- **free copywriting assistance**. If you don't have a winning card already, I'll help you create it — free. No other deck does this.
- **guaranteed top 20 position**.   If you pay for your card 60 days prior to publication, you get a guaranteed spot in the top 20 cards (our decks average 88 cards). Other decks give the best positions to the big guys or to those who pay more; we give them to whoever pays first, not extra.
- **free closing assistance**. Getting leads is no good if you can't close them; that's why I provide tips on how to generate maximum sales from the leads you get.
- **100% deck-responsive names**. Other decks use inferior subscription or compiled lists. Not me. The people who get my deck have all responded to a deck offer in the last 90 days. You go to people who want deck offers, who respond to deck offers, and who buy deck offers. And every 90 days the list is different! That's why advertisers stay in every issue and why we have so few spaces available. (By the way, our current response record is 7,500 responses — a whopping 7.5% — to a card in a recent issue!)
- **on time mailing**. Our decks go out when we say they'll go out. Recently, other major decks in the industry have been as much as *three months' late*. Not us. We flog you to get your art in on time... so the deck can go out on time. So you get your leads on time.

Yes! We can provide your camera-ready art; (there is a charge).

Closing date for this year's last mailing is:

November 23
(mailing January 4, 1993).

Mailings take place every 90 days, in April, June and October. Call for complete details.

Card deck advertising can make you rich. If you want either large numbers of qualified leads fast or to sell to a national audience fast, call Jeffrey at (617) 547-6372. If you're simply interested in receiving the deck, you may also request a copy.

If any of these conditions apply to you... you need an electronic moving message display unit NOW!

- you've got cash registers;
- you've got a waiting room where your customers wait to see you;
- sidewalk traffic passes your establishment;
- you've got a streetside location;
- you go to trade shows
- you need to communicate messages to your employees (like safety messages to assembly line personnel);
- you've got windows potential customers see...

> *Moving signs have been the rage for years in Europe and Japan... and they're increasingly popular here. Been to Las Vegas lately? You know what I mean!!!*

These are the kinds of places electronic moving message display units make sense.

You've already seen them... in airports, banks, malls, airports, in schools, industrial settings... why the restaurant down the street from me has been pulling in customers with its moving sign for years.

Now it's time for you to start benefiting from them.

- They're easy to set up and move.
- They're easy to use.
- You can change your messages promptly and easily.
- You get true colors, lots of dazzling special effects, both text and animation features.

With your moving sign, you can:
- announce specials, mark-downs and sales;
- run contests, news items and trivia;
- talk directly to your customers;
- build the value of all your sales (when you've got a potential customer waiting... use your sign to sell him something else!).

Warning: maybe you've been thinking about getting a moving sign and have been checking out the cheapie models in discount stores and merchandise clubs. Don't even think of getting your sign there. You want extra colors, at least 5000 characters of memory, special effects, the ability to run multiple lines of text simultaneously, easy message-editing capability... and all the other features you need to give your sign the most impact and have the greatest effect on your customers. Cheap signs just don't have what you need. For just a few more dollars, you can get all the special effects and features you need. Don't short-change yourself on this valuable marketing tool!

For assistance in getting you the right moving sign at the right price, call Bill Reece, Nat'l Sales Manager, at (617) 278-4344 or by fax at (617) 547-0061. He'll help you find the sign that's just right for you... including making recommendations on a custom sign .

Dealer Opportunity: We are now setting up dealers nationwide to represent these signs. Interested in adding these easy-to-sell moving signs to your line? Or selling them alone? This is the right time to get into this profitable business... before the field is oversaturated, as it surely will be. For complete, no obligation details, contact Bill Reece above.

Once you've got your moving sign, get Jeffrey's special report on how to use them most effectively to make money faster.

#R83

#R71

HOW YOU CAN OVERCOME WRITER'S ANXIETY AND PRODUCE EFFECTIVE LETTERS, MEMOS, REPORTS, PROPOSALS, ETC. Virtually everyone in American business is called upon to write something for the job. Yet the vast majority of people hate to write — and do it badly. Here Jeffrey interviews New York writing coach Jim Evers, author of *The Hate To Write But Have To Writer's Guide*, to get specific suggestions on how you can overcome your writer's anxiety and produce effective business writing. $6

#R72

HOW TO TALK SO MEN WILL LISTEN. Women regularly report that talking to men (bosses, colleagues, Significant Others) is like talking to a brick wall. They talk, but does anyone really *hear* them? Now Oregon specialist Marian Woodall tackles one of civilization's oldest problems and, as usual, offers detailed suggestions on what women can do to get their points across — and what men should do to hear women. A perfect report for women who want to communicate more effectively with men... and men who really care about women! $6

#R73

HOW TO DETERMINE THE RIGHT COMPUTER OR PRINTER FOR YOUR BUSINESS AND WHERE TO BUY THEM FOR THE BEST PRICES. This report is for people who may be selecting their first computer and printer, or for seasoned veterans who want to make sure they get just the right kinds of machines for their needs — and don't overpay for them. Jeffrey interviews Maine computer expert Ted Stevens on how to determine how to get the right computer and printer for your situation and where to get the best prices for them. $6

Want to get started getting the lowest computer and fax prices? Call Ted direct at (207) 783-1136.

284

#R74

HOW TO MAKE MONEY WITH REAL ESTATE OPTIONS. Here Jeffrey interviews real estate expert Tom Lucier, author of the new book *How To Make Money With Real Estate Options*. Tom provides step-by-step details about how investors with limited funds can profit from real estate — without *owning* any real estate... thanks to real estate options. Shows you how to get the right properties, pay the lowest option fees, and create the right kind of option to purchase agreements. Crucial information so you can make money in real estate despite the current real estate market "melt-down." $6

#R75

THE TOP FIVE SALES-KILLING MISTAKES YOU'RE MAKING IN TELESALES... AND HOW TO AVOID THEM! Jeffrey interviews Art Sobczak, the super-smart publisher of *Telephone Selling Report* newsletter, about the five biggest mistakes telephone sales people make that kill sales — and how to avoid them. Must reading if you're trying to sell a product/sell by phone. $6

#R76

HOW TO LOWER YOUR PROPERTY TAXES THIS YEAR — AND KEEP THEM DOWN YEAR AFTER YEAR! Jeffrey interviews Gary Whalen, author of the new book *Digging For Gold In Your Own Back Yard: The Complete Homeowners Guide To Lowering Your Real Estate Taxes*. Million of Americans are paying too much property tax. This could be you. Here Jeffrey draws on Gary Whalen's experience to show you how to pay the lowest legal real estate tax. $6

#R77

CONSULTANTS: EIGHT CRUCIAL THINGS YOU MUST DO TO MAKE AT LEAST $100,000 EVERY YEAR. Smart consultants now have mid-six figure and even 7-figure incomes. But most consultants earn a tiny fraction of these high flyers. Why? Here Jeffrey lays out the reasons most consultants consistently fail to reach their income objectives and lays down specific rules you can follow so you'll make at least $100,000 every year from your practice. $6

#R78

THE TEN THINGS YOU MUST DO TO BECOME A MILLIONAIRE SELLING SERVICES. Millions of Americans sell services but most of them aren't anywhere close to being millionaires. This is because they don't understand how to use their service business as a lever to make themselves really rich. Here Jeffrey shows exactly what service sellers must do to become millionaires. Clear, easy-to-follow steps that could make you really rich, even in the deflationary 'nineties! $6

#R79

HOW TO GET RICH USING CARD-DECK ADVERTISING. Many more people than currently advertise in card-decks should be in them, Jeffrey asserts. They're a superb and cost effective way for generating a large volume of fast leads and making sales; a crucial part of a sensible marketing program. Here Jeffrey points out just what businesses must do to use card-decks effectively so they get the most leads and make the most sales from them. Getting rich from card-decks is possible for many businesses. Jeffrey's suggestions show you how to do it. $6

#R80

HOW TO CREATE AND MAKE MONEY FROM AN INFORMATION PRODUCT... FOR LIFE! Tens of thousands of 'how-to' booklets, books, audio & video cassettes and Special Reports are produced annually — but most of their creators don't make much money, much less turn their creation into a life-time income. Here Jeffrey, the doyen of America's info-producers, lays out the necessary steps that ensure that *each* information product produces maximum income for life. $6

#R81

THE 10 THINGS YOUR (NON-PROFIT) MARKETING SHOULD NEVER BE! Are you working for a nonprofit organization? Then chances are your marketing is rudimentary and inefficient. Here is Jeffrey's hard-hitting look at the mistakes nonprofits make and precisely what to do to correct them. With virtually all nonprofit organizations facing tough budget times, it is immoral to fail to learn exactly how to use the limited dollars you've got for marketing more productively. Here's what you need! $6

#R82

MAXIMIZING MEMORY POWER: MAKING SURE YOU NEVER FORGET GOOD OL' WHAT'S HIS NAME. Jeffrey interviews Bob Burg, creator of the six-cassette tape album "On Your Way To Remembering Names & Faces", about how to solve the important business problem of remembering names and crucial information about the people you meet... people you want to remember and do business with. The perceptive Burg offers an easy-to-follow six-step method that gives you just what you need so you never forget crucial information about the people you're meeting. $6

#R83

HOW TO MOVE A WHOLE LOT MORE OF YOUR PRODUCTS AND SERVICES.... THANKS TO MOVING MESSAGE SIGNS! Jeffrey interviews moving message sign king Bill Reece about how to use these signs to move more products and services faster. These signs have been popping up everywhere... in airports, banks, school cafeterias, at trade shows... everywhere! Now learn how to select the right sign for your business and how to turn it into a fascinating client-centered marketing tool that gets your message out 24 hours a day for just the cost of the electricity. Whatever you're selling, Reece clearly shows why there's a moving message sign in your future. $6

Note: You can profit from moving signs in two ways: use them to attract business and

move merchandise faster or sell them to make money. Either way, call Bill Reece direct at (617) 278-4344 or by fax at (617) 547-0061. He has dozens of different moving sign varieties available from smaller ones that will fit nicely into your store window... right up to the big monster in Times Square. He can do it all. Just tell him what you want!

New! #R84

HOW TO MAKE $100,000 EVERY YEAR FOR YOUR MLM OPPORTUNITY USING CARD-DECK ADVERTISING
Most people in MLM make pitiable amounts of money. The disaffected drop out of one program, latch on to another, hopeful all over again, only to find they're not making money in that either. Here, however, Jeffrey shows you how to use card-deck advertising to generate thousands of leads quickly at minimum cost and build a 6-figure MLM income. Up till now card-decks have been too expensive for most MLM people, many of whom run small organizations. Not any more! Indeed, Jeffrey even shows you how to get 100,000 cards for no direct cost... $6

New! #R85

THE INGENUE MARKETER'S GUIDE TO CERTAIN FAILURE... OR, IT WOULD BE A LOT FASTER AND EASIER SIMPLY TO THROW YOUR MONEY OUT THE WINDOW
This article is principally for non-profit organizations but the lessons are relevant to all ingenue marketers who need to be aware of the mistakes they're making so they can correct them and start running a marketing program that achieves substantial results. If that's your objective, you'll be certain to want to read this step-by-step report. $6

New! #R86

WHEN YOU CAN'T WRITE THE MARKETING COPY YOURSELF, OR HOW TO GET THE BEST RESULTS FROM YOUR COPY WRITER

Most business people are terrible writers, and as a result they produce terrible marketing communications which don't get them the clients they need. Here Jeffrey interviews nationally known copywriter Dan McComas, director of the National Copywriting Center, on how to find the right copywriter and how to work with him/her to get the results you want. $6

Note: ▬▬▬▬▬▬▬

Want to get started producing superior copy faster?

Call Dan McComas directly at
(301) 946-4284!

New! #R87

HOW TO GENERATE FAR MORE LEADS FOR SELLING YOUR PRODUCT AND SERVICE AND HOW TO DETERMINE WHICH OF THEM ARE WORTH YOUR TIME AND MONEY

Most business people get too few leads, too few good leads, and thus spend far too much time with both too few people and the kinds of people they shouldn't be trying to work with at all. Here Jeffrey, one of America's most aggressive lead generators, shows you how to generate all the leads you want... and how to decide which of them you should be spending your time with. $6

New! #R88

DO YOU *REALLY* WANT TO BE RICH? TAKE THIS REVEALING QUIZ AND FIND OUT...

I've often wondered how many of those people talking about wanting to be rich actually will do what it takes to become rich. If you're wondering about yourself, take my handy quiz and find out if you *really* have what it takes to get rich. $6

... HERE'S WHAT YOU NEED IF YOU'VE GOT LESS THAN AN HOUR TO GET SMARTER...

Right between Special Reports (Jeffrey's unique contribution to get-ahead literature) and full-scale books, are Crisp publications. You've probably seen them. Thousands and thousands of businesses and professionals have made them best sellers. What's different about them is that they take less than one hour to read (Mike Crisp bills them as the 50-minute publications), have sensible, easy-to-follow information you can put to work immediately... and are good value. I've listed below as many as I could pack into just two pages. With Crisp, the title says it all... you don't need a lengthy description. (All Crisp item numbers begin with CR. Please make sure to include complete number on the order form on page 32.)

#CR1

LEADERSHIP SKILLS FOR WOMEN by Marilyn Manning, Ph.D. Provides details on the essential factors that help women become business leaders. 88 pages. $10.95

#CR2

DELEGATING FOR RESULTS by Robert Maddux. If you're overwhelmed, you need to delegate. Here are the key elements of successful delegation. 80 pages. $10.95

#CR3

INCREASING EMPLOYEE PRODUCTIVITY. Of course you want to get more benefit out of your employees. Lynn Tylczak shows you how. 100 pages. $10.95

#CR4

AN HONEST DAY'S WORK: MOTIVATING EMPLOYEES TO GIVE THEIR BEST. My friend Twyla Dell knows that if your employees aren't motivated, they can't produce. She shows you how to motivate your employees to increase their productivity. 80 pages. $10.95

#CR5

MANAGING FOR COMMITMENT: BUILDING LOYALTY WITHIN AN ORGANIZATION. This practical book by Dr. Carol Goman shows you how to build a level of commitment and loyalty with today's new, more independent workforce. 96 pages. $10.95.

#CR6

TRAINING METHODS THAT WORK by Dr. Lois Hart. Want to sharpen your training skills? In just 96 pages you'll learn how. $10.95.

#CR7

RECRUITING VOLUNTEERS: A GUIDE FOR NONPROFITS. Carl Liljenstolpe knows that your nonprofit needs extra volunteer help. Here's how you get it. 100 pages. $10.95

#CR8

STEPPING UP TO SUPERVISOR. Revised edition by Marion Haynes. If you want to become a supervisor or have just become one, here's what you need to make a success of your position. 280 pages. $17.95

#CR9

NO MORE MISTAKES. Twenty four techniques for doing things right the first time. 48 pages. $5.95 (I'm applying for a govt. grant to give every congressperson a copy!)

#CR10

PLAN YOUR WORK — WORK YOUR PLAN. James Sherman shows you how to plan and get what you want. 96 pages. $10.95

#CR11

DEVELOPING POSITIVE ASSERTIVENESS by Sam Lloyd. If you're the mouse who can't roar (or know one of these poor creatures), learn how to develop the positive assertiveness you need to get ahead on the job or in life. 80 pages. $10.95

#CR12

MANAGING ANGER by Dr. Rebecca Luhn. Here you get the methods you need to manage your emotions in a positive manner. 90 pages. $10.95

#CR13

GUIDE TO AFFIRMATIVE ACTION. Pamela Conrad gives you guidelines supported by case studies to ensure that managers make correct decisions on affirmative action, equal employment opportunity, age and sex discrimination and sexual harassment. 96 pages. $10.95

#CR14

YOUR FIRST THIRTY DAYS: BUILDING A PROFESSIONAL IMAGE IN A NEW JOB. Elwood Chapman shows you how to adjust with greater confidence. If you're new, get off to the right start. 96 pages. $10.95

#CR15

QUALITY INTERVIEWING. Robert Maddux' best-selling book helps you master interviewing skills that will lead to sound hiring decisions. 72 pages $10.95

#CR16

PROFESSIONAL EXCELLENCE FOR SECRETARIES. Marilyn Manning provides the information a professional secretary needs so office work gets done promptly and right. 80 pages. $10.95

#CR17

GIVING AND RECEIVING CRITICISM by Patti Hathaway. There are right ways and wrong ways to give it... and to take it. Here they are. 96 pages $10.95

#CR18

WELLNESS IN THE WORKPLACE: HOW TO DEVELOP A COMPANY WELLNESS PROGRAM. Merlene Sherman provides the components of an effective health program with case studies, resources, diagrams, inventories, examples and strategies. 100 pages. $10.95

#CR19

BALANCING HOME AND CAREER: SKILLS FOR SUCCESSFUL LIFE MANAGEMENT. Pamela Conrad's revised edition is for busy people who have to juggle. Includes chapters on home, business, travel and relocation. Shows you how to put quality time where you want it. 80 pages. $10.95

#CR20

OVERCOMING ANXIETY by Lynn Fossum. Anxiety is one of the most common problems medical doctors encounter. Learn what anxiety is and is not and how to overcome it. 96 pages. $10.95

#CR21

PREVENTING JOB BURNOUT by Dr. Beverly Potter. Burnout is a terrifically common problem in all businesses these days. Here are 8 proven strategies to beat job burnout and help you deal with the pressures of your job. 80 pages. $10.95

#CR22

FIRST AID ESSENTIALS. Written by the National Safety Council, you get the latest information on how to deal with a wide variety of injuries and emergency situations. Quick emergency index so you'll know what to do when problems arise. Should be in every business — and home. 222 pages. $11.95

#CR23

MAKING HUMOR WORK. Dr. Terry Paulson shows you how to use humor in the workplace with problem-solving, defusing resistance to change, disarm-ing anger, and improving memory. 108 pages. $10.95

#CR24

FORMATTING LETTERS AND MEMOS ON THE COMPUTER. Dr. Eleanor Davidson has written this for computer beginners. Offers tips and exercises for designing letters, reports and memos on the computer. 90 pages. $10.95

#CR25

BUSINESS REPORT WRITING by Susan Brock. A super quick guide for writing business reports and proposals. Teaches how to organize, research, develop and edit winning documents. 90 pages. $10.95

#CR26

SPEEDREADING IN BUSINESS by Joyce Turley. Of course, you have more to read. So, you either skip it (and stay uninformed)... or learn speedreading HERE! 96 pages $10.95

#CR27

EXHIBITING AT TRADESHOWS. Susan Friedman shows you how to gain a competitive edge at a tradeshow in a cost-effective manner. 90 pages. $10.95

#CR28

CALMING UPSET CUSTOMERS by Rebecca Morgan. You're going to have them, so let author Morgan show you how to deal with both a disturbed and an upset customer. (No, they're not the same!) 74 pages. $10.95

#CR29

STARTING YOUR NEW BUSINESS by Charles Martin. If you're just getting your toe in the water, get this. In addition to a thorough discussion of the basics, includes superb annotated bibliography pointing you to lots of other helpful materials. 110 pages. $10.95

#CR30

EFFECTIVE NETWORKING by Venda Raye-Johnson. Shows you how to use networking to share information, resources and support to build and maintain effective career and personal relationships. 96 pages. $10.95

60 Money-Making Minutes with Jeffrey (on tape)

#T3

HOW TO GET FREE TIME ON RADIO AND T.V. AND USE IT TO GET YOUR PROSPECTS TO BUY WHAT YOU'RE SELLING. Listen as Jeffrey gives you the secrets of getting valuable free time on radio and television so you can sell your products and services without spending any of your money. Getting on *just one* program could return your investment dozens of times! $16

#T4

HOW TO CREATE MARKETING DOCUMENTS THAT GET YOUR PROSPECTS TO BUY WHAT YOU'RE SELLING ... NOW! Since you spend thousands of dollars on your marketing documents, don't you think you should know what will get people to respond to them faster ... to buy what you're selling **NOW**? Here's just what you need to know. $16

#T5

ESSENTIALS OF MONEY MAKING MARKETING: WHAT YOU'VE REALLY GOT TO DO TO SELL YOUR PRODUCTS AND SERVICES, EVERY DAY! Jeffrey shares his secrets of successful marketing, what you've got to do, when and how you've got to do it to sell your products and services. $16

#C3

ALL THREE OF JEFFREY'S 60 MINUTE AUDIO CASSETTES (T3, T4, T5). Just $38. You save $10!

Got three bucks?

Then take advantage of these deals:

#F2

MAIL PROFITS. If you expect to succeed in mail-order, you need this publication. Now you can get two free issues of America's premier mail-order publication. Each issue packed with details on what it really takes to make money by mail. $3

#F3

TELEPHONE SELLING REPORT. If you sell by phone, you can profit from Art Sobczak's infinitely intelligent publication. Each monthly 8 page report gives ideas you will use to close more sales and set more appointments by phone. $3 gets you three issues ($25 value)

#F4

99 WAYS TO SELL MORE BY PHONE: WHAT YOU CAN DO AND SAY RIGHT NOW TO GET MORE 'YES'S' BY PHONE. This just-published 40 page booklet by Art Sobczak lists 99 proven techniques (with exactly what to say and how to say it) for closing telephone sales. These techniques have already closed millions of dollars worth of business. Unbelievable! Just $3.

Special: if you'd like to hear some free tele-tips from the tele-master himself, call Art Sobczak's tips line: (402) 896-TIPS (8477).

#F6

RADIO & TV INTERVIEW RE-PORT package. Send $3 and get complete details on how to get interviewed — for free — on thousands of radio and television stations. You can do the radio interviews from your home or office! Perfect if you're an author or publisher or represent a cause that people are interested in or should know about.

#F7

JEFFREY GOES MLM. I'm an MLM sceptic... or was, until I started getting monthly checks (my first one was 9 cents!) from an old line company that sells thousands of products all of us use every day: household products, hair, skin & health care, nutritional products, food, water filters, home care, gifts and even gourmet products. Now you can join my fast-growing organization and start making money, too. Send $3 for complete details.

#F9

IDEA DIGEST. Considering starting a low-capital, home-based business? Then send me $3 bucks and get three free issues of Gary Davis' well-known IDEA DIGEST publication. Packed with articles and information sources to get your home-based business off to a fast start.

> *"I have already purchased six of your special reports. They were all excellent, and I am certainly satisfied with the quality of your products."*
>
> *Timothy Turner, Raleigh, NC*

FREE INFORMATION!

#F1

JOIN THE HUNDREDS OF PEOPLE WORLDWIDE WHO ARE SELLING JEFFREY'S BOOKS AND PRODUCTS AND MAKING MONEY NOW! Do you offer workshops and talk programs? Publish any kind of publication? Do you have a catalog or regular mailing program? Then you should be selling Jeffrey's books, tapes and special reports and making easy extra income.

Write "F1" on page 32, and you'll get complete free details about how you can profit from America's most relentlessly focused and detailed money-making products. Jeffrey is recognized world-wide by people who know that his name on the product means it works. This means easy sales for you!

Dealer already? Call and get Jeffrey's newest dealer catalogs. It's time to upgrade to your new catalog!

MOVING SIGN DEALERSHIP

Here's just one of the dozens of varieties of moving message signs we can get for you...

Now you can cash in on America's next marketing revolution... Customized Moving Message Displays

These electronic message display units are popping up everywhere. They're already the rage in Japan and Europe. You can make big money selling them to: retail stores, professional offices, airports, banks, bars, schools, trade shows... anywhere people congregate and need to see marketing messages.

We're looking for dealers who are good with people, well organized, efficient and want to **MAKE LOTS OF MONEY**. We pay good commissions and will work with you to create a money-making marketing strategy. Sell these signs alone or add them to your existing product line. Either way, they make you money.

Call National Sales Director Bill Reece now for complete details. (617) 278-4344

All others: call Bill and let him show you how these signs can make your business more money. Stop using stationary signs. *Moving signs sell faster!*

MOVING MESSAGE SIGNS: PEOPLE SEE 'EM. THEY WANT 'EM. IT'S AS SIMPLE AS THAT.

MLM $! Join These 7 Network Marketing Programs... Make Money Now!!! Call for complete details...

1
JOIN NUTRITION EXPRESS!
Make Money from over 200 quality nutritious foods, weight control, personal care, homeopathic, herbal and household products! *You'll be glad you joined Nutrition Express* because of the most *generous and profitable* pay plan in the industry... because the product line is of exemplary quality which creates enthusiasm and product loyalty in your group... people reorder the consumable products constantly MAKING YOU MONEY EVERY TIME. **Call now and get your free Starter Pak**, a proven 'no selling' mail program, free booklet and learn how to make money with NUTRITION EXPRESS fast! No meetings! No selling! A complete system! Contact Richard Brooks at 318-992-5790 or write: Cypress Support Services, P.O. Box 1201, Rhinehart, LA 71363.

2
JOIN ADNET! Profit with both LEADS AND INCOME from the program for MLM professionals. ADNET helps you be successful in any Network Marketing program. ADNET sends you 30-40 highly qualified MLM leads every month! And make your business more profitable by adding an additional profit center. ADNET advertises for you in USA Today and Entrepreneur magazine. **You'll also get free advertising!** Fast start bonus! Profitable with only three people in your group! Call Peter Regan **now** at 413-445-5357 to join ADNET or write: 7 Onota Lane, Pittsfield, MA 01202

3
JOIN UNITED DENTAL PLAN OF AMERICA! *Exceptional income possible* marketing this incredible new dental service! Everybody needs quality dental care — You can earn top income by selling this to both companies and individuals! Virtually no competition! Unbeatable values! This is NOT insurance. Complete Family Plans just $150 per year! Individual Plans only $85 per year! All oral exams and x-rays... No Charge! Cleanings just $20.00! 25-60% Discount off **all** other dental procedures. No Waiting! ... Even on orthodontia, cosmetics and implants! 33% Commission plus same on renewals! Multiple sales to companies are LUCRATIVE! **Call** Bill Crocker NOW at 617-547-8340 for **FREE** details or write Bill at: UDPA, 2592 Mass. Ave., Cambridge, MA 02140.

4
JOIN JEWELWAY INTERNATIONAL! This is one of the *most lucrative* programs available to join today! The FINE JEWELRY mega-industry has a huge market niche for high quality 14K Gold FINE JEWELRY at substantial savings! People buy FINE JEWELRY in a recession *where value is offered... we have it!* GROUND FLOOR! LUCRATIVE! No inventory—catalog sales. No quotas. Call to get your 100 page color catalog with 1000s of high quality FINE JEWELRY. Pays $1000s infinitely deep WEEKLY! **Upline forced to help you!** Call Kathy Byrnes at 313-772-8968 or write: JEWELWAY INTERNATIONAL, 22439 Doremus, St. Clair Shores, MI 48080.

5
JOIN INFINET TRAVEL CLUB!
Go anywhere in the world and never pay full price to get there... ***ever again!*** PLUS, earn FREE vacations and cash... quickly and easily just by recommending INFINET to anyone you know. Members get:
* FULL SERVICE Travel Agency
* **SAVE 5 – 60% off everything you book!**
* GUARANTEED lowest available airfare
* 50% Hotel Discount Program
* Up to 60% off last-minute travel
* PROVEN Referral System! Spreading the word is easy!
* **ENORMOUS earnings potential — Everyone loves to travel**
* ABSOLUTELY no selling or travel experience required for success!!!

Save money on every vacation! Call NOW: 800-966-CLUB for free info. Tell them Jeffrey Lant sent you and save $30 off your membership. (Reg. $79, yours now for $49)

6
JOIN MARKET AMERICA! Make money with us when you join with your *many* (not just one) distinctive product lines to represent. You'll profit when you and your group sells complete product lines including diet/nutritional products, jewelry, personal care products and more! Benefit from a very motivating, powerful pay plan! This translates into HIGH PROFITS! And high sponsoring closing ratios! **You'll be glad you joined MARKET AMERICA** when your four figure *weekly checks* come rolling in! You'll collect on unlimited levels... your upline rejoins in your downline *to help you make money faster!* Get qualified leads from company run infomercials! Call John Jette today at 508-937-2910 or write: MARKET AMERICA, 26 Varney Street, Lowell, MA 01854.

7
JOIN CONSUMERS' BUYLINE! 'CBI' is "The Original" and Best American Discounting Service! *You'll be glad you joined* CBI with its GUARANTEED low prices on over 600,000 products and services or DOUBLE the DIFFERENCE BACK! *You* have the right to earn steady monthly income in the process! SEE PAGE 292 FOR COMPLETE DETAILS. Then call Greig Hollister at (404) 768-0838.

HERE ARE THE WAYS TO BUILD YOUR MLM ORGANIZATION FASTER... AND START MAKING YOUR ANNUAL 6-FIGURE MLM INCOME

Most people in MLM piddle along, making pitiable amounts of money. They jump from "opportunity" to "opportunity", always hopeful, never making enough money to pay for all the stuff they're forced to buy.

If this is you, take heart. I've now got these 4 ways to help you build a big organization fast.

1) **For the littlest guys**. If you're someone who just wants to get a toe in the water, doesn't want to spend too much money but wants to generate new leads, you want a place on the MLM card Gery Carson runs in my card-deck and other decks. For just a few dollars, you can run a line (about 10-12 words) on your opportunity. All the leads go back to Gery who sorts them out and ships them to you. You'll be the only representative of your opportunity, and you'll get leads for a very reasonable price. Contact Gery Carson, Carson Services, Inc., P.O. Box 4785, Lincoln, NE 68504, (402) 467-4230, Fax (402) 467-4292. Also get Gery's fine publication MAIL PROFITS. See #F2

2) Want **more leads faster**? Join Jeffrey's TNT Team. Here you and your opportunity join 4-5 others on a bingo card that runs in Jeffrey's card-deck. What's different about both this program and #3 below is that Jeffrey will join your organization and help you generate leads. All leads go to Jeffrey for processing. He'll send them to you weekly. Note: people who start in this program usually decide to go on to #3 option below (as you can see from page 24)! You probably will, too... This option was created to get you a substantial number of leads for a reasonable price... and to develop your organization so you can process and close these leads promptly. Second note: you can co-op your participation so that you get your leads free. Ask for details.

3) Want **even MORE leads**? Great! Join Jeffrey's TNT team, take a full run in the card-deck (100,000 cards) and get a free listing in this catalog... just like the people on page 24. You'll get at least 750 leads... and possibly 2,000 or more! All the leads will go to you directly. Note: you can also take a split run (50,000 cards) in Jeffrey's deck as an intermediate step. But if you do this, you do not get the free listing in this catalog! You can also co-op this option!

For complete details on items 2-4 on this page, contact Jeffrey directly at (617) 547-6372 or Fax (617) 547-0061.

4) If these three options don't satisfy you, but you still want to generate hundreds of new leads to build your MLM organization, no problem. Just buy a card in my card deck at the regular price ($1199 for 100,000 two color cards; $650 for 50,000 cards). All leads go to you, and you have no involvement with our MLM team. Note: as always, if you pay for your card (full run) 60 days prior to publication, you get a Top 20 position... if any are available!

Special note: Don't forget. Generating leads is only half the battle. Closing them is the rest. For aggressive, client-centered response packages, call Dan McComas at the National Copywriting Center, (301) 946-4284.

JOIN JLA VENTURES… AND PROFIT FROM BEING CONNECTED TO AMERICA'S MOST AGGRESSIVE MARKETING TEAM

My company is growing… and I'm looking for new ventures to invest in and help develop. As you can see from this catalog, I already have divisions for publishing (JLA Publications), catalog (you're looking at it), card deck (Jeffrey Lant's Sales & Marketing SuccessDek), copywriting (National Copywriting Center), and MLM. In addition, I maintain an entity called JLA Ventures which currently sells electronic moving message display units.

WE ARE NOW LOOKING FOR ADDITIONAL PROJECTS TO GET INTO AND MAKE MONEY FROM…

These projects may involve selling an investment (like no-load mutual funds)… or an office product (like the moving signs). We're looking for items with a high profit potential for which leads can be generated through my card deck and this catalog and which can be closed through telemarketing and direct response follow-up. We are particularly interested in products/services that people may buy on a continuing basis, but we are willing to consider items people only buy once… so long as there is significant profit in the sale.

We are particularly interested in working with people who already have a good track record with what they are proposing, who are financially secure and knowledgeable about their products/services. We are not interested in getting involved in anything which cannot be promoted either through my card-deck or catalog.

To get started, outline your idea in just one or two pages and send with any promotional information to Bill Reece, New Projects Manager, JLA Ventures, 50 Follen St., Suite 507, Cambridge, MA 02138 or fax to (617) 547-0061. Remember to include the retail cost of the product/service and the profit margin.

Caution: Do not propose any MLM projects. If you have these, contact Jeffrey at 617-547-6372. Information products like books, booklets, audio and video cassettes are also not appropriate for this division. If you have these and think they're appropriate for my card deck or catalog, contact Jeffrey directly at (617) 547-6372.

Note: if we are interested in your proposal, we will get back to you. Unfortunately, we cannot acknowledge all proposals or return materials to you unless you include a self-addressed stamped envelope.

Get the Lowest Air Fares

New! #B106

FLY THERE FOR LESS: HOW TO SLASH THE COST OF AIR TRAVEL WORLDWIDE. The title says it all on this new, much-needed 312 page book by travel whiz-author Bob Martin. You find out precisely what you need to know to get the lowest air fares all the time. Martin provides insider knowledge on flexibility, off-peak flights, flying weekdays and week-ends, travel seasons, promotional fares, how to work with travel agents, air taxis, charters, consolidators, coupon brokers, ticket auctions and hundreds of other ways to save money now. If you fly and want to cut your costs, you need this book. It's as simple as that. $20.45

Select The Best Computers For Home & Office

New! #B107

THE COMPUTER BUYER'S HANDBOOK: HOW TO SELECT AND BUY PERSONAL COMPUTERS FOR YOUR HOME OR BUSINESS. If you're in the market for a computer, better shop with R. Wayne Parker first. In 237 information-dense pages, he tells you exactly what you should know about computers, how to define your needs, the best home computers (pay attention parents!); business computers; standards and compatibility issues; where to buy the most computer for the least cost; the software you need… and how to get up and running fast. You get helpful lists of mailorder computer dealers, a glossary of computer terms and the publications you should be reading to keep abreast of developments. Whether you're buying your first or thirteenth machine, this'll be real helpful. $19.95

Making At Least $100,000 A Year In MLM

New! B155

HOW TO EARN AT LEAST $100,000 A YEAR IN NETWORK MARKETING. If you expect to make **real** money in MLM, connect with this six-tape audio training series by authority Randy Gage. You'll discover the entire system from prospecting a potential distributor to securing a line for walk-away income 50, 60 and 70 levels deep! How to build a line once and get paid for decades. How to reduce drop-outs by 80 to 90 percent; how to effectively sponsor; why you never lead with the products; the science of building a large group; building security with out of town groups; how to turn yourself into a key player… and much, much more. Thousands take Randy's national workshops on this subject. Now you can get his precise, money-making information and start profiting fast. Just $63.95.

Finding Facts Fast

#B29

All of us are dependent on information, knowing where to find it and where to find it fast is important. That's why you need **FINDING FACTS FAST**, the best little book ever written on quick, economical information gathering. $7.45

Finding A Job

#B83

HOW TO GET INTERVIEWS FROM JOB ADS. If you're unemployed and looking for work, or know someone who is, get this comprehensive book by my friend Ken Elderkin. It tells you where to look, what to select, who to write, what to say, when to follow up, how to save time and a whole lot more. The best jobs go to people who know the system and use it to their advantage. Be one of them. 249 pages. $19.95

Launching Your New Product

New! #B111

HOW TO BRING A PRODUCT TO MARKET FOR LESS THAN $5,000. Author Don Debelak tells you in 298 pages how to test your product idea, market your product and keep costs low, prepare a business plan and get financing. As Debelak points out, each year over 250,000 inventors and entrepreneurs spend as much as $50,000 on their dream product — without a single customer ever hearing about it! Now you don't have to be one of them… for just a few bucks find out if your product idea will work; when to get a patent and when not to; how to minimize all your costs throughout the whole process; how to predetermine manufacturing costs; how to conduct an evaluation after initial sales… and much, much more. $20.95

Mail-Order Money

New! #B139

THE COMPLETE MAIL ORDER SOURCE BOOK. This new 288-page book by John Kremer is a must if you want to make money in mail order. I've been an unabashed admirer of John's books for many years. He produces the kind of nitty-gritty, focused, unrelentingly detailed books I like… and this one is no exception. You get everything you need to start a direct marketing campaign right away and detailed check-lists on what you've got to do and when you've got to do it. If you're not familiar with Kremer's painstaking work, you should be. $24.95

Prestigious… At Last!

New! #B114

STATUS FOR SALE: THE COMPLETE GUIDE TO INSTANT PRESTIGE. The human animal, as author Wayne de Montford-Yeager

293

knows, is a status seeker and always has been. In this, one of the most clever books I've seen lately, he tells you how to elevate yourself by providing page after page of ingenious suggestions. You learn where to get the best quality real and reproduction antiques; portraits of yourself and your animals; how to change your name to something grander and who provides the speech course you need to sound better. You find out how to get an honorary doctorate, a diplomatic passport, a foreign title, how to get in reference books and prestigious clubs, how to get a coat of arms, and much, much more. You may have seen articles about Wayne and his book lately; he's been getting a lot of press. But then... he's been using the guidelines in THE UNABASHED SELF-PROMOTER'S GUIDE, which is what any prestigious person would do! And all for just $11.

Since you can't take it with you...

New! #B115

THE COMPLETE PROBATE KIT: STEP-BY-STEP COVERAGE OF EVERYTHING YOU NEED TO KNOW ABOUT PROBATE. Authors Jens Appel III and Bruce Gentry have provided not only a 196 page book but pages of forms you need to handle probate. You get the basics of probate planning, how to settle your estate, real and personal property issues, state by state requirements, and more. Over 5,000 estates enter the probate process every day. Make sure if you're involved in the process, you use this book so you and your beneficiaries can gain greater control of the financial fate of your estate. $25.95

Before You Fire Him/Her...

New! #B117

PROBLEM EMPLOYEES: HOW TO IMPROVE THEIR PERFOR-MANCE. Are you a boss? Have you got a problem employee? If you're not ready to fire the offending creature just yet, use this 260-page step-by-step approach by Dr. Peter Wylie & Dr. Mardy Grothe. Learn what won't

work... and what will; how to analyze your employee's performance, how to handle employee meetings, how to begin the interview, how to get your employee to talk, how to get your employee to do a "self analysis," how to get your message across, and how to present your analysis of your employee... and negotiate a performance agreement. Finding a new employee is time consuming and expensive. Use these techniques to see if you can salvage the present situation. Just $25.95

Winning Your Small Claims Case

New! #B119

SMALL CLAIMS COURT WITH-OUT A LAWYER. Attorney W. Kelsea Wilber has written the book you need if you're going to small claims court and want to win without a lawyer. In 211 pages, you get the details you need about: deciding if you have a case, when, where and how to file a lawsuit, how to prepare for your day in court, easy ways to serve a summons, and collecting your money after the judgment. You get sample letters and forms and a complete listing of individual state-by-state information. $22.45

Incorporating Your Business

New! #B124

HOW TO INCORPORATE: A HANDBOOK FOR ENTREPRE-NEURS AND PROFESSIONALS. This 235-page paperback by Diamond and Williams tell you how to select the right form, what to do before you incorporate, how to handle the financial structure, dividends, the articles of incorporation, bylaws, corporate operations, taxes, and more. $25.95

Getting Rich with TV Ads

New! #B126

HOW TO MAKE YOUR SALES EXPLODE WITH TELEVISION ADVERTISING. Lots of particularly small business people think they're too

little to benefit from tv advertising. Author D.B. Carson shows otherwise. This very helpful step-by-step book tells why you should be advertising on television, shows you how to understand your market, budget, plan your television creative strategy, develop the right message, write the script, select a production company (and not overpay), find the talent you need, shoot and edit your spot, develop a media plan... and much, much more. This book is long overdue and is perfect for breaking you into television advertising. Just $38

Making Money in Mutual Funds

New! #B153

BUSINESS WEEK'S ANNUAL GUIDE TO MUTUAL FUNDS. If you're investing in mutual funds like I am, you need this 154-page guide to finding the best funds for you, complete data on over 1100 funds, how funds invest your money, and a whole lot more. Individual stock picking is too risky for most investors... but you still want to get the advantages of the stock market. Therefore mutual funds make sense... and this book makes sense of mutual funds. $29.95

Getting Listened To... At Last!

#B84

HOW TO TALK SO MEN WILL LISTEN. Marian Woodall, whose books I've recommended for years, has done it again. This is for you, ladies. If you've wondered why so many men really don't get it when you talk, get this book and follow its 108 pages of sensible suggestions. It'll help you with bosses, committees, adult children, even spouses and boyfriends. Marian shows that the genders communicate differently and offers detailed guidelines on how you can finally get your message across. Look, these methods must work, right? Marian constantly persuades me to put her books in my catalog... and she's never even taken me out to lunch! $10.00

Getting The Money You're Owed

#B46

You've got uncollected and uncollectible invoices sitting in your drawer right now. Makes you sick, right? Well, if you used th e techniques in **PAYMENT IN FULL: A GUIDE TO SUCCESSFUL BILL COLLECTING**, some of them wouldn't be there. If you'd use it now, you can still collect on some of them. $27.95 is also a pretty fair price to pay to cut the anger you feel about the deadbeats who're ripping you off.

What You Need To Know To Launch Your Invention

#B40

FROM CONCEPT TO MARKET. Gary Lynn's 243-page book tells you how to protect your idea without submitting a patent, how to license a new idea, market your innovation, start your own company, raise money, build a prototype, write a business plan and produce your product. Developing a product is one of the best ways to get really rich. Making a small investment in Lynn's extensive research tells you how to devleop it right and launch it fast. $22.95

New #B149

MARKETING YOUR INVENTION. Once you've got your idea, you've got to market it. Start off right with Gary Lynn. Then move on to this new 240-page resource by Thomas E. Mosley, Jr. Find out whether you should manufacture your invention or license it to an outside company; why most inventors should not become entrepreneurs, and everything you need to know about the business of *inventing*. If you expect to make money from your invention, you need these two resources. This one is just $24.95.

Selling More

New #B150

THE COMPLETE SELLING SYSTEM: SALES MANAGEMENT TECHNIQUES THAT CAN HELP ANYONE SUCCEED. Author Pete

Frye's new 192 page book is for you if you haven't yet figured out that to make money in sales means developing a *sales system* and following it religiously. Here you get both the structures and strategies you need to succeed in sales. Sensible answers to key questions like: "I can't get my sales people to do what I want them to do;" "We get a lot of people through the store every day, but not enough of them buy," "Whenever I question a salesperson's performance, I get an argument," and "I sell through independent reps — it's impossible to manage the process." This is a no-nonsense book designed to do one thing: SELL MORE. When that's what you want, send me $26.95 .

All The Accounting Information You'll Need

New! #B151

SMALL TIME OPERATOR. If you've never heard of this book, you must have your head in the sand. Author "Bear" Kamaroff's become famous for the kind of practical advice he dishes out on starting your own business, keeping your own books, paying your taxes and staying out of trouble! 190 fact-filled, easy-to read pages provide complete information for sole proprietors, partnerships, corporations, independent contractors, freelancers, employers, home businesses, consultants and all other self-employed individuals. If that's you, rush me $18.95 and keep this essential resource close at hand!

Key Information on Patents, Copyrights & Trademarks

#B66

PATENTS, COPYRIGHTS & TRADEMARKS. If you're going to use any of these three things, you need this useful 236-page paperback by Foster & Shook. Crammed with useful information about what's patentable, how to conduct a patent search, apple for a patent; what's copyrightable, your copyright rights; how to register your work; how to protect your trademark; frequently asked questions and their answers; myths, etc. Save yourself a bundle by sending me $24.95 for this exhaustive resource.

Speakers' Resource

New! #B55

SPEAKER'S & TOASTMASTER'S HANDBOOK. If you speak… if you introduce speakers… you need Herbert Prochnow's pile of 500 humorous stories, 500 epigrams & quips, 100 stories and comments, 292 humorous definitions, 190 statements on important subjects by great thinkers, 209 wise & witty proverbs, 160 unusual quotations from world leaders, etc. You'll be a lot smarter (and get better speaking reviews) if you send me $22.95 for this book.

Continue on… there's more to come!

Building a Lucrative Catalog Sales Business

#B68

STARTING & BUILDING YOUR CATALOG SALES BUSINESS. This is Herman Holtz' latest volume, and you'd better get it if you're not already making millions in the catalog sales game — but want to. 271 pages tell you what types of merchandise sell well by catalog; how to write catalog copy that sells; necessary elements in any catalog mailing; what you need to know about mailing lists; pricing details and much more. You can lose a bundle fast with a money-losing catalog. Use Herman's latest to make sure *you* profit. A steal at $33.

Staying Covered for Less

#B85

INSURANCE SMART: HOW TO BUY THE RIGHT INSURANCE AT THE RIGHT PRICE. Jeff O'Donnell's new 236 page book covers EVERY type of insurance — including homeowners, car, health, business, life, farm & ranch, and medicare supplement. There isn't a single reader of this catalog who wouldn't be better off using what he says to get the best coverage at the lowest cost. Also explains forms & terminology, tells you how to file a claim, provides consumer protection information & more. $17.95

Creating A Business Plan

#B154

You know you need a written business plan, and you know you don't have one. That's why you need **THE BUSINESS PLANNING GUIDE.** It's not just a book. It's your basic business tool and roadmap. Packed with forms, checklists and immediately usable examples, this will give you exactly what you need: a specific, written business plan. In about 130 pages, you'll get your MBA in small business management. Over 250,000 businesses are already profiting from this book. You should, too! $23.45

When You Need Someone To Spend Your Money On...

New! #B90

HOW TO BE OUTRAGEOUSLY SUCCESSFUL WITH THE OPPOSITE SEX: HOW TO SOLVE EVERY PROBLEM YOU'VE EVER HAD... MEETING, DATING, OR MARRYING THE MAN OR WOMAN OF YOUR DREAMS. Why is this book here? If you're alone... or looking... I really don't need to tell you, you know. Besides, it's written by my shrewd, yea brilliant colleague Paul Hartunian who's parlayed his own encyclopedic knowledge on the subject into appearances in a string of nat'l tv shows. 141 pages. And a lot cheaper than calling those 900 numbers! P.S. If you order before 01/01/93, Paul will include a FREE copy of his Special Report "The 5 Things You Have To Do To Impress That Special Someone." $22.95

Getting Organized... At Last!

#B102

ORGANIZED TO BE THE BEST! Subtitled "New Timesaving Ways to Simplify and Improve How You Work", this 434-page book has been selected by NINE major book clubs as a special pick. No wonder. It's awesomely detailed! Author Susan Silver takes on the gigantic task of organizing America — and you! And succeeds! Details about organizing your desk and its paper jungle; getting files up-to-date; organizing IBM personal computer & Macintosh files; work and project management shortcuts; special tips for collectors who "can't" throw anything away... and much, much more including tip after tip for organizing your work environment. People just love this book. If organization isn't your strong suit, get this crucial resource. $15.95

Getting Merchant Charge Card Status

#B10

STRATEGIES FOR GETTING CHARGE CARD MERCHANT STATUS AT YOUR BANK (EVEN IF YOU'RE A MAIL ORDER DEALER). This 49-page booklet by my friend John Cali tells you how and where to get a Merchant MC/VISA account and how to handle your credit card orders. Particularly mail order merchants (who know just how difficult it is to get MC/VISA status these days) will want to get this very useful resource which is always kept updated by its author. I referred one friend to it who had had incredible difficulty in getting such an account. By following the steps here he had one in just five days. Cheap at $21.95.

Free Help From Uncle Sam

New! #B152

FREE HELP FROM UNCLE SAM TO START YOUR OWN BUSINESS OR EXPAND THE ONE YOU HAVE. If you're interested in getting money from the govt. for your business, you need this "must own" 304-page resource by William Alarid and Dr. Gustav Berle. Contains over 100 government programs for small businesses plus dozens of examples of how people have taken advantage of this help. 22 loan programs; 10 loan guarantees; 5 direct payments; 109 grant programs; 26 information services; 11 counseling services. And much, MUCH more! Just $17.95.

Running An Effective Partnership

New! #B129

THE PARTNERSHIP BOOK. If you're going to have a partner, you need this 221-page resource by Clifford & Warner. It's subtitled " How to Write Your Own Small Business Partnership Agreement." For years, it's been the most thorough guide to how to set up a partnership — and make it prosper. All aspects covered, including choosing a legal form, getting your business started, the partners and their relationship, terms, no-no's, partnership decision making, financial considerations, changes, growth & new partners, and much, much more. If you want your partnership to work, you want this book. It's as simple as that! $27.95

Do-It-Yourself Marketing Research

#B121

DO IT YOURSELF MARKETING RESEARCH. Too many businesses simply "market" without researching or planning. Their poor results should cure them of this folly, but too often do not. However, if you want better results, use this detailed 251-page resource by Breen & Blankenship. It's got just the information you need to handle your own marketing research... and improve your results. Includes information on collecting the information, conducting a focus group interview, making sure you question the right people, how to develop a good questionnaire, summarizing the results of your study... and much more. $49.95

Publishing Your Newsletter

#B19

Howard Penn Hudson is America's newsletter guru. If there's something to be known about newsletters, he knows it. That's why you should use **PUBLISHING NEWSLETTERS: A COMPLETE GUIDE TO MARKETS, EDITORIAL CONTENT, DESIGN, PRINTING, SUBSCRIPTIONS, AND MANAGEMENT.** Take my word for it: this is the best book on newsletters ever written. $16.95

#B108

NEWSLETTERS FROM THE DESKTOP: DESIGNING EFFECTIVE PUBLICATIONS WITH YOUR COMPUTER. If you're even thinking about producing a newsletter and using your computer, get this detailed 306-page book by Roger Parker right away. I've often recommended Roger's books; they are always good value. Here he gives you the details you need to plan your newsletter, select a grid, create a nameplate, work with body copy, add reader cues, place and manipulate visuals, add graphic accents, and a whole lot more. You're going to spend a lot of money producing your newsletter. Let Roger help you do it right! $28.95

Order Form on page 298.

BARGAIN BOOK PAGE.
EVERYTHING ON THIS PAGE COSTS YOU LESS... AND EVERYTHING ON THIS PAGE IS IN VERY LIMITED SUPPLY. IF YOU WANT SOMETHING ACT NOW... OR IT WILL CERTAINLY BE GONE!

Special on Jeffrey's books

I have a few copies left of the last edition of **CASH COPY** and both the current and past editions of **THE CONSULTANT'S KIT** and **DEVELOPMENT TODAY**. These books have some minor cover damage... but the contents are fine. They're $20 each postpaid. If you want one, call, since they won't last long. Too, every once in a while I have damaged copies of some of my other books; if you want something else, call me. I might have it!

Warehouse Discovery!

The other day my warehouse assistant discovered one case of the previous edition of **THE UNABASHED SELF-PROMOTER'S GUIDE.** These books are all in perfect condition... but, of course, some of the reference material is outdated. Still, if you want a fabulous bargain, send me $12.50 (postpaid) and ask for "The Unabashed Collector's Item." These books, by the way, will go fast!

One of a kind close-outs.

The following are all new books that I no longer need in my collection. I'm selling them for $10 postpaid each. Values here up to $40. Call before you order, because these will go fast... and I only have one copy of each! If you'd like other bargains, drop by and check out a huge supply we have of this stuff. I'll put new items in future catalogs...

ENTREPRENEURIAL MEGABUCKS: THE 100 GREATEST ENTREPRENEURS OF THE LAST TWENTY-FIVE YEARS/A DAVID SILVER

SEVEN STRATEGIES FOR WEALTH & HAPPINESS: POWER IDEAS FROM AMERICA'S FOREMOST BUSINESS PHILOSOPHER/JIM ROHN

HOW TO EARN MORE USING THE PROFESSIONAL EXCELLENCE SYSTEM FOR MANAGING PROFESSIONALS/ PETER H BURGHER

INFORMATION TECHNOLOGY/THE TRILLION DOLLAR OPPORTUNITY/ HARVEY POPPEL

GETTING THE JOB/HOW TO INTERVIEW SUCCESSFULLY/MARY MEYER

COMPANY MANNERS/AN INSIDER TELLS HOW TO SUCCEED IN THE REAL WORLD OF CORPORATE PROTOCOL & POWER POLITICS/LOIS WYSE

HOW TO ADVERTISE/A PROFESSIONAL'S GUIDE FOR THE ADVERTISER: WHAT WORKS. WHAT DOESN'T. AND WHY/ ROMAN AND MASS

WINNING BACK YOUR MARKET: THE INSIDE STORIES OF THE COMPANIES THAT DID IT/JAGDISH SHETH

THE SUPER MANAGERS: MANAGING FOR SUCCESS, THE MOVERS AND THE DOERS/ROBERT HELLER

GAME PLANS: SPORTS STRATEGIES FOR SUCCESS/ROBERT KEIDEL

GUILT: LETTING GO/FREEMAN & STREAN

THE DYNAMOES: WHO ARE THEY ANYWAY? FEATURES THE ACE 100 TOP ENTREPRENEURS UNDER 30/BRETT KINGSTONE

QUICK SOLUTIONS: 500 PEOPLE PROBLEMS MANAGERS FACE & HOW TO SOLVE THEM/THOMAS QUICK

HOW HOT A MANAGER ARE YOU?/ ERNEST DICHTER

INVENTING THE FUTURE/ADVANCES IN IMAGERY THAT CAN CHANGE YOUR LIFE/MARILEE ZDENEK

STRAIGHT TALK ABOUT SMALL BUSINESS/KENNETH ALBERT

If you'd like more information on any of these, call 617-547-6372 and I'll read the table of contents, etc.
Remember, these are one of a kind offers!

297

Order Form

*Special
Edition for
Development
Today*

Photocopy or return this page to: Dr. Jeffrey Lant, Jeffrey Lant Associates
50 Follen St., #507, Cambridge, MA 02138

CLEARLY write down the item number(s) of what you order here. Each number is composed of a letter and a number. Please make sure to give both!

———, ———, ———, ———, ———, ———, ———, ———, ———, ———, ———, ———, ———, ———, ———, ———, ———, ———, ———,

Remember, if you're ordering my Special Reports (#R1 – #R88), you get **any three for $14**. Individual Reports are $6 each.

Total your order here $ _____. Are you a Massachusetts resident? ❏ Yes ❏ No
If so, add 5% sales tax here $ _____.   Total enclosed $ _____.

| Your Day Telephone |
| ( )_____ |

Shipping. If you are ordering books, tapes and Special Reports by Dr. Jeffrey Lant, they are sent the day you order (unless you are using a post office box address that is not guaranteed by a MC/VISA/AMEX). Other books are sent to you direct from their publishers by fourth class/book rate shipping. Allow four-six weeks. If you want them faster, add $3 per item for first class or UPS shipping. Remember: to ship UPS, I must have a street address!

Canada and overseas. If you want your items shipped to Canada, add $1 for *each* item ordered and $1 to the total for our bank's fees, even if you pay in U.S. dollars. If you want shipment to any other country, you must pay by credit card. I'll charge your account surface or air shipping, as you like. Check ❏ surface ❏ air.

Premiums. If your order totals at least $150, you can select any one of my three 60 minute audio cassettes as my gift to you. The three titles are listed on page 287. Write down the one you want here # _____. If your order totals over $275, you get your free audio cassette and any one of my eight "Get Ahead" books (#B1 – #B7 & # B9) or **Development Today** (#B8). List the item number of the one you want here _____. Remember to get these free premiums, you must order from this catalog by 01/01/94.

Payment & Billing. Unless you are a government agency, college, library or other official public organization (in which case, include your Purchase Order # here _____), COMPLETE PAYMENT MUST ACCOMPANY YOUR ORDER. I cannot invoice individuals and private businesses. If paying by check, make it payable to Jeffrey Lant Associates, Inc. If you are using a post office box number for shipment, I require a Master Card/VISA/AMEX number and expiration date to guarantee your check, or else I wait for the check to clear. Sadly, several rip-off artists use post office boxes to defraud reputable merchants like me, so I have to inconvenience good people like you. You can also Fax your order to me at 617-547-0061.

If paying by credit card (or using a post office box for shipment):

✓ ❏ MasterCard   ❏ VISA   ❏ AMEX   #_____

   Expiration date_____   Signature_____

For faster service, place your order by telephone twenty-four hours a day at (617) 547-6372. (Yes, I really do answer my own phone.) Before calling make sure your credit card is handy. The order tape doesn't last forever! **Speak clearly!**

Your books and materials will be sent to the address on the shipping label below, unless you indicate otherwise. Please be clear about where you want your items sent.

Send materials to:

Name _____

Organization _____

Street Address _____

City _____ State _____ Zip _____

Telephone (_____) _____